BOB MACY

BOB MACY

The Man Behind The String Tie

Pat McGuigan, Chris Querry, & Bryon J. Will

AS TOLD BY BOB MACY

TATE PUBLISHING & *Enterprises*

Bob Macy

Published by Tate Publishing & Enterprises, LLC
127 E. Trade Center Terrace | Mustang, Oklahoma 73064 USA
1.888.361.9473 | www.tatepublishing.com

Tate Publishing is committed to excellence in the publishing industry. The company reflects the philosophy established by the founders, based on Psalm 68:11,
"The Lord gave the word and great was the company of those who published it."

Cover design by Amber Gulilat
Interior design by Lindsay B. Behrens

Published in the United States of America

ISBN: 978-1-61346-372-7
1. Biography & Autobiography / Lawyers & Judges
2. Biography & Autobiography / Political
11.06.30

ACKNOWLEDGEMENTS

Thanks to Darlene Whitehead for all her hard work in helping me complete this book.

A very special thank you goes to Chris Querry for being my friend when I needed one the most.

And a very special thank you goes to Bryon J. Will for graciously giving permission to use so very much of his previously written work.

TABLE OF CONTENTS

Chapter 8

Chapter 9

Chapter 10

FOREWORD

They Call Him "Boss"
by Wilford Brimley

I have been asked to write a few words at the beginning of this book about Robert H. Macy, the district attorney for many years of Oklahoma County.

Bob Macy is, first of all, my friend—one of my dearest, dearest friends. I first got to know him twenty to twenty-five years ago when we talked about a project not unlike this.

Bob Macy is honest to a fault. He is possibly the most honest man I have ever known in my life. He is capable. He is direct.

In spite of the fact that he and I are the best of friends and we care a great deal for one another, I don't ever want to stand in front of him in a court of law. Because in that situation, nothing counts to Bob Macy except the truth, the right for the sake of right, and justice—equal justice for all. I have sat in the courtroom with him on many occasions. I have watched him prosecute some of the vilest human beings I have ever been in the presence of. I've seen him keep his composure, I've seen him so well prepared, and I've seen him conduct his trials and his legal matters in a manner that is awesome.

You see, every once in a while, the word *awesome* does come into play. It comes into play when you are talking about someone like Bob Macy. I've walked down the hall with him in his county office building, and I've heard everybody from the guy downstairs in the garage to the people on the first floor and people in the elevator, regardless of their department or their capacity as employees of the county refer to Bob Macy as "Boss." I remember very well on many occasions going in the building with him and hearing people say, "Good morning, Boss!" and "Hi, Boss!" or "How are you, Boss?" and simply "Good to see you, Boss!" He is one of the most loved and cared-for men I've ever been around. Bob Macy is truly a public servant. He is so because he chose to be, he was prepared to be, and his record stands on its own merit. I'm so proud of him.

I am grateful for his friendship. He has been an example to me in many areas. I have to take a few words here to write about Brett, his loving and devoted son. They have a relationship that is enviable to anyone who ever sees it. I'm very fortunate because I've got some sons like that, too. If everybody had a son or even a friend like Brett Macy, it would be a far better world.

To Bob: Good luck with this latest project. You can bet your string bow tie I will read this book. I'm grateful to you for your life, your service, and your friendship. Thanks, pal!

—Wilford Brimley
Fall 2009

PREFACE

To the reader:

I retired in 2001 after twenty-one years of service as the Oklahoma County, Oklahoma, district attorney. During my tenure in office, I tried over sixty murder cases, in addition to numerous serial rapists. Any time that I find myself in a social position, I find that the public wants to know more about the cases I have tried and other cases of the justice system. I hope that this book will explain some of the complexities and personalities of my tenure in office.

Furthermore, I hope this book can explain some of the complexities of living life in a way that does not compromise one's integrity. This book is less about me than it is about my friends, and I have many of them. Some people say I have surrounded myself with a certain kind of people, people who have the same passions I do. The truth is people gravitate toward passions rather than toward people. I was fortunate to exhibit the passions that others believed in also, and to that, rather than to me, they gravitated. I was and am still extremely fortunate to have many of those as my true friends, people who look past the failures and the mistakes to want to continue walking down the path with someone they consider a friend as well.

I'm hoping this book will be seen as entertaining and as enlightening, and I hope most of all that it will encourage people to follow their passions particularly in helping those who need a helping hand and a person to stand up for them.

—Bob Macy

EDITOR'S PREFACE

Though this book has been in progress for over ten years, it has only recently, in the past couple of years, taken on a serious focus. Bob Macy is in his golden years era and, with that, he has come upon some hard times with his health. In as many years, he has broken both hips and, though still strong, recovers slower than past times. He has more time on his hands and has dedicated hours too many to count to finishing his account of his life. Several people have helped Bob with this, and many will go unnamed not because they are too embarrassed to have their names brought to light but because the focus of the book is really on the reader, not even Bob Macy.

Bob's life has been "one hell of a party," but there's so much more to it than just that. This is not even a biography as such; it's Bob's memoirs. Biographies tell only a story, and he has a wonderful story to tell of his life. But it doesn't stop there. At every turn, there is a lesson that needs to be revealed to the reader. His story is full of surprises, over-comings, survival, dedication, and a ferocity to do what is right for the right reasons that is lacking in our people today. One couple who read just a few chapters of an unedited version remarked, "We want our children to read this." Our world is full of people who feel sorry for themselves because they don't have the latest toy or gadget. But they've never considered living in a house with no running water or indoor toilets or heating and cooling. They expect to go to college. They expect to have a good-paying job handed to them. They expect to be catered to. And when that doesn't happen, they complain and rebel and end up getting in trouble with the law. Work is a dirty four-letter word, and life owes them more than a living.

Bob Macy was never given anything, never was owed anything, and never relaxed from hard work. He was never promised anything, and he had enough hard times and disappointments to sour even the most optimistic of the younger generation. But he survived and excelled and not just for himself but for people who could not see their way out of the dark, who had been victimized by man, society, and their own fears. Bob met his fair share of challenges, and he rebelled. He met the challenge of discrimination and intolerance and rebelled against it. He met the challenge of disappointment and rebelled against its permanent effects. He met the challenge of victimization and rebelled against its empowerment. He met the challenge of being told "no" with the rebellion of, "We'll see about that." He met the challenge of losing his faith in mankind with a rebellion against those that beat down the good man. He met the challenge of his belief in what is right set against the wrongs of the world, and he rebelled by winning.

But this is less a story of Bob Macy the man as it is the lessons of Bob Macy we all can learn from. I have been privileged to come to know Bob Macy in these years, when the ego of a man is tempered by his physical weaknesses and the truth behind those eyes shines clearer than even his words can say. This is not an exposé; there is, in fact, nothing to expose, nothing hidden. I've tried to put as many of his thoughts directly on paper as possible. The quotations are his, from his own memory and from his lips. The comments about what the quotations mean come from me, a man who has come to respect a legend and who has been fortunate to see beyond the legendary to the man himself. And it has been a pleasant journey. He is a man of compassion, the holder of the largest heart I have ever met. He is a humble man, whose compassion is misunderstood as ego. He is a man of unquestionable ethics and morals and carries with him a sense of right and wrong that never blurs the line between. I can truly say that every man whose butt has been kicked by Bob Macy needed and deserved to have his butt kicked because he disregarded a moral right or crossed the line. Macy is still fierce in his belief that right is right and nothing, not ever a thing, will confuse right and wrong. He is still a man driven by his passion to serve, to help, to rescue, to teach, to love, and to stand up for what he believes and for the people who haven t the strength to stand for themselves.

This isn't a biography. It's a journey to come to know a man who values friendship and the best that men can be at whatever they do, no matter the cost and no matter the disadvantages. This is less about his successes than it is about how he became successful. He met the challenges head on and prevailed because he saw no other way. There are lessons to be learned here. There is inspiration.

CHAPTER 1

When the World Changed

Bob Macy reluctantly rolled out of bed at 4:15 a.m. He slipped into a shirt, jeans, and moccasins and stumbled to the barn through the dark Oklahoma morning. He fed and checked the water for his three horses, seven steers, ten chickens, twelve cats, goat, and pot-bellied pig. Sandy, his German Shepherd, accompanied him wherever he went and almost seemed to direct his chores.

Macy remembered that morning in particular. "Everything was quiet," he recalled, "peaceful and beautiful until I woke up the roosters." He chuckles a bit. "They are the ones who decided to wake up the world." He continued smiling as he talked. "I looked up at the star-studded sky and thanked God for my many blessings." After finishing his daily chores, he showered, shaved, polished his cowboy boots, and put on a freshly starched shirt highlighted with his traditional string tie. He remembered he grabbed a handful of vitamins, downed them with a glass of orange juice, threw his briefcase into his truck seat, and stuck his .45-caliber Sig Sauer pistol in his belt. By the time he left his house, it was 5:30 a.m.

As with every morning, he turned south down Midwest Blvd., a country road bounded by farm fields and tall trees, just late enough to allow dawn to peek over the horizon to the east. As he thought about his daily schedule, he kept a cautious eye open for deer, coyotes, and bobcats that routinely cross the country roads that early in the morning.

"As I turned onto Highway 66," Macy said, "traffic was minimal but fast moving. At I-35, the traffic picked up a little, but few Oklahoman Cityans go to work before 6:00 a.m. And by the time I got on the Centennial Expressway, I was greeted with the beautiful, panoramic view of the state capitol complex and the skyline of Oklahoma City. That sight always excites me."

Why would Bob Macy, a native of Indiana, be excited to call Oklahoma City, the capitol city of the Sooner State, his hometown? He explained the reason. "In 1957, I joined the Oklahoma City Police Department. In those days, an officer was required to know the entire city. On any given shift, he might be assigned to patrol and protect any district in the city. I learned to know the streets, the neighborhoods, the businesses, and the character of this great big, overgrown cow town. It had become, in my mind, my town."

The day before, Macy had attended a funeral for the victim of a horrible murder—a lady, Anita Bebout, who had been doused with gasoline and set afire. Her little girl had also been terribly burned. When he was leaving the woman's funeral, a man came up to Macy, the Oklahoma County District Attorney, and said, "Mr. Macy, those of us here are just average, normal citizens. We don't understand violence. We don't know how to deal with violence directed at us or our loved ones. That is why we elected you. We expect you to bring the murderers, rapists, robbers, and burglars to justice."

Macy said that made him stop and think for a minute. "I had never thought of my job in quite those terms," he reflected. "That man was absolutely right. It was my job as the chief law enforcement officer of the county, along with all the other peace officers, to seek out and incapacitate or eradicate the vicious cowards who preyed on the law-abiding citizens of my county. I knew that part, but I didn't realize I had to make sense of the violence to the victims."

Later, the April 18 encounter at the funeral led him to reflect in a speech:

> Like it or not, we are your hired guns. We are paid to stand between the good and the evil in our society and to lay down our lives if necessary to protect the lives and safety of our citizens. We want you to be able to walk upright before your God and to be safe and secure in your homes and businesses and any place in between. It is better that we die on our feet than to have the citizens of our country live on their knees in fear of the violent psychopaths who seem to abound today."

Bob Macy, District Attorney of Oklahoma County, had long ago taken a stance against crime. But this speech made his stance a promise.

On the casual drive into the office, Macy was grateful for the way his workday, a Wednesday, was beginning. "I turned off the expressway, drove up a couple of blocks, and entered the underground parking at the Myriad Center. It was just before 6:00 a.m., time to meet the many religious and civic leaders of my city, for a time of prayer preceding the annual mayor's prayer breakfast.

"I had a full day scheduled. The prayer breakfast would be over by 8:30 a.m. At nine, two homicide detectives were to brief me on a murder case. I had a luncheon meeting, and that afternoon, I was to meet with the president pro temp of the Oklahoma Senate to argue for adequate funding for my office. If time allowed, that evening my son, Brett, and I planned on practicing roping for a team roping event we entered at the 89ers Rodeo that Friday night."

As was customary, the annual mayor's prayer breakfast, sponsored by the Full Gospel Businessman's Fellowship, was a sellout. "Thousands of Oklahomans attended," he remembered, "including the mayor, the governor, congressional members, legislative leaders, the chief of police, other law enforcement leaders and the civic leaders of Oklahoma City. Every powerful and influential city and state leader was in the same room at one time." This thought would cause Macy to have ominous recollections for years.

After a good breakfast, an excellent presentation, and many prayers, Macy remembers getting a page from his secretary letting him know his nine o'clock appointment was already there waiting. Macy left and drove the short distance to his office on the fifth floor, and greeted the two detectives and his first assistant, Pat Morgan. The time was 8:58 a.m. Macy's day, and his life, was about to change. His meeting, which should have been a routine moment in a life that was rarely routine, had begun.

"It was exactly 9:02 a.m., Wednesday, April 19, 1995, that my world changed forever. The walls in my office vibrated violently from side to side. Windows shattered. Ceiling tile fell. Employees were knocked off their feet. Only because nearly all of my attorneys were in court farther from the blast did we avoid casualties."

Macy's chief investigator, Clint Dedek, ran into his disheveled office yelling, "They've just bombed the federal building. The county building may be next." Macy instinctively knew that might be right. He and his staff quickly got everyone out of the building then made arrangements to get all of his employees home or, at least, out of the downtown area. "Only then did we respond to the blast site," he said.

With rank-and-file employees dispatched to safety, Macy and several of his closest aides ran toward the smoke arising from the federal building just a few blocks away. He remembered seeing people standing on the downtown sidewalks with dazed looks on their faces. Within just minutes of the explosion, Macy and his aides arrived at the site of the A.P. Murrah Federal Building, or the remains of it. The whole north side was sheared off and lying in rubble at the base.

Macy described what he saw in his words. "The devastation was unreal. Television and pictures were incapable of conveying the true horror of the sight. As a career officer, I have seen a lot of death and mutilation. In 1986, on August twentieth, Clint Dedek and I were the first people in the building behind the tactical team when Patrick Sherrill slaughtered fourteen workers at the Edmond post office. I had to participate in notifying ten of the families of the deaths of their loved ones that day. I thought that was the worst day of my life, but it didn't even come close."

Before long, Bob Macy, though hardened by years of service, realized, "The magnitude of the atrocity of April nineteenth shocked and numbed me. My life will never be the same. You can only imagine the impact it had and will always have on some of the sensitive, loving individuals who responded and who had never before been subject to this kind of mayhem. Many of the dead were literally blown to pieces." This was the beginning of a time of service at the mouth of hell. "I spent the next four days and nights trying to help at the site of the blast."

Macy had a highly visible media presence as the prosecutions of the bombers advanced. But in the early days of rescue and recovery, he was hardly seen on camera. When asked if he purposely avoided the media during that time, he replied, "There weren't any cameras down near the pit where I was."

"In those days," he added, "I worked side by side with agents from the Federal Bureau of Investigation, the Bureau of Alcohol, Tobacco, and Firearms, the Drug Enforcement Agency, the Immigration and Naturalization Service, Customs, and Secret Service, as well as the Oklahoma Highway Patrol, Oklahoma State Bureau of Investigation, police officers, and firefighters from Oklahoma City and the surrounding communities, medical examiner's personnel, and the crane and heavy equipment operators." In the midst of the blood, the rain, the dust, the tears, and the destruction, Macy made friendships that will last forever and that he will cherish until his last day.

His son, Brett, an Oklahoma City police officer, paged him immediately to make sure he had survived. Within minutes, Brett and his fellow officers, firemen, highway patrol troopers, sheriffs, and civilians, were down inside the building, which was still smoking and shaking, with debris and desks and filing cabinets tumbling down, trying desperately to save lives. Nobody was running away. Everyone was running toward the building, laying their lives on the line for their fellow men. "What very few people realize," Macy commented, "is that, following the blast, the Murrah building was structurally unsound. What was left of those nine stories could have come tumbling down at any time, and all of the rescue workers would have been buried in the debris." True to Macy's character, he is more proud of his son's efforts than of his own.

The manpower of a city converged on the shattered building. "Heavy equipment supervisors saw the blast and started their cranes rolling to the scene in minutes," Macy explained. "Doctors and nurses came running. No one even seemed concerned with the danger, though one nurse and a reserve deputy were killed by falling debris. We actually had more volunteers than we could use, in spite of the danger. Acts of uncommon valor were happening everywhere. Some of it was captured on film. Most was not. Some heroes received recognition. Most did not. Many, including my son, witnessed untold horror in the area where the bomb had done the most damage, including the nursery. Firemen had to hold a lady while a doctor amputated her leg without anesthetic in order to free her. Others witnessed seriously injured victims they couldn't reach and about whom they still have nightmares. DEA agents found the body of their fellow agent and couldn't get him out for a day and a half because a beam had his body pinned in."

Macy remembered that team of DEA agents, assisted by others from the ATF. "They kept going back into the debris day after day, in spite of the extreme danger, until all of their personnel—one agent, one office administrator, and three support staff, including one secretary six months pregnant—had been removed, unfortunately, all dead." Macy wound up working with that team to recover the bureau's fallen. Macy looked down at his hands cupped in his lap. "When we finally got the DEA agent out, he was placed on a gurney. We escorted the body to the medical examiner's location, all of us with our hard hats in our hands. As the other officers saw that an officer had been recovered, they formed a procession, stood at attention, and saluted as we passed by." As time went on, work stopped when possible as each body was recovered and the rescuers stood in respect. "That says something about the people of this state. That says everything about why I stayed here."

Pat Morgan, Bob's assistant, looked at the building from the north side as the rain started to fall the first evening and wondered how the rescuers were holding up. Bob can't recall that evening without being overcome with emotion. It's hard not to cry with him as he recalled that night with tears starting to glisten his eyes. "We all knew the rest of the building could come down at any time and kill everyone remaining there. The first night, Wednesday the nineteenth, we had a thunderstorm. It was raining and it was cold and the wind was howling and the building was creaking. Most of us were soaked to the skin, but there was still hope of recovering someone alive... so no one left."

In a speech long after the bombing, Macy related, "Since the 1950s, I have been in love with Oklahoma and with Oklahoma City. It is my home. I don't want to live anywhere else. Other places may have more ideal climates or mountains, or beaches, or ski slopes. But that isn't what counts. What really counts is the people, and I believe that the greatest people on the face of God's green earth live in central Oklahoma. Since 1980, they have honored me by electing me to serve as their district attorney. On that Wednesday, a date that would go down in infamy, a band of cowards slithered into our city and coldly murdered 168 of our citizens, most of whom were women and children." Macy's love of the people and his faith in the righteousness of his work never caused him to tone down his speech when referring to criminals who preyed upon the helpless.

Recalling the statement made by the citizen after Bebout's funeral, in numerous speeches in that spring and the summer of 1995, Macy grappled with the twisted rationales of the murderers.

> We now hear that the cowardly killers are mad at the federal government and want to strike a blow at that government. But they didn't kill that government or even a high-ranking government official. They killed nineteen babies and scores of daughters, wives, sisters, mothers, and sweethearts. They killed dozens of fathers, husbands, sons, brothers, and loved ones. They killed grandparents and uncles and aunts and nephews and nieces and just good friends. They killed Sunday school teachers, Boy Scout leaders, little league coaches, religious lay leaders, and fine role models for our children. They killed twelve law enforcement officers, including a DEA agent, five Secret Service agents, INS agents, and Customs agents, all men who had dedicated their lives to protecting the lives and property of American citizens. They also killed secretaries, office managers, clerks, cashiers, and daycare attendants. They killed ten of my friends. They cut our very hearts out, but they couldn't kill the spirit and the will of the people of Oklahoma. In the dark hours, days, and weeks following the blast, Oklahomans came together and united to meet the demands of the crisis. And we will survive and go on and build a better Oklahoma for our children who did not perish in the blast.

As his time at the site itself ended, Macy returned to daily duties with a grim and determined focus. For fifteen years, he had done his best to do that job for the citizens of Oklahoma County. He recalled a certain letter he received. "It really made me feel good when, following the Memorial Service four days after the bombing, I received a letter from a lady in Blanchard. It was only a couple of lines. It said, 'Mr. Macy, I just wanted to tell you that when I saw you on TV Sunday, I finally felt like it was going to be OKAY. God bless you and your staff. You will be in my prayers.' That letter really humbled me, but it reinforced the obligation that I had to the citizens of my county, state, and nation."

Bob remembers the survivors with more than compassion. He remembers their strength and resolve to continue with their lives. And even for him, a routine to his life returned but always with the survivors in mind. He spoke frequently with federal law enforcement officials and local colleagues. He spoke many times with Attorney General Janet Reno, who became a friend.

Macy knew there would be two prosecutions arising from the bombing of the Murrah Building. The federal government planned on taking jurisdiction for the use of explosives to damage and destroy federal property, an action that resulted in the deaths of 161 persons. Then, at the appropriate time, Macy planned on taking jurisdiction and filing charges for the killings of the seven victims not on federal property at the time of their deaths. He was fiercely determined to "seek the death penalty for those persons who conspired, constructed, and set off the April nineteenth bomb" and to file charges of first degree murder for all of the 168 victims.

In the months that followed, Macy traveled to Washington, DC, to meet with U.S. Representative Henry Hyde of Illinois, chairman of the House Judiciary Committee, and with Newt Gingrich, the speaker of the House of Representatives. The two men pledged to support a federal habeas corpus bill then pending in the conference committee. The measure was designed to dramatically reduce the amount of time it then took to get a criminal appeal through the federal courts. Throughout, Macy's intent and mind was set on the victims, their families, and the survivors. Not long before, Macy had helped push through the state legislature a bill to shorten greatly the amount of time necessary for state criminal appeals. The net result of both bills was to reduce the time for death penalty appeals from twenty-five years to as little as three or four years. His focus remained firm on his fellow Oklahomans he represented. He believed, "When we identify and convict and get the death penalty of the cowards who set the bomb, we Oklahomans want short appeals and quick executions." His intent was not to resurrect the pioneer justice of the land run days. But his intent was surely to serve justice and a formidable statement to outlaws and criminals of all sorts. It was as if he was saying, "We Oklahomans take our home, our lives, our liberties, our families seriously, and we hold them in utmost honor." The biblical notion of *lex talionus*, "an eye for an eye," held merit in his esteem. In speeches of the time, he made promises he intended to keep. "As God is my witness, I promise you that I will use every ounce of my strength, experience, and intellect to see that the guilty parties are prosecuted, convicted, sentenced to death, and timely executed."

Macy was no stranger to death penalty prosecutions and litigation. By the spring of 1995, he had already personally prosecuted and convicted more than sixty murderers, sending forty-five of them to death row. "All of those killers put together," he reflected, "did not kill as many people as the cowardly scum who set off the bomb on April nineteenth, 1995."

Again and again, he praised the resiliency and strength of his fellow Oklahomans and of the rescuers who swarmed the city to recover the bodies of the dead and who helped his town get back on its feet. He often recalled a quote he read from the British theologian, Brooke Foss Westcott: "Great occasions do not make heroes or cowards. They simply unveil them to the eyes of men. Silently and imperceptibly, as we wake or sleep, we grow strong or weak and, at last, some crisis shows us for what we have become." Macy believed the events of April 19 "showed what we in America's heartland have become. I am proud to be an American and doubly proud to be an Oklahoman."

In the fallout of the bombing, there were rumors and allegations started by those who enjoyed conspiracies and loved to disrupt the order and work of the rebuilders. There were allegations that ATF knew in advance of the bombing and pulled their personnel out of the building. Macy calls this "a damnable lie." He continues, "Several of the ATF personnel in the building were injured. One agent on the ninth floor had his office blown away right in front of him. The regional agent in charge was on the elevator when the bomb went off and dropped six floors but survived and went on to rescue others."

Macy was very suspicious as to who planted these rumors, especially on the heels of an NRA fundraising letter referring to the ATF agents as "jack-booted government thugs" and radio commentator G. Gordon Liddy's remark about head-shooting government agents. Macy was protective of the women and men he knew in the ATF, DEA, INS, FBI, and the Secret Service. He told conspiracy theorists, reporters, and average citizens alike that the federal agents "are my friends, dedicated to making this a better world for all Americans. When you attack them, you attack me, because we are one in our life's mission."

As he grappled with the minutia of his many cases, continued with his prior cases and prosecutions and his routine work as the district attorney, the agony of the bombing and its carnage was ever present. During the days and weeks following the blast, a lot of things had to happen before his routine got back to routine. He attended twelve funerals, each offering a tremendous amount of pain, suffering, and grief. The entire time, Macy shared the grief and suffering and pain of others as well. A few of his friends shared similar burdens of dealing with grief while laboring to finish a job they considered the most important in their careers.

Don Webb, agent in charge of the local office of the Drug Enforcement Agency, lost five employees in the carnage—one agent, the office administrator, and three support staff. Seven employees of another good friend, Joe Gallo, special agent in charge of the local Secret Service office, also died. Both men, he recalls, were legitimately away from their offices but felt guilty because they were not with their employees when the blast happened.

Webb made a strong point in his conversations with Macy, one Macy would often repeat in the difficult days that lay ahead. "Bob," Webb said, "when you and I signed on for this war, we accepted the fact that we could die violently and unexpectedly at any time. These ladies, the secretaries and support staff, were only trying to supplement their family income. They didn't sign up for the war, and it's not right that they should die like this." Macy agreed and resolved, "to assure that this kind of atrocity doesn't happen again, it is absolutely imperative that the bombers pay the ultimate price … their lives." He argued the trial should take place in Oklahoma City. After all, that's the venue the bombers chose.

It never was just a job for Bob Macy. He did less in choosing the task that led to his career than it chose him. It was his mindset, his nature, his passion, the driving force that compelled him from his youth, but it was never his *job.*

CHAPTER 2

And So It Began ... Born on the Fifth of July

Indiana is typically hot in July. But the summer of 1930 was one of the most difficult years for the people of the state. Wall Street had collapsed the year before, taking with it many jobs and prospects for jobs. On the horizon in the Midwest was the Dustbowl, preparing to inundate the Midwest in dust and desolation, reducing even more the potential for jobs. This was the world to the young Macy family. There were no jobs and no place to live for Harold "Red" Macy and his young wife, Ethel.

"Red," whose real name was Harold Clifford, sported an anchor tattoo on his forearm from his past navy days. He set his jaw to make a life for him and his new wife the only way he knew: a combination of hard work, determination, honesty, and perseverance. He earned the nickname of "Red" because his temper often turned his face that color. Nonetheless, he was entirely devoted to his young wife, Ethel, usually seen wearing faded and baggy dresses, proud but poor. Red was born in Shelby County, Indiana, on February 10, 1905. According to Macy family lore, his ancestors, Baptists suffering from religious persecution, came to the shores of America shortly after the Mayflower. Family lore reveals the Macy people settled originally on Nantucket Island. Family history continues to disclose he had kinfolk on both sides of the Civil War but back in the Carolinas in the colonies' days, they were whalers. When they came west to Indiana, they traveled there in covered wagons and became farmers.

Today, Tom, one of Red and Ethel's sons, still retains many of the family heirlooms and possessions. Even now, a grandfather clock, an object of fond childhood memories as one of the few possessions Red and Ethel owned, is marked with a rut, a groove rubbed into it by the wheel of that covered wagon on the trail to Indiana.

It wasn't long before the couple started to build a family, even in those hard times. First came Bill, followed shortly afterward by Bob. Robert Harold Macy was born on July 5, 1930, in his grandmother's house with the help of a midwife, his parents too poor to afford a doctor or hospital.

In the spring of 1932, Red and Ethel moved their growing family into a small house at 6630 Ferguson Street in Broad Ripple, Indiana, just outside of Indianapolis. Ferguson Street was literally "on the other side of the tracks." This house, on a street that had no sewer lines, no water lines, and no pavement, remained Red and Ethel's first and only house. The house itself was missing a roof over the porch, and the interior was about as sparse. But the family continued to grow.

Bob had two more brothers, Dick and Tom, and one sister, Betty Lou, who came along sixteen years after Bob. "From the time we were born until we left home, it was four boys all in one room," Macy recalls. There was a tiny closet in their bedroom with a nail from which they hung their clothes. The boys, by necessity, shared nearly everything. "We had an old battered dresser with four drawers. Each of us got one drawer, and in that we kept just two pair of clothes each." After Betty Lou was born, she slept alone in the living room of the four-room house on an old couch.

Bob's earliest memories are of the hard, back-breaking work his parents did to keep food on the table and to provide the best they could for the family. Red was a kind and loving husband and father who was not afraid of hard work. He was the sixth of nine children and one of two brothers who stayed on the farm to help his parents after everything burned when he was ten years old. Hard work came naturally to him. Red Macy had dump trucks after the Great Depression and the New Deal came along. He worked for the WPA during the day and then picked up milk after work. "I remember," Bob recalls, "he had long, long days."

But certain things stand out in his memory. "I remember that old house. It was really a shack. In Oklahoma, it would be called an oil-field shack. They built it near the levee down on the White River. The house had four rooms and a path down the middle of it. There was one electrical outlet in the living room from which hung a single light bulb. There was a levee there along the river's edge. It would flood every two or three years. We were the last house outside, down from the dam."

Outside the drafty house, they had what was called a Roosevelt outhouse. During the Depression, the government built the simple outdoor toilets using 2 x 4's and 1 x 4's. On the back porch was a hand pump for water. "Inside I remember a pot belly stove we had to keep warm. It had a brass ring around it and was actually somewhat ornate. It was our only heat. The third room was the dining room. My parents, I'm not sure how, got all their junk into an armoire that had been thrown away. We had three chairs that were battered and worn. The fourth room was a little kitchen that had a little table and three or four chairs. And we had an ice box that had to be supplied with ice blocks. We had a kerosene stove fed by a one gallon jug, and I remember that everything tasted like kerosene."

Just as Indiana suffered from the heat in the summer, the state is known for its harsh winters. "In the winter, the shack was so ramshackle that the wind often blew out the matches when we tried to light the stove. The stove ran on two or three chunks of coal at a time." On Mondays, Ethel filled the washtub with water heated on the kerosene stove and did all the clothes washing. On Tuesdays, she ironed all the clothes and on Wednesdays, she cleaned house and did what little grocery shopping she could afford. Much of their food came from their garden. His hardworking parents always had a big garden. "So we had tomatoes, corn, beans, and my mother canned vegetables. We had fruit trees—apple and cherry. Those we ate from as quickly as they arrived every year." Every Saturday night, we bathed in the corner in the same wash tub of water."

Tom recalls a specific incident one Saturday night. Their mother heated the water so the boys could wash themselves in that old washtub next to the stove with the brass ring and floral design. "It was winter, and the stove was on. If you got any distance away from the stove, you'd get cold. As he was getting out of the tub, Bob faced his rump toward the stove, bent down, and you know the rest."

Bob tends to understate that incident these days. "My bottom touched that old stove. When that happened, I jumped all the way across the room. And for three or four years, I carried around that floral pattern from that stove on my butt." Tom insists Bob still carried that brand on him even when he went off to college in 1948. Even if Bob still carries that scar, that's only one of many, some caused by accidents, such as a rock thrown tearing into his lip and knocking out a tooth, and some caused by his many surgical events. But even after the branding, all the boys slept close to the stove in winter.

Some of the memories are pleasant, and some helped shape his mindset for his future, even without his knowing. "We had a battery-powered radio," he fondly recalls, "and I used to listen faithfully to *Mr. D.A.* And I even remember the beginning: 'And it shall be my duty as district attorney... to prosecute to the limits of the law all persons accused of crimes within this county, and to defend with equal vigor the rights and privileges of all its citizens.'" Only much later in his life did he realize the foreshadowing the radio show would have on his career choice and his life's passions. "We also listened to Walter Winchell; 'Good evening, Mr. and Mrs. America, and to all the ships at sea.' I loved *Fibber McGee and Molly* and *The Shadow*. 'Who knows what evil lurks in the hearts of men? The Shadow knows.'" And with that memory comes a clue to Bob Macy's future. Bob would spend the majority of his life coming to know "what evil lurks in the hearts of men."

In those early days, long before county safety ordinances, the boys used to play and wander through the woods, not always the safest playground. There was some quicksand or soft sand around and once, Tom and Bob had to pull a friend out of the dissolving sand bank just as the boy was quickly sinking. But as all children, they challenged their fates and their safety in typical childhood adventures by exploring the woods and surrounding undeveloped areas. Macy recalls exploring along the White River; where it merged with Williams Creek, they nicknamed Billy Creek. "We used to explore all around in the little bit of free time we got," Bob says. "I was eight or nine, and we thought we were great explorers. The water there was fairly clear, and we used to swim in it to cool off."

The train and the Monon Line crossed the river on a trestle the boys liked to stroll across. When locomotives approached, bearing down on them on the bridge, Bob says, "We'd kind of dare the train. We'd stay on the trestle just as long as we could then jump into the river as it approached. The drop was about twenty feet into the water. I learned to swim by doing that." Then he adds, "I still don't swim very well." One time, as Bob and Tom and their dog walked along the tracks with another friend, Roy, they had a real brush with death. As a train bore down on them, they had to jump off the tracks. But they couldn't jump into the water because of their dog. They managed to leap onto a pier, a crossbeam, below. "Somehow," Tom recalls, "we all survived, even the dog. We were stupid kids. That's for sure." Today, Tom explains all the tracks and trestle have been made into a nice, manicured walking path and trails on the north side of Indianapolis. It is now a picnic and exercise area, no longer the adventuresome yet dangerous childhood playground.

Life was good for the boys on Ferguson Street, at least as far as they knew. Red Macy's character was deeply shaping the kind of man Bob Macy was to become. "For my dad," Bob says, "the thought of doing something illegal would simply never cross his mind. He would never abuse children or stand by and see children abused." Bob's later passion for protecting children and innocent people, obviously, had its roots in Red's examples of how to live as a man, a lesson Bob took seriously. Another crucial influence was his older brother, Bill. When he was old enough, he began to work as a stock boy in a store.

And as all boys of that time, they fought often. Bill, however, didn't get involved in even the childhood kinds of fights. But that wasn't so true for Bob, however. As the years passed, a hierarchy developed in the neighborhood, with Bob at the top and the weak and helpless at the bottom. The task of defending those below the top fell to Bob. He was bigger. He was stronger. He had more resolve to protect the kids who needed protecting. Even after the boys moved away from Ferguson Street, the neighbors remembered Bob as the one who stood up for the little guy, a trait he carried throughout his entire life. He continued to defend and stand up for the little guy, the underprivileged, the weak in the courtroom, the legislature, and on the streets.

"I remember fights, primarily with kids from other schools like Short Ridge. They tormented the poor kids and called them terrible names. A few times, I'd kick somebody's butt in order to stick up for those kids." That became a forming characteristic of Bob Macy the rest of his life. Macy was never afraid or hesitant to "kick somebody's butt" when the time came. And the time came often enough.

That was the practical side of life, but in the summer, conditions turned quite the opposite. "We didn't have a fridge or air conditioning, of course. In the summer, we opened up the doors and windows and hoped that the wind would blow," Bob muses. In those days, houses were built to catch the breeze with cross-ventilation windows. In the Macy household, the entire house caught the breeze, whether or not the breeze was wanted at any particular time.

Living conditions were worse for the Macy family than the average family in that area. But the miserable conditions grew worse, even while Bob was still a youngster. The city, unfortunately, "decided to put a dump right next to the house. After that, all day, every day, they were dumping loads of trash and garbage right next to where we lived. It was awful. There were rats and flies. One time, one of my brothers woke up, and a rat was chewing on his toe."

Tom started reflecting on their real condition and interjected his thoughts. "I hate being poor," he was often heard to say. Up to that time, it had been tolerable living by the levee and the tracks. Then the dump came along and, as Tom remarks, "there were no EPA regulations. They hauled old wagons out there and dumped and filed in the holes." The situation brought with it more than just the rats and flies but cockroaches and other pests as well. Tom said the conditions gave him phobias that he suffers from to this day. Bob remembers, "Dick had, or we thought he had, rabies one time from a bite."

As simply as if reading aloud a newspaper, Bob concludes, "We were as deprived as we could be, and then they turned the lot next to us into a dump. It's actually a miracle any of us survived." At no time then did Bob consider they belonged to the very class of people he fought to defend in school. Life was just that way, and Red taught the boys, by his own example, never to complain. If life isn't the way it ought to be, he taught, do something about it. The boys had hands, feet, and minds, he reminded them. Mouths complain, but hands work and minds think.

Tom tried his hand at recycling clear, broken glass from that dump for ten cents a bushel. All the boys were willing to do anything they could to help Red bring money into the house. Later,

Tom followed in his father's footsteps and went into the trucking business and did much better, now owning a large fleet of trucks.

In grade school, Macy says, "I never worried about my grades. In my schools, everyone was from either the wrong side of the tracks or the right side. I was from the wrong side. Some of the students were very, very poor. Some of the kids were very, very rich. They had cars, nice homes their parents owned or rented." With searing honesty, he says, "We hated the rich kids. I remember thinking at times that, if they were rich, they had to be crooks." No one could possibly work harder than his parents, who had so little. If they had more, he reasoned, they must have acquired their belongings in illegal ways. Eventually, he outgrew those feelings, but those feelings gave him a certain focus and determination that remains with him to this day. His heart and his compassion always rest with the hard workers, those who earn what they have from honest means. "I was good at math and at art. I was a pretty good artist. I did both oil paintings and water colors." Throughout his life, Bob excelled at whatever he attempted in order to prove to himself he was capable. And this determination to do well at whatever he tried was the impetus for his successes.

Macy distinctly remembers one day in grade school when the principal gathered all the children to listen to a speech given by President Franklin Delano Roosevelt on December 8, 1941, the day after the bombing of Pearl Harbor. Though only eleven, he remembered vividly the teachers crying as the announcement came over the radio of Roosevelt's declaration of war. The reason for the crying became evident once they explained the men and women who then would be drawn into combat were the same children who sat in the same classrooms just a few years before. The attack on Pearl Harbor changed the lives of everyone in the nation, including those who were not yet old enough to fight. Within a relatively short time after the announcement, the streets of Broad Ripple were devoid of young men, leaving only the too old or the too young. Wives and mothers went to work in the factories in Indianapolis. Red was in the naval reserve and was called up for active duty. A hearing impairment prevented him from active duty. Nonetheless, he volunteered to do as much of his patriotic duty as he could. He was a member of the civil defense for the town. And he worked hard to provide for his family in these very lean war years by working three or four dump trucks, having to use ration cards for gasoline and tires. Still, they barely made ends meet. That is, until his health failed in 1945, leaving him broke, weak, and unable to provide even the bare necessities for his family. Rheumatic fever disabled Red for almost two years and left him permanently weak after he recovered. Desperately struggling to survive, Ethel took a job delivering newspapers while still taking care of Red, bedridden and unable to bring in money. Red and Ethel's patriotism didn't wane a bit during these very hard times. Bob remembers many times his parents inviting uniformed soldiers who had no place to sleep during their layover to stay in their meager house and share their minimal food. More often than not, Bob remembers waking up to a floor full of sleeping soldiers.

As he grew, Bob considered his mother "a saint," knowing even then she had a profound influence on his character. She gave them a certain amount of time to be boys, though the majority of his time was devoted to hard work. Despite the grinding poverty, there was always food on the table. As they grew up, all the boys had jobs, and that made their mother proud. She used to say, "I've got four boys, and there's not a lazy one in the bunch." Their hard work paid off in their later lives, but it also helped while they were still at home. Some of the war years were particularly tough for the family. Bob remembers his mother "would get up, empty Dad's chamber pot, clean him up, clean up in the kitchen," and then fix paper bags containing lunch for the boys. For years, she did that and worked a long paper route. "She'd drive to get the newspapers, load up the vehicle with papers, just absolutely filling up her car. Then she'd drop off the papers for the paper boys and do her own route. After all of that, she'd be back home in time to get us going."

Even with all their troubles, Bob and Tom remember their family refused welfare and his father got mad when people offered it to him. Bob thought his dad might have been "cocky and self-confident," but he understands his father better now than he did then. Still, there is some sadness. "I think he worked himself to death, to tell you the truth." All the boys took after Red in their health issues. Bob has had a lifelong battle with health issues, some even being life threatening early in his life. Tom's health took an early poor turn as he developed rheumatic fever, eventually undercutting his natural athletic abilities. But even during his father's long bouts with illness, Bob continued to learn valuable life lessons from him and his mother as well. Red never let his illness beat him down or cause him to surrender, and Ethel never complained of their lot in life.

High school came, and Bob got a job in the movie theater in the evening hours. "After football practice, I'd go home, change into a white shirt, and literally run down to the theater. That was what I did seven nights a week. On Fridays and Saturdays, I worked more because there were matinees. I'd work 1:30 p.m. until 9:30 or 10:00 at night. Other days, I'd work starting at 5:30 p.m. or so until 10:00 or 10:30 at night." The motivation was simple; he made forty cents an hour.

This job presented Macy with an example he saw as directing his life: Freddie Sorrells, whose father-in-law owned the movie theatre. Freddie was a short WWII veteran who often spoke to school assemblies in order to recruit for the military. Certainly, Sorrells's career in the military attracted Bob's attention. Bob was a lieutenant in the high school ROTC. After one such assembly, Bob approached Freddie, asking for a job, and Freddie hired him as an usher. Macy would get out of school and run to football practice. As soon as practice was over, he'd run home to get his white shirt and then run to the movie theater to work until late at night. Often after his shift, Freddie and his wife took Bob out for a hamburger and a chat. Freddie was a Mustang P-51 pilot who had been shot down three times. It wasn't so much the war stories Freddie told Macy that endeared him to his boss. Instead, it was the lessons about patriotism, perseverance, dedication, and goal setting. Freddie saw beyond Macy's worn attire and lack of social skills into his still developing, but quite noticeable, character. Macy considers Freddie Sorrells, even today, one of his heroes, not so much for his wartime heroics but because he took the time to teach a struggling young man how to stand straight and remain standing straight and true to his values in the face of adversity.

All the boys hustled to bring in some money. Bill sacked groceries. Dick worked in a produce market and then became a fine plumber. Tom worked at the hardware dealer. Whatever they didn't need for their own expenses, they'd pool to help their parents. Bob and Tom both agree they hated the poverty, but that was the situation they lived in at the time. They weren't as concerned of getting out of poverty for themselves as they were for not wanting to raise their children, should they have any, in poverty as they were raised. Their dad always trucked but didn't make much money. But in spite of the poverty and the bouts of illnesses, Red was "incredibly ambitious." Eventually, Red owned five trucks. But his trucking work went in cycles. He went from five trucks down to one truck.

The small and simple house on Ferguson Street provided barely enough room for the six, but there were lessons on life and love enough for all. Bob and his brothers supported their parents through the rough times by bringing home whatever they could earn, and they never resented their parents for not being able to provide more nor did the boys ever ask for more than their parents could provide.

It was in high school that Bob discovered the unanticipated skill on the football field that would, eventually, open the door to higher education. He always knew he would finish high school. Red made it through tenth grade and had to drop out to work to support his family. Requiring the same for his children was not an option. "One thing was a given. My parents stressed that we *were* going to graduate high school—all of us. Dick got his GED after going into the Air Force at sixteen, but the rest of us got through high school." The boys worked their way through Broad Ripple High School. Beyond that, college was not even a fantasy that Bob dwelled upon. No one in his family had ever attended college, and something like that was not even in the realm of a dream for any of the poor Macys.

But then came football. The coach was Ed Dietrich, who asked Bob to try out for the squad. Bob discovered how much he liked football. "I wanted to play. I must say, it gave me a legitimate reason, an opportunity, to knock the heck out of people—rich people," he says, again with crystal-clear honesty. "I told you we lived down by the levee. Some of the rich kids used to taunt the kids who were poorer. As I went along, I got the reputation for sticking up for the little guy in those situations, and I did." Football was part of that. And the rest of his life proved his passion had a strong foundation.

"I played football in the leather helmet days." Under Coach Dietrich's tutelage, Macy played defensive tackle that first year, and, like every other player at that time, he played man-to-man. The game suited Bob physically. "I was as lean as a snake," he recalls. "I got in the habit of running everywhere I went. I'd get up and run in the morning." In her own way, his mother, Ethel, supported Bob's growing love for the game. After those mid-day paper routes getting the newspapers delivered during football season, Ethel "would be back and then head down the road with my sandwich." Running to get to the workout, Bob practiced from two o'clock to five o'clock.

Before long, Coach Dietrich and the boys on the team noticed something special about "Big Macy," as he was called. "In practice, the running backs and tackles would run straight at each other. One reason I did well is that I really liked to take them down!"

Bob remembers, "I think I played defense the whole season that first year. Then, I remember when I was a junior, by golly, I found out I could run. And *they* figured out I could run. They made me fullback and did some switching around at various positions."

Coach Dietrich's play schemes were simple. "To the right, the plays were designed for power. To the left side, the plays were for speed." Big Macy was good at both and they found themselves winning during their second season and Bob's love of football grew.

Bob spent his days running from home to school, back home, to jobs, to practice and, generally, everywhere. All that practice caused him to soar to stardom on the football field and, in the meantime, he tried to refine his skills as a wrestler. He competed in both track and field events, doing well in high jump and shot put and running the 440-yard dash. Again, he was proving to himself he could be the best. Soon enough, Macy was going to prove to the world he could be the best at whatever he tried.

As Bob earned the name of "Big Macy," his little brother, Tom, proudly carried the name of "Little Macy."

"Tom made me proud because he was proud to be called 'Little Macy.' He had rheumatic fever and lupus growing up yet he was still a great athlete. He played baseball until he was older and even played in the semi-professional Industrial League Baseball. Those were sponsored teams, where they had uniforms."

As tough as Bob was Tom was, in some ways, the toughest. "Sometimes he would kick butt. The expression we had was, 'Tom? Tom lives on Tough Street. The farther you go, the tougher it gets, and he lives in the last house.'" Nonetheless, they did all they could to help out around the house. They spent some of their time in the woods shooting squirrels, skinning them, cooking them, and then eating them. "We ate squirrels and rabbits all the time," Bob adds. "If you could kill a squirrel, you wouldn't have to eat the family's chicken, and that helped out the family."

As the high school years passed, Bob hired out as a farmhand working on the land in the country. Tom, born in 1936, liked hanging out with Big Macy and went to work with him often. Bob and Tom worked on their uncles' farms every summer, making $10 or $15 a week, though they might save only $50 for the entire summer.

Even in the midst of the hard labor, Bob's artistic bent continued. He did a painting of one of the barns, a piece his sister-in-law, Sylvia, still has. Before long, Bob was alternating "vacation" hitches at the properties of two uncles, Herbert Macy and Harry Richardson, who was married to Red's sister, Oneta.

Uncle Herbert, Red's older brother born in 1902, was a sharecropper, Bob remembers. He has some distinctive memories of the work he did for Herbert and his wife. In the summer of 1947, Bob, working at the farm, tried to help his uncle shoe a horse. Tom, as usual, was there to help Bob and Uncle Herbert shoe that large horse. Tom was holding the twitch on the horse's lip to keep him still when, all of a sudden, the horse reared up. Tom, all of about ninety pounds, went airborne and landed in a lump several feet away. Tom got right back up, and they continued shoeing that big horse. Nonetheless, Tom was certainly "Little Macy."

Uncle Herbert would try almost anything—and make the boys help. He'd castrate an animal and then dab a little bit of tar on the poor animal's incision. After the castration, the boys watched as the horse ran into the fields moving from horse to horse. According to Herbert, "He's out cancelling his dates."

They also worked at properties owned by Uncle Harry and Aunt Nita, first at Greenfield and then at Dublin. Bob recalls that life wasn't too pleasant at Harry's place. "Aunt Nita, truth be told," Bob confides as if they were listening, "did most of the work." Bob adds it was all right for most of the time, but his uncle's sloth and laziness meant he and anyone else on the premises had to do a lot of the work there.

Time passed slowly as they worked, pumping water into a hog tank, milking the cows, and putting the milk into fifty-gallon cans so a truck could pick them up. Daylight came in the summer as early as 5:30 a.m., and then sunlight lasted for fourteen hours.

Tom recalls, "We worked like the dickens six days a week. On Sundays, there was only a little let up, as Bob had to mow on that day. Our uncle would lay around the house on Sundays. Before too long, I got tired of that and went to work delivering newspapers." In spite of all the laziness of his uncle, both sets of uncles and their wives were good enough farmers to make a living, especially with young hands around to do the lion's share of the work. But Bob never complained. He was used to hard work.

Bob began to ride a horse named Scout at Uncle Herbert's place, which was four or five miles from Red and Ethel's place. Bob still has exceptionally fond memories of Scout, and working from horseback grabbed him right away. Soon, he discovered his remarkable affinity for horses. That affinity landed him a job working after high school graduation at the Trader's Point Horse Club, where he found himself drawn even deeper into a lifelong passion for horses.

On a practical level, it wasn't hard for the lad to figure out that the money earned through all his hard work those late years in high school helped his family. It also meant there was one less mouth to feed when he was away.

Bob was hitting his stride, growing into manhood even as he harbored doubts—"an inferiority complex" he calls it now, about his abilities, one of the reasons he tried until he excelled. But Sylvia, Bob's sister-in-law who married Bill in 1949, says Bob was already a notable personality by the time she entered the family. At the time of this writing, she mentioned to me, "I thought Bob was good looking when I met him. I thought he looked like Rock Hudson." During that conversation, she kidded Bob to his face. "All the girls were in love with you." Bob scoffs at that and says he didn't think he was either popular or handsome in high school. Remembering those years, all he did, he says, was work and play football. But Sylvia insisted as she told me, "He *was* good looking." Sylvia and Bill would have celebrated their sixtieth anniversary in 2009, but he passed away in 2004. Today, she is characterized as the matriarch of the extended Macy family.

There is no doubt Bob Macy was extremely attached to his family, and they relied on him as much as he relied on them. Most young men in his situation would have wanted desperately to get away from the terrible conditions. But that wasn't part of Bob's thinking. As long as the family needed him there, he was willing to stay and help out.

When not wrapped up in sports or summer work, he spent all his free time with his family. For all the family's poverty, Tom and Bob say they got some peace and quiet at home because their family owned two lots, providing some space between their house and the neighbor's house. The neighbor used to wake them up pretty early because he had a sawmill powered by the rear wheels of his car and chow dogs that were not the least bit friendly.

Bob said he and his brothers were close in most ways. He remembered an incident when "Bill got mad at a guy down the way." That fellow owned a grey 1940 Chevy two-door coupe. Bill had an old Chevy of his own, one that he bought and fixed up with wheel covers from money he made plumbing. One day, the neighbor ran into the back of Bill's car as Bill was driving down the road with a carload of family members. Bill was so mad he went after the guy with a 2x4. Bob was also mad and joined in as Bill "explained" the situation to the other driver. Part of the reason they were so upset, as they told the guy, was because of Bill's wife, Sylvia, who was pregnant and in the back seat. Bob says, "It worked out, but we scared the heck out of the guy." He sardonically adds, "Bill loved cars and took good care of them. He liked to race a little." Maybe that, along with an inherited trait from Red, had a little something to do with Bill's anger.

Looking back to 1948, the year of his graduation, Bob insists today that he expected to work hard and eventually settle down in the same area as his parents. Red and Ethel lived in the same house on Ferguson Street until he died of emphysema in 1965, less than fifty miles from the farm where he was raised. Bob expected to do the same. That's usually what was done in those days with just a high school education. With all the soldiers returning and getting a college education, prospects for a poor farm boy were limited. "I never dreamed of going to college. It was simply beyond me. I thought it's not going to happen."

The summer after his senior year, he took a job building burial vaults. He was, even then, still working for Uncle Herbert. Bob was making pretty good money, but "I didn't have anything to look forward to but building a burial vault." Still, he tried looking to the future.

Based on Bill's success, "I thought plumbing might be a good living. But then, I also saw Dick doing well in the Air Force, so that might be a possibility." When not at the farm or Herbert's, Bob worked, shoveling sand and concrete into those forms to make the burial vaults and was making some pretty good money. He earned $40 a week for a sixty-hour week, in those days a pretty good sum for a man his age. His athletic ability landed him a spot on the semi-pro team in the Indianapolis Industrial League. "I didn't make any money, but I sure enjoyed it." Then, on top of everything else, he got a job at a lumberyard "and thought I was doing pretty good."

Before long, a whole year passed. Bob was out of high school but not in college, still mulling over what job or jobs he might do to make a living and get a little ahead in the world.

But the truth is that, when football season rolled around, everything changed for Bob Macy. It took some prodding from friends and a girl he cared about to convince him of that.

Up at Earlham College, a small Quaker school, in Richmond, Indiana, "there was a guy I'd played with in high school. His name was Vern Porter." Porter and Pappy Wann, one of his former teachers, told Bob's brother, Tom, that Bob should go to Earlham and try out for the football team. He remembers fondly, "It was the most unbelievable thing to me, to be contacted about playing football some more, and in college! All my life, I had been feared and tormented by kids who had more. I was working five or six jobs to make ends meet at that point. It was August 1949."

Adding to the mix of issues and motivations, Macy says, "About that same time, I was pretty fond of a girl named Clare Hannah. She was one year older than me. She believed in me and said I had too much talent to let it go to waste. She said, 'You need to go to college.'"

With Tom echoing what he'd heard from Clare, Pappy, and Vern, Bob decided beyond the horizon looked brighter than the horizon itself. Having thought it over and reached a point where he was willing to explore what Earlham might hold for him, Bob jumped into Vern Porter's car, and the two of them rode to Earlham. And what was beyond the horizon changed his life.

CHAPTER 3

Learning How to Live: The Earlham Years

"Guarded well by elms and maples, shrined in every heart, our beloved alma mater, Earlham fair thou art." - Earlham College

Earlham College was a nationally recognized Quaker liberal arts institution that followed, and still follows, the principles of equality, nonviolence, and social justice. At the time of his visit, Bob Macy had little idea how much of a role Earlham and those principles would play in molding him into the man he was to become, building upon what he learned from his father and his youthful environment.

It was mid-September 1949. Upon arriving at Earlham, Bob paused for a moment to take in the breathtaking beauty of the trees and foliage on campus. The campus was nestled among 320 acres of grand landscaping. The leaves were beginning to change with blazing red, orange, and green, and this was the kind of sight Bob's eyes had never seen. Even if he had seen this picturesque sight before, he hadn't had time to take in its beauty. At the center of the campus was "the heart"—where tables and seats had been set up for the new student enrollment with undergraduates assigned there to assist the new students in picking out their classes. Macy remembers, "I was amazed at the friendliness of everyone there." It seemed to him that no one knew he was poor or didn't care, even though the only pair of jeans he owned were tattered and worn.

Vern was a returning football player, and Bob had never even seen the campus. As they approached the athletic department, a silver-haired gentleman intercepted them, asking if he could help them. They said they were looking for the football coach. The distinguished looking gentleman smiled, introduced himself as Dr. Merle Rousey, the athletic director, and pointed to the nearby coach's building. He walked to the door, opened it, and said, "You've come to the right place. Come on inside."

Rousey asked Vern his name, recognized it on the list, checked it off, and turned to Macy. "And who are you?"

"I'm Macy, sir."

"I don't see your name on the list. What's your status?"

"I didn't go to college last year, but I heard you were looking for football players. I would like a chance to try out." Macy went on to explain he played fullback at his high school and was a leading ground gainer. At that, Rousey perked up a bit. Rousey explained he was newly hired at the school but had suffered a terrible losing season the year before. In fact, the school lost every game. He was desperate to turn this next season around. Porter and Rousey talked for a bit about Macy's talent outside of Macy's earshot. After a couple of minutes, Rousey approached Bob with a question.

"How fast do you run the hundred-yard dash?"

"I have no idea."

"Pick out a pair of shoes, and let's see what you can do."

Bob ran the hundred-yard dash in 10.7 seconds, quite respectable in those days, and that started Bob Macy's college career.

That evening, the boys were invited to dinner at Rousey's house. Rousey was dressed in slacks and a sports coat, and Bob had the only pair of jeans he owned, a worn-out shirt, and a pair of boots almost as bad. In spite of how he looked, Rousey was willing to give young Macy a try. He offered him a four-year education and a scholarship to front the money to pay for school. In return, Macy had to commit to playing for the team, keeping his grades up, and working forty hours a week for the school, none of which seemed too much of a promise for Macy to make.

Macy's transformation from a young, hardworking man to a college freshman was rapid. "I checked it out and decided Earlham was a fit for me; rather, I was a fit for Earlham. I turned around and went home to get my clothes and other essentials on a Friday, and I was back at school on Monday ready to start."

On the trip back home, the boys hardly spoke a word until the excitement sank in. Vern slapped Macy on the leg and exclaimed, "By God, you did it!" No one from the Macy family had ever been to college, and the excitement wasn't spared on his parents. They couldn't believe Bob was actually going to college. Neither could he, and he wanted to get back to Earlham as quickly as he could, just in case this really was a dream. His family gathered up his clothes and a little bit of money they could spare and, by Monday, Macy's college adventure was about to start.

After the whirlwind enrollment, new students began their Earlham journey with an assigned room. Bob's new home was in the male dormitory, Bundy Hall. At one end were six lavatories and the showers. To his amazement, he'd "never been in a house with running water and an indoor toilet before." As he walked into his new residence, he noticed that the dorm room was organized into three sections. The middle room had doors leading to the other rooms and was the one with the least privacy. He recalled with that same sense of amazement, "I'd never not had to share a room with anyone before."

To each side, right and left, were private areas that were clean and neat, each equipped with its own bed, dresser, closet, desk, and lamp for studying. The laundry and room-cleaning services, provided once a week by students who took school jobs to assist in paying their tuition, were free for all students. Macy had never seen anything like the accommodations before. He had a room to himself, a chair that was all his to use, and laundry picked up and dropped off at his dorm.

Earlham also provided meals at the cafeteria. It had its own dairy and farmland rich with vegetables, beef, pork, and chicken when needed. "I could eat as much food and drink as much milk as I wanted!" Bob recalls, now smiling. "I think I gained fifteen pounds before the start of the football season." The job assigned to Bob during enrollment was at the milking parlor, a job not entirely new to him.

Shortly after the room assignments were made, Macy met his first roommate. "My first roomie," Macy tells, "was a junior named Byron 'Barney' Shelton. He was my exact opposite. He was not athletic and was built like a skeleton. But he was one of the finest, brightest men I have ever known."

Before long, Barney told Macy of a conversation he heard between two students. One said, "That Macy sure has a chip on his shoulder." The other replied, "Yeah, but he's a heck of a football player." Macy asked Shelton how he should take the conversation. Shelton told him to take it as a compliment. "There aren't that many good football players," he added. The chip on Macy's shoulder was nothing more than his "inferiority complex" at not being accepted, but he knew, deep down, he could make good at Earlham.

Not long after getting settled, it was time for football. The players met on Comsteck Field, the practice area for the team. It was a mixed group, at best. There were approximately thirty-three players, ranging widely in age and in experience. In September 1949, in the aftermath of the post world war military discharge and prior to the Korean Conflict, many of the players at Earlham were older fellows, military veterans with football experience. The rest of the prospects were young men like Macy, straight out of high school. Their coach, Don Comley, was a former professional football lineman who totally intimidated his young charges.

One thing caught Macy's attention immediately. "I realized for the first time that a substantial number of the players were black." It hit Macy that he had never, ever, competed or played alongside a black man. Earlham was liberal in that sense. "The school recruited blacks, and the fellows they got were stellar," Macy says. He notes, "Earlham was a good preparation for life." Years later, when he worked with some of the first blacks on the Oklahoma City Police Department, he had positive personal experience from Earlham he could draw from.

"About half the guys on the team were black. And when I started to play in the backfield, all the other three guys in the backfield were black. They were all fine men."

Macy remembers, "I got to know the guys when I played football. Thurman Washington, the quarterback, got a degree in accounting and was one of the toughest men I ever knew. Bob (Bobby) Ewing was the left halfback. After college, he had the chance to be the first black guy to go to Indiana trooper school. He did something else, though. The right halfback was George Cooper."

The first few practices were different from his high school practices, to say the least. The older players tended to be lethargic, while the younger ones were full of fire. That led to some interesting on-field confrontations.

The team captain in 1949 was an older veteran named Dick Pollen. He was "big, bad, and lazy," Macy remembers. During an early practice, Pollen was on the line across from a young fireball named George Oberle. The ball was snapped, and Oberle laid a mighty blow on the older man.

Pollen started at Oberle for a little bit and then said, "Boy, save that stuff for Saturday."

Oberle retorted, "What's the matter? Can't you take it?" The next snap, Oberle again laid a hard lick on Pollen.

This time Pollen shouted, "Boy, save that stuff for Saturday!" Oberle just grinned. That set something off. Pollen uncoiled, knocked Oberle flat on his back, stood over him glaring, and said, "Boy, I told you. Save it for Saturday!" That ended that confrontation and made the point clear. This was going to be a group of men who worked together as a team.

The first season, Macy earned his way onto the first string as a fullback in the backfield. He was the one white guy in that speedy and effective quartet. Washington was the quarterback, Cooper on the right, Ewing on the left.

Macy laughs as he tells this story. He says he came to know the men on the team, both black and white, when "someone once told me that black men were my inferior. I retorted that they were smarter than me in class, could kick my butt on the field, and were the darlings of the parties. I was only a wallflower, so if they are inferior, then I'm in a heck of a mess."

In those first two seasons of football at Earlham, "in some towns, we found out they wouldn't serve the black players when we stopped to eat. When that happened, we'd just go on down the road. That was Indiana in 1949. We never really talked about this, but we never hesitated. We'd just go somewhere else to eat."

Earlham developed a good offensive line, and, as competition began, they racked up some high scores. The team played its heart out and, as Macy puts it, "won nearly half of the games," and they worked as a team. Macy, Cooper, Washington, and Ewing all had especially good seasons. Macy remembers, "There was nothing quite like being a football star at a small college. It gave you the opportunity to be, and feel like, a leader, a star. At least, that was the case every Saturday."

He also recalls, "We had good crowds at our games. Most of those away games, with only a couple of exceptions, were within driving distance. I remember, too, we had a good cheerleading squad."

Long before the anti-tobacco consensus formed in America, Macy recalls, "Playing football, and the coach's influence, kept me away from tobacco. I wanted to do well, and I didn't want anything to hold me back." Even long before Coach Comley, Macy had the determination to be the best he could be. It was a good winning stretch in the young man's life. "Earlham had lost every game the year before I got there. It was so special to play on a team at a small school. I enjoyed it so much. It was, you could say, the right time for Earlham and for me, too."

While at Earlham that first year, Big Macy wrote several letters home to his folks and went back home a few times to visit, always sleeping on the floor when he got there. His mom always wrote back, but his dad was often too sick to do much writing. But there were times both his mother and father came to watch him play football.

Following the first football season, Earlham comptroller Paul Furnace called Macy into his office. Bob learned that Furnas not only was the school's financial advisor but also that he owned twenty-seven Morgan horses. He kept the magnificent creatures on campus for equestrian studies and, in their conversation, he inquired about Macy's experience with horses. After a lengthy chat, Furnace told Macy he was aware of the young man's financial situation, so he offered him the responsibility of operating the stable. Bob gleefully remembers today, "I thought I'd died and gone to heaven!" Not only was he playing football for a college he already loved, but he was also offered a job satisfying his second love, the one he had developed while working for his uncles, that of taking care of horses.

Macy confesses, "Somebody once asked me, years later, if it was okay for me to have that job and play football. Well, I can't conceive of a bunch of Quakers like that not doing something totally legal."

During the first semester, Bob made extra money by picking corn that fell from the corn wagon in the fields. He was able to sell half of it back to the farmer for extra cash for clothing and necessities. But the job offered by Furnace actually allowed Bob to start repaying his school expenses.

Macy was soon in charge of the Morgans, three stallions and several geldings and mares. Morgan horses were developed and nurtured in American colonial days because they were good utility horses, big enough for farming but small enough for surrey.

When Macy started, the youngest stud, called Robin Hood of Earlham, was five years old, a deep chestnut color with a white blaze on his forehead. He was a magnificent animal that the school displayed whenever possible. But all of the stallions and some of the mares were high-strung and ridden, at first, by no one but Macy. He rode English tack, which made it an easy task for the horses to buck him off. Consequently, he tried to break the young colts with minimum bucking and in a method suited to their disposition.

In early interviews for this book, as Macy described the ways he tried to "gentle break" the horses, I asked if the technique he used to train these colts was similar to what is now known as "horse whispering."

He answered, "We didn't call it that, but I guess it was." He used touch, soft talk, and eye contact with them. "Let me tell you about that. I worked at a riding stable with hunters and jumpers. I learned I was good with horses. I've always been good with them. I had worked with horses in steeple chase and fox hunting situations at the club, became good at training the horses, and then came my opportunity at Earlham."

Later in that first school year, a farmer whose property was near to Earlham offered Macy the use of two jumping horses. In addition to exhibitions, the young scholar used them to teach jumping classes.

Macy was in his element. He spent as much time as possible with the colts during winter months and, in the spring, got the horses ready for the classes. Spring activities involved not just the horses; Bob also ran track. In field events, he participated in the high jump.

His best jump of five feet and six inches was not enough to win at the big meets but was better than some competing jumpers from other schools. In other events, "I was decent. I could run the 220 or the 440 and was fast at each. I could do the 880 if they really needed me but only if I had to! The truth is I was extremely fast the first fifty yards, and then I would start slowing down considerably." The first fifty yards made him tremendous on the football field.

That first year brought many interesting people, men and women, into Bob's life. He later described them as "wonderful human beings." One was Dorothy Perkins, whose father owned a large ranch in Elk County, Kansas, and the hardware store in Howard, the town closest to the ranch. She invited Bob out to her father's ranch that first summer. But before he could go, Bob had to have medical treatment, repair for an abdominal hernia. It had been smarting for years, and he finally could no longer ignore it. It was the first of many nagging health challenges Big Macy would have to face as the years passed.

The summer in Kansas was a joy for Bob. He spent the entire time there working on the ranch, falling in love with the land and the rural world the longer he stayed. But, as much as he loved Earlham, he dreaded returning in the fall. The Perkins' were wonderful people and outstanding in their community, and they treated him with respect and kindness. For perhaps the first time ever, Macy felt he was really where he should be. He knew, however, his time at Earlham was not over. He was still full of passion for playing football and, even more, learning. The opportunities at school were undeniable, and he returned to college.

For his second year at campus, he moved out of the dorm and into the Earlham farmhouse, where he could be closer to the animals in his care. Bob loved living in the horse barn, waking up to the smell of fresh hay and horse flesh and the sounds of the horses rustling around in their stalls in the morning. Getting up to feed them was less a chore and more a fulfillment of love. Each horse would hang its head over the stall gate and look in the direction of the feed door, waiting for Bob's appearance. Occasionally, they would whinny or snort when he appeared.

Bob had to arise at four thirty to begin the day by feeding the horses and then head out to classes until two o'clock. After class, he had to get seven to nine horses ready for riding lessons then brush and feed all of them prior to going to his room to study.

He also had thirty-seven head of Holstein cattle to milk daily, but he recruited his pals, Murray Mills, Bill Loucks, and Bob Fowler, all football players, as farmhands to help with the cattle chores. The winter, especially, at the Earlham farmhouse was hard work for Macy and the boys. The Holstein cows were large and unwilling to participate in the daily milking ritual without protest. The cows were not stupid. They soon learned to hook their feet across the straps that held them and kick the milk cans across the barn. The winter weather dried out and cracked their teats and the milking machine irritated them that much more. But this was a very responsible task. Earlham College took the milk, pasteurized it, and processed it into ice cream, cottage cheese, and milk for the student body. The program of providing the food for the students worked very well, at least for the tall and lanky Macy. When he arrived at Earlham, he was 185 pounds. By the time he was a junior, he weighed 215 but still retained his speed on the field.

To make class on time, the foursome would get up at four in the morning to begin their rather daunting routine of feeding horses, milking cows, finding time for a shower before classes, getting to school on time, and, after all that, practicing for the sports they played. As busy as they were, the men had time to become close friends and associates. Even their families became close. Loucks and Fowler had parents who were on the board of directors of the college, Mills' parents owned Maple Hurst Dairy, and Red Macy drove a truck. In spite of their obvious differences, Bob Fowler and Red Macy sat together at the home football games.

Murray Mills was another one of Macy's roommates, a man who was athletic, well dressed, and well liked. Bob remembers, "I spent one summer vacation with Murray and his family on a thousand-acre dairy farm in Indianapolis, a place called the Maple Hurst Dairy. Murray had three brothers, Morris, Howard, and Amos, and one sister, Helen. His mom and dad, Bernice and Howard, Sr., were the hardest-working people I had ever known. Bernice would be out late every night, holding eggs up to the light to make sure they were good."

Loucks was from New Jersey. He was slender, tall, around six feet, five inches. "If he had money, he sure did not flaunt it," Macy recalls. "He made one fine athlete at Earlham, playing football, baseball, and basketball. Bill made all-conference in football two years in a row." Macy continued, "Bill was in love with Betty Hunter almost from the moment he met her at Earlham. They were college sweethearts all the way through until graduation." Bob attended their wedding.

Fowler invited Macy to spend a couple of spring breaks on his Athens, Georgia, "plantation," as he called it. He had four brothers, and the five boys averaged six foot, five inches tall. Two of them attended Earlham, along with their older brother. One of their siblings, Jim, was a naturalist who later gained national recognition during his many years on *The Wild Kingdom* television program hosted by Marlin Perkins.

Macy remembers one evening at the Fowler home. At supper, "everyone was holding hands while saying grace. That was new to me. I got enough nerve to ask Jim about that later."

Jim said, "There is no religious significance to it, really. It's just the old man wants to give everyone an equal break." The idea amazed Bob, joining hands, saying prayers, and sharing equally. Up to that point, Macy hadn't been exposed to very much religious practice. He had an innate sense of right and wrong and lived according to that, but his family never had much opportunity to attend a church. But, as with anything new, Macy's curiosity kicked in.

But the world he was so familiar with called again the end of his second year, and Macy and another college friend, Earl Hancock, drove to Howard, Kansas, where Macy had spent the summer before. There, they rented a truck and made money all summer hauling hay. They used any free time they had to ride horses and, as Bob puts it, "playing cowboy."

In the spring of 1950, Macy applied for a student military deferment so he could finish college. Somehow, the deferment card was lost in the mail, so Bob stayed in Kansas and enrolled at a local school, the College of Emporia. He soon found out, however, he could not play football there because of his status as a transfer student from Earlham. By this time, though, football was in Macy's blood, so he arranged to practice with the Emporia varsity every afternoon.

As he had the summer before with the Perkins family and at Earlham, Macy found an agricultural work that he loved. Every morning, he awoke at 4:00 a.m. to feed five hundred cattle before heading to the Emporia campus for classes. By this time in his college career, Bob started to see his horizons open for him. Prior to college, he planned on being satisfied with his lot in life, a carpenter, a plumber, a truck driver. But now, he started to dream about what lay beyond the horizon. He even envisioned himself owning a large cattle ranch or a massive horse stable. Earlham had taught him not just about how to make a living but how to live life.

Though he tried to save money that summer, it wasn't enough to finance his return to Earlham. During that summer, he became friendly with the banker in Howard, Cap Morss. The two met for coffee several times and chatted but had never done any business. But now times were desperate, and Macy went to the bank to see Morss. "I need a favor," he told Morss. "I need $500 to pay for getting back to school. I have no collateral, but I'll work hard to pay you back."

Morss must have seen something special in the young man. Macy says the old banker looked at him and said, "I've learned that a man with collateral is no better or worse than a man without collateral. I trust you." Morss loaned him the $500. "I never forgot what he said. I worked hard, and I paid him back before the next semester was over." The real question was whether Macy learned honesty and trustworthiness from Morss or the other way around.

Macy rode the train back to Earlham to prepare for the next semester and to start his work at Earlham's barn again. Enrolling for a new semester, he picked up where he left off, back to feeding the cows, taking care of the horses, and participating in athletics.

"In three of the four years at Earlham, I ran the stables and took care of the horses. I had to feed and water them twice a day and brush and clean them up when we rode or used them. I was busy all the time; I saddled and got the horses ready to go for the riding classes. I'd race over to the football field during the season and then back there to unsaddle the horses."

"The winter weather was memorable," Macy recalls in an understatement. "I remember a couple of the winters the snows came at Thanksgiving, and the snow was still on the ground in February. One year, the snow was so bad that those who had gone to their homes could not get back to campus for many days. Sometimes in January, the snow was twelve inches deep, with drifts higher than your head! I stuck around most of the winter breaks like Christmas. They took care of us on campus, and sometimes I went to people's homes for holiday meals. Well, it was about two and a half miles to the riding stables from the campus. There were times in those winters that the snow was so deep that it took all afternoon to get there, do the work, and return to campus."

Hanging around the cold weather helped Macy forge some other good memories of less-than-stellar athletic prowess. "In the winter, sometimes members of the basketball team would be away due to the holidays. We had only a few players, and I got some extra playing time. I was not very good, but I got a lot of playing time simply because they needed me."

He remembers "a game where we got a good lead but didn't have enough players. So the coach had us running the figure eight endlessly—that's where you cross and trade off the ball—to try to wind down the clock! Well, the coach finally called out to, 'Give Macy the ball.' Then, I got the pass; I took the shot and made it. The joke was I had the best percentage of shots of anyone on the team. I made 100 percent of my shots that game. Of course, I attempted only one shot."

After his return from Emporia, Earlham's football team emerged as a new powerhouse in regional small college ranks. Fowler, Loucks, and Dudley Moore made all-conference. New quarterback Bill Cope was named the outstanding small college quarterback in the country. And the team grew in stature, experience, and teamwork, all traits that impacted Macy then and in later life.

Macy recollects, "Loucks and Moore were receivers. They could catch anything that got within twenty yards of them. Cope was a scrambler and a little guy. It was my job to keep tacklers from catching Cope so he could throw his pass. I really like my job," Macy adds with a mischievous look in his eyes. "I really liked knocking opponents flat on their rear." Earlham was in the Hoosier College Conference, a gathering of schools of roughly the same size as Earlham's "Fighting Quakers." In 1952 and 1953, they performed very well. In those latter campaigns, Bob Meyne was the coach, while Merle Rousey continued as the athletic director.

In some ways, the game went through some changes while Macy competed. "When I first started, we used the platoon system and fielded the team in groups to allow time to rest. Then, in those last two years I played, a limited substitution rule came along." That rule limited the substitutions to four players at a time. "After that,"

Macy remembers, "there were several of us who played both ways for most of the game. I was on offense but played defense quite a bit, too."

There was one game that stands out in Macy's memory some sixty years later. The game was against Anderson College. He tells the story this way.

"We had an important game against Anderson, just a short time after we learned the coach's daughter had been exposed to polio after babysitting Mr. Rousey's daughter. Meyne was petrified with fear for his daughter. He was really torn up about it. I had never seen anything quite like it and wouldn't have such feeling myself until I became a father years later."

Macy continues, "Coach called us together and he said, 'Boys, I can't really be of any help to you today. My heart and my mind aren't here right now.' Well, we got well behind in the game. It was twenty to six in the third quarter. So he called for a timeout, and we all jogged to the sidelines. He was sad, and all he said was, 'Boys, I'm sorry. If you're going to win the game, you'll have to do it yourselves.'"

It was one of those moments, and now Bob Macy was living it. "It was the darndest thing. We all looked at each other. Somebody said, 'Let's just do it.' Two or three plays later, we scored. Then, on defense, Anderson's first or second play from scrimmage, Bill Loucks intercepted an Anderson pass and darn if he didn't run it for another touchdown. We made the two-point conversion, and the score was tied." The seemingly impossible now seemed possible, and with that momentum, perhaps inevitable. "In the huddle, after that, there wasn't a word. Nobody was talking. We scored again and won the game by eight points. It was truly amazing."

Another teammate on that good Earlham squad was John East, a strong, tall and lanky player who also saw a lot of playing time, primarily at offensive tackle. East was a natural leader, albeit with a highly intellectual bent, who later served in the U.S. Marine Corps before being stricken with polio a few years before the vaccine became widely available. Confined to a wheelchair for the remainder of his life, he went on to become a respected writer and professor at East Carolina University and served one term as a U.S. senator from North Carolina. Friends dubbed him "Helms on wheels," a tribute to the state's long-serving Jesse Helms.

Macy recalls both East and Priscilla, known as Sis and later John's wife, with particular fondness. Sis told him in one memorable conversation, "Bob, you could have dated any woman at Earlham."

Macy, though, remembers. "I didn't have time to chase any girls. I spent most of my time taking care of horses. Other than that, it was study and football." Still, the inferiority complex prevented him from asking many girls for dates. He was afraid of being rejected. But that didn't keep him from falling in love at least twice a month with some beautiful, young coed. He never had enough money to take a girl to the movies in town or to dinner. About the best he could do was to take her to the horse barn and show her the horses. Bob continues to reflect, "It was a good time in my life. I fell in and out of love once a month, it seemed. I had girls I dated, and then there were girls who were just my friends. I came to respect them all."

He developed a close friendship with one girl in particular. "One girl who became a dear friend was Susie Long. She was a Jewish girl, one of the cheerleaders." Bob laments that they probably loved one another back then, but he was too afraid of rejection to really even ask her out, and they were "too stupid" to know it. Years later in 2001, when he returned to Earlham College for a reunion, he remembers hearing a woman call out across the room, "Where's ole blue eyes?" And he said seeing Susie again after all those years was certainly a time to warm an old man's heart. From the interviews gathered for this book, it's apparent Bob would not have had to do any chasing. All he would have had to have done was stand still long enough for one of the girls to chase him.

Reflecting back on his time there, Macy claims it was an idyllic life in some ways. "Living on campus was like being in another world. Our laundry was done as part of the living arrangement on campus. They gave us three wonderful meals every single day. All of our real needs were provided or fulfilled. On dates, there was not a lot to do because most of the students did not have their own cars or did not drive them. There weren't many vehicles on campus." Entertainment was what you made for yourself. "You could go to the library on campus to read together or talk quietly. There was a telescope to look through, and that was pleasant at night."

Earlham wasn't a monastery, of course. And Bob Macy wasn't a monk totally sequestered in his cell. "Right next to the campus, there was a huge cemetery. Between the campus and the cemetery, there were double and triple rows of trees. That was a place where some of the girls and boys would go to kiss. If you weren't careful walking along that row, you might step on somebody! The tombstones and graves were so big that it was a place you could sit down and smooch or hold hands.

"There was a movie theater in Richmond, and you could walk there from campus. There was no smoking on campus, except in certain areas of the student union or in your car. And there was no drinking. They were strict on that. You could get kicked out of school."

Not all the athletic glory came on the gridiron. Macy tells this story. "I wrestled as well, and I was pretty good at that. My normal weight was 215 pounds, but I wrestled as low as 191 pounds. In 1952, I came in second in the Hoosier Conference. The only reason I didn't win that year was because I had taken off too much weight, five or six pounds, and it made me too weak. I was good enough in wrestling those last two years that I went to the Olympic tryouts in Chicago." Once again, Big Bob excelled at anything he attempted. And just for fun, in college intramurals, he also played some slow and fast pitch softball.

Just about everything at Earlham impressed the young man. "I'll tell you that it took a lot of people to run that campus. When it closed down, it didn't really close down. They had farms for dairy, beef, pork, chickens. No matter what went on at campus, somebody took care of the livestock. As for the horses, even though they were able to run in the pastures in the summer, they were taken care of as well." There was little need for anyone to leave campus; it was almost completely self-contained and supported.

It was different from anything he had experienced growing up yet it was affirming. "Most of our competition was right there in Indiana. On the team and at school, we had a carryover of the same moral values I'd gotten at home. There was no smoking or drinking, except smoking was allowed in certain places in the student union. The school had very high morals and ethics.

Earlham truly reinforced what it meant to live a meaningful life."

As the years at Earlham rolled by, Macy became more involved in college affairs. He served on the Bundy Council, Ionian Literary Society, joined the Letterman's Club and, in another formative experience, helped build and then attend services at the Quaker meeting house. Prior to Earlham, Macy had not been active in any church functions or services. That spark of religious interest at the dinner table grew into a great desire to know God and to serve man in a godly way. He took a degree in religious studies and threw himself into local church activities that have remained a habit with him still.

His mother and father rarely had time or energy enough to keep bread on the table, much less to attend church. Nonetheless, they instilled in him and his brothers certain moral and ethical beliefs. "The right thing to do" was ingrained from his early childhood. But in 1950, the Earlham community built a Quaker meeting house. Local contractors and citizens, including Macy and his schoolmates, helped with the labor. After finishing the project, Macy joined the church and attended regularly, thus giving him the church structure he enjoyed for the rest of his life.

The Quaker church, as Macy came to know it, was a diverse denomination. On the one hand, business and community leaders attended services similar to what could be found in any denomination. On the other extreme, many of the Quaker meetings did not have a minister, but services and business matters of the congregation were handled by a clerk. Quaker churches were built with facing benches so that everyone in a service faced the center. There were no rituals. Once the meeting started, anyone could take the floor and speak his mind on any matter. One might read from Scripture, another sing a hymn, while still another might call attention to a sick member who could not gather his own crops. Often, the prayers were said in each person's heart in total silence. After a true Quaker meeting, Macy says today, "There could be no question that the Lord was present." Many of the members were biblical scholars and professors at Earlham.

One aspect of the Quaker religion that fascinated Macy was known as "the inner light." This was the belief that in the heart of every man there burns an inner light that is good and that the solemn duty of every man is to bring forth that light. In retrospect, it is easy to see why "the inner light" belief so intrigued Macy. All his life, he sought to bring forth his "inner light" that so directed his thinking and actions innately. His passion for doing right, one might suggest, was fed from these early Quaker beliefs. Ultimately, he came under the mentorship of D. Elton Trueblood.

Trueblood was a prolific writer and an outstanding speaker and lecturer. He was also Macy's personal advisor. On several occasions, Macy drove Dr. Trueblood to other college campuses to speak. The two of them kept in close contact over the years after Macy's departure from Earlham.

Macy says he learned valuable lessons on speaking and the need to speak to others from Dr. Trueblood. When speaking at other campuses, Trueblood would arrive two hours early and stop at the student union. There, he would intermingle with the students and, in a matter of a few minutes, they would talk with him freely. Then, Trueblood would find a private place to organize his thoughts and prepare his speech. The students, Macy recalls, were mesmerized by this man from out of town who came in and spoke directly to their hearts. This was, to the younger man, a valuable lesson that he reflected on and used in later years. Speaking to the hearts of his listeners became a pivotal trademark in Macy's later speeches.

Perhaps more in academics than anything else, Macy matured. "I did well in science, had to take geology and found myself fascinated by it. My other interest became philosophy, or philosophy of religion. I didn't decide until I was a junior on my majors. I took fifteen hours a semester of classes. The whole situation at Earlham was divine intervention in my life." In fact, religion turned out to be one of Bob's majors. At Earlham, all freshmen had to take a particular battery of courses, one of which was Philosophy of Religion. Bob never studied philosophy or religion and had only a very slight introduction to religion until his time at Earlham. But this one course fascinated him so much that he eventually took a degree in religion and one in geology. During his first religion course, he, along with the other five or six students, was asked what he would do if he found out he had just six hours to live. He told the class he would go to the barn, feed the horses, saddle one of them, and ride off into the sunset. When it was his friend Bill Loucks' turn, he said he would run after Bob screaming, "Macy, come back. Macy, come back," like the Brandon Dewilde in the classic western movie *Shane.*

His other major was geology, not because he had any plans for a future career but because the professor, Don Coats, made the world come absolutely alive for him. He was able to envision how the world was made, how mountains developed, how rocks formed, why streams ran a certain way, cutting certain paths through certain rocks. "The next minute, he could make the Pleistocene era come to life in front of your eyes. He helped me understand how and why oil was made. I got to where I had all kinds of important geological data memorized under his influence. In addition to all that, he was a real gentleman." Macy's world, to this point in his life, was relatively small and secluded, and the notion that a world existed outside his recognition and outside his vision made him want to look beyond the horizon that much more.

Other students and professors also had a profound impact on Macy. Although he was a Quaker then and attended the Society of Friends' services at Earlham, Macy became acquainted with, and developed into friendships, members of many different denominations. One close friend was a Jewish pre-med student from Philadelphia. His father was a prominent physician who decided to bring his son's horse to Earlham and pay for its keep. This student, Bob Capper, was fascinated by Macy's tales of the ranch life he experienced in Kansas. Macy told of his encounters with bobcats and coyotes, but Capper didn't believe Macy because his father had insisted that coyotes were extinct and had been for years. No amount of talk from Macy would convince the younger Capper otherwise.

Macy and Capper spent many hours riding horses and discussing the Jewish faith. They also lingered on matters touching the recent reestablishment of a Jewish homeland in Israel in 1948. Macy found himself again wanting to defend "the little guy" against religious and ethnic persecution.

"There was Dr. Rawsey. Besides being a school leader, he ran the intramural football. He used to say that was fun but of no real practical value. On the other hand, he said badminton and volleyball were in a sense practical sports and valuable because they were things you could keep playing your whole life."

Relations with the nearby town of Richmond were symbiotic. "We had not only resident students, like me, but a lot of commuter students who went to school, worked at local jobs, took night classes, and then went home. In some ways, it was a Quaker town. The Quaker meeting I attended was actually in Richmond, off campus."

The time at Earlham passed too quickly. Graduation came in 1953, and Bob Macy had to say his farewells to the campus and to the friends he made. Some of them stayed behind as he went on to military service and the rest of his life. Remembering his dear friends at Earlham, Macy says rather solemnly. "They were more than classmates and teammates; they were dear to me." Nearly a year later, in April, he enrolled in the U.S. Aviation Cadets, taking with him the lessons on living he gained from Earlham and the lessons that broadened his understanding of his fellow man and giving him a new confidence as he faced the future.

Bob Macy had learned how to live. He was about to learn how to lead.

CHAPTER 4

Learning to Lead: Airman, Engineer, Officer, Lawyer

Back at home, time continued on while Bob was away, and the boys were leaving home one by one. Bob, of course, went to Earlham in 1948, Bill also left home in 1948, Dick entered the Air Force in 1951, and then Bob followed into the service in 1954.

It was August 31, 1954. Bob Macy was assigned to ground duty in the 463rd Troop Carrier Wing in the new U.S. Air Force after dreams of becoming a flier fell apart. Like so many Oklahomans of his generation, it was the military that brought Macy to the Sooner State. So many people had left during the Dust Bowl and the war the two decades before.

He remembers, "They cut me my orders, sending me to Ardmore, Oklahoma, to the Air Force base." Before traveling to Oklahoma, he stopped in Indiana to visit his family and pick up his orders. Red's health was declining from the emphysema, and he'd never fully recovered from his lengthy illness in 1945. Still, he continued to work. After three or four days driving in his 1949 Buick Super, Bob approached his assignment, stopping close to Ardmore to ask, "Where the heck is Sulphur?"

From there, "They gave me instructions to take this narrow road, paved, then gravel. I traveled state Highway 81 south to a main intersection, where I had been told to turn right. The road was so narrow in those days that, if you met an oncoming car, you had to turn off the road." In the heat of a typical Oklahoma summer, he began to worry the directions had been wrong.

Bob finally came to "a little bridge that was well built; apparently the Corps of Engineers had put it in. Everything else was so primitive on that road, and it was hotter than you-know-what." He laughs and says, "I'll tell you, I thought they sent me to the end of the world. Then I came up to the entrance to the base. It was actually very nice."

From the first, despite the ultimate disappointment of his time in the aviation cadets, the opportunity that first drew him into the service, Macy and the military mixed pretty well. He recalls, "Although Earlham helped me immensely. I had an inferiority complex all my life. I'd begun to conquer it, but the Air Force was so good for me in that regard. When I went into the aviation cadets, my confidence grew a lot. Part of it was my physical ability. We had base competitions of various kinds, and I always did well. For the first time, I strongly felt like this was an opportunity to prove I was as good as anybody else."

Macy explains his point this way. "When I first went to Earlham, as I've said, I was very lacking in self-confidence. I guess you could say I had a chip on my shoulder. But at college, I started feeling accepted by students and faculty. I really believe Earlham taught me how to live, and then the Air Force built on that." Graced with physical strength and agility, an agile mind, and an engaging personality, Macy was slowly learning to lead.

Several months before arriving at the gate in Ardmore, Macy signed up in hopes he would learn to fly airplanes. He traveled by bus to Lackland Air Force Base in San Antonio, Texas, which was the headquarters and training center for the Air Force. Everyone on the bus, he recalls, agreed the lengthy trip was sweltering, sticky, and unforgettable—an experience that exhausted all the recruits. But that was only the beginning.

When they finally arrived, separated from the others, the aviation cadets were ushered into barracks, ordered to shower, and then told it was lights out. The next morning came too quickly, even for a young man used to getting up well before dawn to do his chores. Macy and the others were issued fatigues and fed breakfast, had their heads shaved, and made ready to begin their military journey.

As he stood in a long line of similarly dressed recruits, Macy remembers all the recruits had to surrender their jewelry as a means to make all the two thousand cadets stand as equals. Bob remembers looking at all the cadets in formation that day, knowing that all of them had been thoroughly tested, passing background checks to gain high security clearances, and recruited into the cadet ranks as he had been.

Aviation cadets were recruited hard and selected carefully. The training in preflight was hardcore with strict discipline, and physical training was rigorous. They all worked long, hard hours with minimal rest. His memory is blunt and somewhat stark. "It was constantly stressed that we were hired killers." They were told, "As George Patton said, 'Don't die for your country. Let some other S.O.B. die for his country.'" Yet he was eager to become part of the next generation of combat aviators, all in excellent physical condition and generally between twenty-one and twenty-five years old.

They were separated into four squadrons, supervised by a group of second lieutenants. The recruits were given full, strenuous days of long and hard calisthenics. They were required to remain silent, not allowing any conversation. The order of each day was close order drill, constant calisthenics.

Again and again, he says, came the bellowing reminder from the second lieutenants, "You are hired killers. You were hired and trained to eradicate those individuals who would destroy our country." Despite relentless drills, constant instruction, and the rapid pace, Macy found he acclimated well to military life. He loved the hard work and was well used to working that way. His time at

Earlham, with the heavy football and wrestling load, prepared him well for the physical activity.

He remembers details vividly, closing his eyes for a moment while describing his military attire. "The aviation cadets all wore freshly pressed uniforms, and we had suspenders. We wore khakis that were starched. We had a belt around the waist and suspenders were attached to the belt at your waist and then went down inside the pants' legs to your ankles so there were no bulges in your socks."

This training was very challenging, even for a gifted athlete such as Bob. "We were up at dawn and lined up in full-dress uniforms. Breakfast and the meals in general were starchy." After the early weeks of training, out of two thousand cadets, Macy received the second highest rank of captain and squadron commander. This was another step toward developing self-confidence by prevailing against top flyer competition.

But, in spite of his successes, Macy, who had vision problems, learned that there was no way he could be accepted into flight school. Although his time as squadron commander was only eight weeks, Macy excelled. By his own recollection, Macy demanded near-perfection, and the men responded, resulting in his squadron's high-performance ranking in every category.

At the end of three months, qualifying candidates were promoted to primary training and slated for reassignment. As a qualifying step, all the cadets underwent an intense physical examination. Macy, informed of imperfect vision, was disqualified from flight training. The news, striking like a dirty fighter, crushed dreams of flight. His choices became limited. On the one hand, Macy could stay in the cadet program, become a radio observer, and get on track as a commissioned second lieutenant to serve out the rest of his four-year enlistment. On the other hand, he could resign from the cadet program, become an enlisted man, and serve just two years of active duty. The Korean War had ended with no perceived threat of hostilities in the near future. Red Macy's poor health had developed into emphysema, and sensitive to his family's needs, Macy opted for the shorter enlistment.

Macy then accepted an assignment as a ground trainer, eventually spending much of his time trying to help the little guy, the misfit, the malcontent. That was how he got to southern Oklahoma and the gate at Ardmore.

He reported to the office of Major Charley Murihad. "When I went in the first time, I marched in and saluted real sharp." Murihad looked up, saw it was the new guy, and said, "Macy, knock it off." Murihad told Macy to relax and sit down, beginning an affable and productive relationship. "I was assigned to him, as he was the base executive officer. Anytime I needed anything, he helped. He was a career guy who had specialized in those P-47s, the Thunderbolts. It was a small unit, our group, a lieutenant, first sergeant, and later two or three enlisted guys who worked for me."

Macy and Murihad got along just fine, but he really became fast friends with the younger lieutenant he worked with directly. Lt. Dee Wheatley III was known to pals as "D-3." Wheatley was a six-foot, six-inch Texan. Macy laughs as he remembers. "He was full of it but actually the nicest guy you'd ever meet." Wheatley delegated a lot of authority, and that was fine with the young man. "Macy, you run this outfit, and I'll sign the papers." He adapted to the heat and the lifestyle of Ardmore quickly and adapted to the leadership role he assumed even faster.

In every six-month period, their unit provided sixty hours of in-service training for Air Force enlisted men. "Our job was that we organized and designed the training. We kept them, the airmen, on their training regimen and timetable. My job was basically to run the school. I was responsible to see [that] the training actually got done."

Macy recalls, "One particular example was the firing range reported to me. We used .45 automatics, M1A1 carbines, and a .30 caliber rifle. I prepared the small arms training in those days."

It was hard but good work. In down time, Macy got to experience for himself the dreams of flying that had drawn him away from early aspirations of naval service into the new Air Force, born out of the old Army Air Force. His eyes kept him from pursuing flight status, but they didn't keep him on the ground. As he remembers now, "D-3 flew a C-45 twin engine. It was just the next step down from a C-47. We called it the 'tail dragger.' D-3 was rated and had his wings. I have real pleasant memories of flying all over Ardmore and Ada and that area."

Of all his memories of flight, the most pleasant was going with D-3 to Sheppard Air Force Base in Texas. "How beautiful that was, like a great big Christmas tree from the air. We didn't set down, so we just took a round trip in the air. We took those flights in the area so he could keep his wings. I loved it."

At Ardmore AFB, "the planes our guys worked on, did ground fly simulations for, had big booms on each side. They used to always break down. We had the 119s, what we called the 'flying coffin.'" Thanks to D-3's tutoring and his own inclinations, "I flew the flight simulators just fine. I had absolute confidence that if I'd ever needed to fly one, I could have."

Eventually, D-3 went to another assignment and, "there was a guy named Kelso, a lieutenant, who was a nice guy but didn't measure up to D-3." At first, "Kelso was scared to death, afraid of his own shadow." Soon, the two got along fine, after Kelso began to defer to Macy's judgment in most matters. Macy's leadership skills were being honed.

Macy rarely drank liquor and gave it up entirely years later when he became district attorney. But in those days, he wound up getting some practical training in the rougher edges of life while in the military and at the Ardmore base. "I was an Airman second or third class. I wasn't making much money," he notes. That's why he welcomed the opportunity to become the bartender at the base's non-commissioned officers' club. He also served as the facility's bouncer and therein lays another story. It was a good life for a transplanted Indiana boy, but "at the bar, seems to me like we had a lot of fights. Off work, some of the guys would drink themselves into oblivion. It was beer and mixed drinks. I could mix fast and pretty well. Usually, it was just me working. There would be thirty-five to forty guys and gals, some of them wives." Macy learned that where there were boys and booze, there would be fights.

"At that time, there was a circuit of pro wrestlers who traveled around to Ardmore, Ada, Seminole, and some of the smaller towns. As bartender at the NCO club, I got to know all the first sergeants. That's how I got into the wrestling. One of the sergeants asked me if I'd be interested in bartending and then wrestling on the side. Truth is, it all added up to give me a decent standard of living. That last eighteen months or so at Ardmore, I traveled that circuit." Although thin, Macy was muscular and learning to be pretty tough. "Pauls Valley," he tells, "was also on that old wrestling circuit. I could only wrestle three or four nights a week, and the other nights I bartended. There were always some pretty, young ladies hanging around the arena. That was nice. I had wrestled at 191 pounds back in college. A lot of the guys were just actors, but some of the guys were real athletes and very skilled."

One night, things went a bit awry. "You had to watch what you were doing. You could get really worked up. We called it 'working hot' when the pace got heavy. I remember a guy, a good guy, named Honest Abe. We were 'working hot' and I slammed him and the poor guy broke his leg in three places. I felt just awful about that."

Macy had dark hair and, on the small town wrestler circuit, he was known as "Pretty Boy."

"They always cheered for Pretty Boy. A couple of times, I really got it put on me. I got hit in the chops. We'd throw each other around and run around." It was more hard work than fun.

As for whether or not the matches were fixed, he smiles and replies, "Well, we had an understanding about who would win. The nights were interesting. We had preliminaries for thirty minutes or until there was a fall. Then, the main events were for sixty minutes or until there were two falls. It was hot and sweaty work for a whole long, long evening. We'd split whatever we took in, maybe $100 per guy. Most wrestlers were not military men. We tied in with other circuits. Many of those fellows were drifters. It was fun, but some of those wrestling audiences could get plumb crazy. There was a little bit of Bobby Knight and performance art in all of that."

He also learned to convey confidence and strength and a certain menace when necessary. "Later, when I was a lawyer, there were a couple of times that attorneys on the other side of cases would threaten to kick my butt. You know, I never worried too much about that because I'd had on-the-job training butt kicking in the Air Force!"

In 1955, Tom Macy got out of high school. He quit at the hardware store, connected with Bob, and drove him back to Ardmore after one break in the military. Tom had a 1949 Buick at the time. After a short time at the base, Bob and Tom drove to Howard, Kansas, Bob's old home away from home.

Bob knew several people in "that little bitty town" that still had hitching posts. They stayed at a hotel, where they had to share bathrooms with other guests. They wound up, in a roundabout way, getting work putting up hay, at 1 cent a bale each. They could make ten dollars a day while Bob was on leave. After a few days of hot and hard work, they quit haying to drive a truck at night. "It was less money but not so hot," Tom recalls. Bob had to go back to the Air Force, but Tom stayed a little longer.

Bob Macy, a lowly airman, was running ground training for the entire base, or "at least, it seemed that way. If I had run it, I could have run it better than they did. When I finished that hitch, I got a really nice letter from the officer in charge. It was good duty."

One benefit of his posting, Macy recounts, was "I could hitchhike on flights going elsewhere and did. I often 'hitched' a flight up to Indiana. Once on a trip up to Indiana, I got strep throat and was pretty sick." On one such occasion, Macy felt a little sick but stuck it out for a trip home to Indianapolis. He felt ill all the way up. On the return trip, an unusual amount of turbulence made him greener by the moment. Back at the base, his roommate, Merv Krueger, insisted he go to the base hospital.

Learning strep throat was the culprit, the doctor ordered a three-day stay in the hospital, a round of antibiotics and, significantly for Macy's future, the watchful eye of "the prettiest nurse" he had ever laid eyes on. Nurse Betty Hendryx gave Macy a square-needled shot in the butt and, he said, "instantly stole my heart." He soon learned she was still in mourning over a beau whose B-29 had been shot down with his body never recovered. Macy waited patiently while she grieved by often communicating with the missing flyer's mother.

Time passed, wounds healed, and the pair became virtually inseparable, although it was against rules for nurses to date enlisted men. As he put it, the ban on dating "didn't slow us down one bit. Betty lived over in Springer. Mrs. Arnold and her daughter, I remember, rented a room out to Betty. She was a civilian nurse at the base hospital."

No one knew it, but a way of life was destined to end at the Ardmore facility. "Eventually, Ardmore Air Force Base closed, but it hung around for a long time. They closed it after a troop carrier plane went down and a group of airmen died." As Macy tells it, "I remember even when I was there, and thereafter, they made the base nice. It had good barracks, a headquarters building, a very basic gym, a theater, a chapel. It was kind of interesting because about the time they got the decent amenities, they closed it."

It didn't take long after his arrival in Oklahoma before Macy discovered the Air Force base's football team. Not much prodding to try out was required, and Macy was delighted to learn he was eligible to play. His eagerness and talent shone through as he gave it his all to qualify.

With the base providing a field and equipment, Macy and his teammates practiced as hard as they played. Sheer talent oozed off the squad, he recounts. Over half his teammates had played pro or semi-pro football. The starting quarterback, Paul Tetzlaff, was a former all-star. The coach, Howard Waugh, was an All-American running back for the University of Tulsa's Golden Hurricanes.

Macy's team played against comparable military squads and won most of the contests. But reluctant to be outdone, some commanders put together powerful and highly skilled teams in an all-out boasting bout. Macy was in his element again and reunited with his first sporting love, having a good season. But then, one October, he suffered a torn hamstring. He knew he had to have surgery or face the prospect of never playing again. Torn between getting it repaired by a military physician, who might or might not have the right experience to counter such an injury or going off-base to a private practitioner he'd have to pay himself, Macy was uncharacteristically indecisive as he faced another health challenge, another in the long series of medical issues that would dog him throughout life.

After much internal debate, he opted to allow the injury to heal on its own. That effectively, and forever, ended his football career. Despite the injury, the military was good to Macy.

Still, he has no real regrets. "Sometimes I think how things might have been different, but you know, I've done so darn much better than I ever would have expected."

With marriage to Betty planned for the near future, "I wanted to go back to Indiana to join the state police. She didn't want to leave Oklahoma. So I worked for a while in the oil fields. Pulled pipes and derrick work." The geology degree from Earlham proved its utility but only marginally.

Macy's days were long, sometimes going well into the nights. It was filthy, hard work, but it was paying the bills. The days were long, working on derricks, pulling pipes, and handling whatever was needed to get the black gold out of the ground. Macy went from one oil company to the next, until settling on Halliburton, an Oklahoma company based in Duncan. He was placed in the engineer development program, finally using his degree. But that didn't pay his bills as quickly as driving the trucks.

Macy learned to drive dump trucks from his dad; so working for Halliburton driving trucks was almost second-nature work for him. What he didn't learn from his dad necessary for the job, he learned "the hard way."

"I worked at Halliburton for several months in field operations," Bob details. "I ran pumping units in the field. I remember the huge truck with two big engines. It drilled down through the layer of sand to the Permian layer. The truck and the Twin T Ten had independently-running diesel engines. It forced fuel down to the sand level then exploded it to get the oil flowing."

Macy was sent to Hugoton, Kansas, to run piping units. The oil fields were booming, and he began working eighty hours a week or more. Halliburton's services were in constant demand, and so was Bob's talent. Despite the frantic pace, Bob saw an opportunity and asked Betty to join him there. She did.

On June 30, 1956, the two drove around town trying to find a preacher to marry them. They finally met at a preacher's house, where they wed with only the minister and his wife as witnesses. After the ceremony, they prepared to go their separate ways, back to their designated jobs. There would be no long honeymoon for the two. Instead, there was work to be done. "We were in love," Bob can't help but smile even after all these years. "She's a heck of a woman."

However, as soon as word got around that the two had been married, Macy's friends coaxed Betty and him out of their residence. They put her in a wheel barrel and made him race her down the main street of little Hugoton. Macy was cajoled into wheeling Betty down the street himself, in a Kansas variation of the old-fashioned frontier "chivalry."

While harassment outside continued, wives of Macy's coworkers were busy taking the labels off canned food goods so that for the next couple of months, every meal was a surprise. Nonetheless, after their wedding, Betty had to leave to return to her job.

On the job, Macy ran a pump truck. He remembers well "the Panhandle of Oklahoma. I loved the people but hated the area. Many long nights, I ran the equipment. I remember a sand dune would build up by the side of the truck while you were drilling. It was so, so cold."

Early one morning on the way to a rig, Macy and a coworker were driving the Twin-T-Ten at about seventy miles per hour when a surprising thing happened. Macy was at the wheel when the steering wheel came loose from the shaft. Because the sand on the roadside was several feet deep, Macy couldn't steer without risk of a head-on collision or a rollover. All he could do was try to pull onto the shoulder. He chuckles a bit when he tells this story. He said he was flailing his arms about holding that steering wheel and looking like something from a Laurel and Hardy movie. He looked over to his frightened partner and said, "Hang on. We're going for a ride."

When the front end of the vehicle headed into the sand, he stuck the steering wheel onto the shaft and turned the wheels to the right, and the truck began to roll. In fact, it rolled three times before coming to a stop. As Bob remembers it, "It seemed like forever before it stopped. I remember the fact that we had several hundred gallons of diesel fuel pouring out over the hot engine."

Macy grabbed his partner and literally threw him out of the truck. Following behind in a pickup truck was Macy's supervisor, who slid his pickup truck to a stop and bailed out, running toward the driver and his partner.

All the supervisor could think to say was, "What the heck do you guys think you're doing?"

Macy said for once in his life, he was speechless. All he could think to do was throw the steering wheel, which he held onto when he bailed from the truck, at his supervisor like a Frisbee. "After the crash, we checked the steering mechanism and found that when they assembled this rig, the steering wheel had not been properly attached to the shaft." Knowing that didn't make the incident any less frightening.

Because of lack of sleep, many drivers, Macy included, were setting the throttle on the truck and standing on the running board to let the wind blow in their faces to keep them awake. He recalls, "You would go to sleep, only to be awakened by your front wheels hitting the bar ditch. One thing I learned was that the hardest times to stay awake were right at dawn." Not surprisingly, by this time, Bob Macy was tired of working eighty-hour weeks. "Our services were in such high demand that we weren't getting much sleep, and Betty was by then having to drive fifty miles to work and back each day. As soon as one truck came in, another went out."

Macy finished the field work in November or December of 1956. After that, "I needed a better, decent job." Part of his oilfield work involved picking up two pipes, weighing 170 pounds each, and connecting the joints. That work certainly took its toll on his back. "Up in Wichita, I'd seen an advertisement for youth work with the YMCA. They needed a program director. They advertised for a young man with Christian ideals." He applied and got the job from Ron Craft, a gentleman he still remembers fondly. Macy "ran the program inside that winter then programs in the city parks the following spring and summer."

"It was nice being out of that wind in western Oklahoma and Kansas! It was good work," Macy states emphatically but adds that the job was boring. His post was "a good job with good people." Somehow, it didn't offer the challenge Bob was so used to in his work history. Meanwhile, Betty found work as an orthopedic nurse at the Wichita clinic.

But something was tugging at him. Police work seemed more and more a natural fit for the young man. He heard Oklahoma City was looking for good officers. He thought to himself, *Who better than a twenty-seven-year-old college graduate and former professional wrestler?* The YMCA job lasted until September 7, 1957, when he decided to return to Oklahoma and join the big city police force. Betty was all in favor of returning to Oklahoma and her family.

Macy went to Oklahoma City with his friends from Ada, Peyton and Tom George, because all three intended to join the police department at the same time. Back then, Macy explains, the hiring for the police department was done at 2nd and Walnut at the Department of Public Safety on the second floor. All three walked in with the confidence that they had what it took to be big city cops.

In fact, they did. But that turned out to be no big accomplishment. Macy recalls that, "If you made it to the second floor, you were hired," and all three made it up the stairs. There was no polygraph required, just some references, and they were hired on the spot. Then they were sent to Battles Uniform shop to get uniforms. They were given two badges and a $90 allowance to purchase everything they needed. And it took every bit of the $90 and then some. They also had to buy their Smith and Wesson .38 Special revolver and ammunition, if they were lucky enough to have any remaining money. And then they went to work that night.

Macy says, in those days, the chief, Roy Bergman, explained they were to receive $295 a month, a full $100 a month less than what he earned as an oil field truck driver. But they could look forward to a $15-a-month raise after six months and another raise to $335 a month after a year on the job. Macy also learned that promotions were politically based, but being a Mason gave an officer an advantage. So he became a Mason.

At times, the work was hard, but the pairing of Macy and police work was a match made in heaven. Still, his original field of academic endeavor, geology, lingered for a while. Macy accumulated twenty-one hours toward a master's degree, studying at Central State College (now the University of Central Oklahoma) in Edmond. But dreams of geologic strata soon faded as Macy the cop excavated crime and rooted out criminals in his chosen new hometown. The die was cast, as Macy's life began another fundamental shift.

Years later, when Police Chief Vern Hoy of the Los Angeles Police Department came for dinner at their home, Hoy asked Betty, "Did Bob enjoy being a cop?" Her answer was intriguing for many of those who know Bob Macy today. "Vern, it was the only time in twenty years he was really happy." Nonetheless, during that time, he got bad pay and hard work doing a job he loved.

On November 19, 1957, Macy was part of the department that afforded protection to President Dwight Eisenhower during what the war hero/president called, "my all too brief trip," to the Sooner State.

Just as promised by Chief Bergman, on February 19, 1958, he was told his pay would increase to $310 a month, and it did upon completion of his six month-probationary period on March 1. That July, he was sent to a two-month school for patrol officers. In September, the pay rose again, this time to $325 a month.

The money, barely enough to support his family, was not what motivated Bob Macy. Being a cop meant helping people who really needed it, and five decades later, that's what Macy best remembers about the job. "Their smiles of gratitude made it worthwhile," he says. Macy again was living his passion, doing what he liked best, and now knowing the reason for doing it. He learned to sacrifice, but this was where he knew he needed to be, doing what he knew needed to be done.

His past was as much a teacher as his police training. The experience as a wrestler in college back in Indiana and on the semi-pro circuit around Ardmore during the Air Force years was a help. Bob had broad and useful knowledge of takedown maneuvers, and he used that to good advantage. He earned a reputation among officers for being fast and effective in tough situations. Though he used violence sparingly, he was ready when necessary in the line of duty and especially when outnumbered. Bob remembers, "I was not going to be defeated. When an officer witnesses or comes upon a crime, he has to bring the criminal in. He can't back out of the situation." He had Red to thank for teaching him determination and perseverance.

But there were the exceptions to the rule. His passion for standing up for the ones who couldn't stand up for themselves was always the driving force of his actions. In his days on patrol, domestic cases were a particular problem and sometimes challenged his sense of peacefulness. If a wife or child was battered or beaten, and the drunken abuser was still there, the fellow "stood an excellent chance of getting his rear kicked before being put in jail," Bob recalls.

There were other situations that helped Bob, in later years, determine officer complicity from the district attorney's point of view. Car chases through residential neighborhoods were harrowing and too often led to violence, as Macy recalls. He puts it this way: "When an officer is involved in a chase and nearly crashes with another officer or some innocent citizen, the adrenaline is pumping, and it doesn't take much 'loud lip' to have blows struck."

Macy recalls one incident in which a chase lasted for thirty minutes, a very long time for a chase in any era, in a poor and crowded area. When the car finally stopped, the violator cussed out Macy and spit in his face. In a second, Macy smashed the outlaw against the car. Macy admits he "would have whipped him good" but for the intervention of other officers.

These memories often tempered Macy's judgment on how to handle complaints against officers. Sometimes, citizens expect more from an officer than he is humanly capable of producing. Years later, in our candid discussions at his retirement home in Newalla, Macy confessed he would have had little mercy for Rodney King, the focus of an infamous incident in Los Angeles. When King resisted arrest, he was beaten by a group of L.A. officers. As far as Macy was concerned, "If a person nearly kills an innocent citizen or group of citizens, he has a butt-kicking coming." Police work was different in those days—in some ways better, in other ways worse than today—but Macy readily discloses "there was a lot of street corner justice dispensed."

For most of his time as an officer, Macy patrolled District 10 for the Scout Car Division. His beat encompassed the city limits south of the Canadian (now the Oklahoma) River and west of Western Avenue. He wore badge number 0689. During that time, Allen Street was mayor of a city much more wide open than its conservative reputation might indicate.

Officer Macy's "beat" was over a hundred square miles and included a place that became, at night, a "hell hole." The area where much of his work centered was called Packing Town, home of the National Stockyards and meat-processing facilities. "My shift was 11:15 p.m. to 7:15 a.m. It was good, hard work."

Though Packing Town had its share of bootleg joints and dives, a center of activity was Cattlemen's Cafe on South Agnew. Today, it is a pleasant restaurant with possibly the best beefsteaks west of the Mississippi, surrounded by shops selling western wear and a popular venue for young country music singers.

In those days, Packing Town was a much rougher place. Before or after the cowboys went to Cattlemen's for a breakfast of brains and eggs, they often downed a pint of bootleg booze. They took advantage of all that the city had to offer, including gambling and ladies of the night.

In the 1950s and for years afterwards, Cattlemen's was operated by Percy Wade and his boys. The story goes that Percy won title to the place in a game of cards. He ran the business in a manner Macy recalls as "wide open, but fair. The doors had no locks, and the place was open twenty-four hours a day, and brawls were the order of the day." Generally, the place had two or more Oklahoma City police officers on the premises, enticed to stop in by the fine coffee and half-priced meals. Their presence kept violence among the cowboys to an acceptable level, but many of the patrons were looking for trouble—and they usually found it. "In an eight-hour shift, an officer could count on at least three good fights" at the old Cattlemen's.

Working in and patrolling the district, Macy became lifelong friends with Percy's son, Gene, and years later gave a stirring eulogy at the man's funeral. Gene's family presented Bob with a saddle he admired from Cattlemen's after Gene's death. That saddle was, as they said, a token of Gene's friendship with Bob. Even then, Bob chose his friends carefully and remained loyal to them. Friends, he still believes, are as valuable as family and, in fact, become family.

"In those days of prohibition, it appeared that nearly everyone was treading on the edge of the law," Macy recalls. Service stations up and down Agnew were fronts for bootleggers. Every officer worth his salt knew the bootlegger boys by car make and by name—Billy Fields, Roy Young, Grady King, Cat Jimenez, Red Holt. The bootleggers often hijacked each other and had some "God-awful fights, but oddly, nobody got killed or severely hurt," to the best of Macy's recollection. All this was a new world for him, but Macy readily adapted to it. He was respected by the patrons of Packing Town for his tough, no nonsense but fair response to their calls. One thing was for sure; Macy never used his badge for power. There were times he had to use some force, but he probably would have stood up for the underdog, whether he was a cop or not.

And there were some close calls. As noted in a September 6, 1959, investigation report, Macy and partner N.V. Wilkerson were on patrol at 12:45 a.m. They stopped a pickup in the 1400 block of South Agnew. As they worked that stop, they saw a Chevy coming at them from the 1700 or 1800 block, traveling north "at a very high rate of speed."

Macy stepped into the street, waving his flashlight back and forth "in an attempt to stop the car." As the vehicle approached, it swerved directly at Macy, who had to leap behind the stopped pickup to avoid being hit. Subsequently, "Officers gave pursuit and stopped the Chevrolet in the 2200 block of Exchange Avenue." They placed under arrest Donald Ray Littleton. Their report describes Littleton as "very belligerent." Leaving the vehicle "properly parked" on Exchange, they took the man to jail.

Taken to headquarters on N. Shartel, he was given a "drunk-o-meter test," with a blood level of 0.135 noted. As the Macy-Wilkerson report discloses, "Enroute to headquarters and after arrival... subject kept insisting that his wife had been running around with a policeman and that he hated all policemen and that if something was not done, he was going to kill every policeman he saw." However it ended for Littleton, he didn't kill any policemen, and Macy and his partner were able to finish the shift and go home.

The normal nature of police work on the streets of Oklahoma City was not as dramatic, but it certainly was not boring. In those days, the calls for service weren't as often, the city not as large, and the officers patrolling not nearly so many. Communication with the dispatcher was infrequent, and situations on the street had to be handled by the officers taking the calls. However, it can be assumed from an examination of contemporaneous commendations and reports prepared for the Scout Car Division, each night presented the officers with a whole new set of rules in a playbook not yet written.

On some days in October, 1959, Macy's logs record that he issued a dozen or fewer moving violations, a half dozen or more calls answered, a couple of assists to other officers, and no arrests. Other days, the activity was more substantial in all categories, with as many as three or four arrests. Then there were days like October

9 and October 23, when he was in court testifying at trial about previous arrests. Macy particularly liked the court testimony because it gave him a sense of justice being served, though the groundwork of catching the crooks was pretty enticing, too.

Another man named Littleton turned up in the records of Macy's police work. Months before his encounter with Donald Ray Littleton, Macy and Wilkerson, on January 31, 1959, nabbed James Baxter Littleton and James Alfred Engst, shortly after the pair robbed the Standard Service Station at 2020 South Agnew. Detective Captain R.S. Worthy commended the two officers for the quick arrest, saying, "We have prevented other robberies which they would have pulled in the future."

On March 12, 1959, County Attorney James W. "Bill" Berry sent a letter to Detective Wayne Harbolt commending a pair of Macy's colleagues for their testimony that contributed to the March 9 "conviction of one of our leading thieves." Berry said he expected the good work of "Officers Cooper and Cassidy" but continued that "the outstanding thing in this trial was the testimony of R.H. Macy. His poise, memory, and manner of expressing himself in regard to detailed evidence was outstanding." Even now, Macy's memory of detail is remarkable.

To be sure, Bob Macy loved being a cop, but perhaps something in letters like the one from Berry reawakened latent yearning in his spirit. Already by September 1958, one year into his time as patrol officer, the thrill of participating in arrests and trials caught his interest that would last forevermore.

The tug he had first felt as a boy in Indiana listening to the radio was renewed, and Macy enrolled in the University of Oklahoma College Of Law. Yet he continued to work full time as a police officer.

In the late 1950s, Bob and Betty were busier than ever but found time for each other. Their family began to grow right around the time Macy entered the law school in Norman. The birth of Sheila, their first daughter, was a joyous time as well as one that increased his responsibility. With a child now in the picture, Macy was ever more determined to make good grades to ensure he could become a protector, both publicly and privately.

Then, in July, 1959, a second daughter, Teresa, was born two and a half months prematurely, weighing only two pounds, twelve and a half ounces. The little girl remained in an incubator for fifty days. Betty went back and forth to the hospital every day, and Bob went as often as he could. Teresa survived. And the bills mounted up. His salary of $335 didn't stand up long against hospital bills, family expenses, and a $61-a-month house payment for their sparsely furnished house. When the Macys first came to Oklahoma City, they lived at 2037 N.E. 37th, but as the family grew, they moved to 2201 S.W. 52nd and somewhat nicer quarters.

But in August 1960, Macy was repairing his home, which had been damaged by a tornado, when he felt a severe pain in his right side. It turned out to be a malignancy, yet another in his series of serious health challenges. As a result, he had to have two major surgeries. The first was an appendectomy. His appendix was home to a fibrous malignancy, and because of the severity and the fear, it had spread to his intestines; half of Bob's colon was removed.

And while in the hospital, Macy was informed of a staph infection that he had contracted from his hips to his knees, a scourge the doctors feared they could not control. Macy was unsure how he was going to take care of his family or even if he would be around to care for them. He ultimately recovered, but it was agonizing and long.

One day, Macy had a visitor during his stay in the hospital. It was a law professor from OU, Ben Stockwell. "He was not someone I knew especially well," Macy recalls with, as he now says, "a frog in my throat." Stockwell inspired Macy by telling him, "About a year ago, doctors diagnosed me with terminal cancer. In fact, it was so bad than when they opened me up, they saw how bad it was and closed me back up. They told me I had six months to live. I didn't give up then, and you should not give up now. You will get through this." In an interview in 2009, Macy recalled with tears in his eyes, "As long as Ben lived, I would get a Christmas card and on it, it always had praying hands." Bob still reflects on how a simple story and a card influenced and inspired him. It's hard to estimate how many people Bob Macy has inspired with his stories of overcoming hardships and illnesses. Certainly, there were many people in his life who inspired him.

As if all the stresses of premature babies and of his own illness were not enough, while Bob was still in the hospital, Betty suffered a blow. Two of her brothers were working on an oil rig that "blew" and burned them severely. For several weeks, she traveled to Shawnee Hospital, then back to Oklahoma City to Bob in the hospital and the family at home, before each of the men was well enough to go home. Teresa was still in the incubator, Bob in another hospital, and her brothers in still another hospital. Yet every day, she drove a 1954 Ford without air conditioning to the three hospitals miles apart. Bob fondly remarks about Betty now. Describing her then and now, he says there is "no woman with greater faith and strength" and that he is "very proud of her."

Upon leaving the hospital, still riddled with infection and far from being healed from the surgery, Macy returned to the classroom at OU. He was approaching his final year of law school and could not afford to drop out. He was determined. To catch the seepage from his infection, Betty bandaged his legs with cloth diapers, wrapping and securing them to his thighs. He managed to finish while enduring painful hours sitting and listening in the classroom.

Despite memories of the pain of that health crisis, Macy's recollections of his time as both a policeman and a law student are overwhelmingly positive. "I'd get off work and then drive down to Norman, in uniform, to go to law school until 1:00 p.m. or so. I always drove U.S. 77 to Norman."

He remembers some of the professors fondly. "Professor Phelps was the teacher in contract law. I sat in the front row in his class and got a B. That actually surprised me, and I told my friends I hadn't expected to get such a good grade. One of my pals teased me, 'I'm not surprised, Macy. It's easy to understand. My God, you sat there on the front row with a .38 on your hip! No wonder you made a good grade.'

"My best professor was probably Bill Bandy, in criminal law. He was always interested in what I was doing. I didn't make exceptionally good grades from him, but his class was great, and he treated me fairly. I had him twice, if I recall. Joe Rarick was an interesting character. If you dozed off in class, which some of us did, he'd throw chalk at you. Dean Earl Sneed was another good professor. I always respected him a lot."

Although mostly men, a couple of women classmates were early indications of a shift in the legal profession. "There were two women in the class. Deanna Burger was a single Jewish girl. Jo Tapp was the other woman, although Jo dropped out later."

And there was one name that brought many of the law students together, George Nigh. George Nigh was a rising star in state Democratic politics who had become, at a young age, the state's lieutenant governor. Then, he was governor for a few days when incumbent J. Howard Edmondson resigned. Nigh was elected lieutenant governor again, becoming the longest-serving "light governor" in state history. Ultimately elected as chief executive of the state in 1978, Nigh served two full terms as governor.

This was an important seed, planted during his law school years, for Macy's future. "It was during my time at OU law school that I got to be friends with the Nigh Group." George Nigh was not a lawyer but had a cluster of close allies in and around the OU law school at the same time Macy worked his way to a degree. The others studying the law were David Hudson, Bob Scarborough, Jim Hasenbeck, and Ted Bonham. "That group and a few others got to be friends." Two decades later, Nigh, still remembering the law school friends, helped boost Bob Macy into his dream job.

When law school ended, "I passed the bar the first time. I'd interviewed for a job as an assistant county attorney, and it was offered to me *if* I passed the bar. I was able to go ahead and practice law for two or three months on a permit basis. I was sure tickled to death to pass the first time because I had Betty and two babies at home. To tell the truth, I had no time to study or prepare." Bob confides that he had encouragement from Betty to attend law school. She always thought, he thinks, that she would marry a lawyer, but she married a cop. He also admits he wanted to please her and support his family, but his passion for the underdog drove him hard. "After I got my law degree, I represented every poor SOB I could." It was some years later when he fully understood how the two, his law degree and his desire to stand up for the underdog, were to be combined into the same passion.

In a speech many years later, Macy recalled his feelings as he worked the streets and studied the law. "As I became more and more involved in arrests and trials, and time after time watched guilty felons go free, I realized that the person who had the most impact on the criminal justice system was the District Attorney of Oklahoma County."

Even then, he felt that was the job for him. Twenty-two years later, on June 16, 1980, those early dreams came true, and he was sworn in as the county DA. But first came a long hitch in private practice and government service, as Bob Macy paid his dues. He resigned from the police department in 1961 and went off to Ada to become the Pontotoc County Assistant County Attorney.

CHAPTER 5

Learning to Serve: 1961 to 1980

As he headed to Ada and Pontotoc County, Macy's hardheaded idealism, he confesses now, caused him some troubles right off the bat in the local prosecutor's office. Macy admits he didn't understand small-town politics and, even if he had, he would have still done what was right. Often, small-town cases are tried on who was hired as the attorney rather than the merits of the case. Ada, at that time, was no different. Macy worked for Pat Holman, who "told me I was way too idealistic, and I guess that was demonstrated in a series of cases soon after I got out of law school."

One tough case involved Ed Brown. As Macy recalls, "He lost a bunch of money in a poker game, so he left then went back with a shotgun and robbed the money back. Well, we put Ed in jail for that." Brown had close ties to the little town's elites. "Pat was mad at me, and I was mad that he was mad. I knew that when Ed went and got that gun, it could have led to a blood bath. I didn't give a darn who Ed was; he'd threatened to kill people, and it certainly wasn't in self defense."

Regardless, "He was friends with the local judge and with the chief of police. They used to play poker once a week. I'm sorry to say it wound up being an example to me of rural justice. If you were part of the in-crowd, you could get away with things. I was not part of the in-crowd. They made me back off that case."

Macy decided to leave the job, but "I didn't leave the office in a lurch. I finished the docket I'd been working on and won every case. Then, I quit." But it was hard for him to leave a job making $5,400 a year when he had been making $4,000 with the police department.

But he remained for several years in private general practice in the town, where the most notable enterprise was probably East Central State College (now a university), a medical center, and a variety of oil and natural gas-related businesses.

As Macy recalls, "Here I was in Ada, America, with two little girls and Betty at home. I was basically broke and barely out of law school." But in some ways, it was an adventure. "I went to an old office building and rented an office. I hired a college girl to work for me, the first of several. Judy Gladen was the best of the bunch. My secretaries worked half days for me. I rented a typewriter then found a desk that someone else had thrown away."

His only son, Brett, the youngest and last of his three children, came along in 1963. Macy remembers a humorous story involving Brett's birth. It was a dark night when Betty went into labor with Brett. Betty started her career at the Seminole Clinic and was intent on having her children there. Brett was premature, just like her other two babies, so she went on to the clinic.

Bob was still in Ada when he got the word she was at the clinic. He remembers he had a black '59 T-Bird and drove so fast to Seminole that he "ran a hole in the wind." Bob had a few good friends on the Highway Patrol at the time, very few, and one of them was Spike Mitchell. But another one on the patrol, H.T. Gay, was not so amiable to Bob or to anyone else. It just so happened that Bob drove past a trooper sitting in the median on his way to Seminole. *If that's Spike*, he thought to himself, *I'm okay. If it's Gay, I'm in trouble.*

The trooper didn't stop him, but Spike asked him a few days later, "Where in the heck were you going the other night?" Bob told him and Spike smiled and said, "I knew it must have been something like that. My cruiser rocked for five minutes after you passed by. Try to take it slower!"

For a long time, Macy remembers, "I didn't have any resources at all. I did everything to make a little money. Wills, contracts, forming corporations, and a lot of domestic stuff and divorces. As the practice slowly picked up, I got a little better office. I actually tried to avoid criminal cases, but I couldn't stay out of them completely."

The work was frantic and, generally, for desperately low pay. In one notable case, he secured a judgment against Frisco Railroad for negligence in a crossing case. "The defense for the company underestimated me, so I slipped up on them. That was the second highest verdict in Pontotoc County up to that point." He fought effectively for other "little guy" clients, including a custodian who worked at the local high school. In fact, he sought out the "little guy" cases, helping to satisfy his passion but not his pocketbook.

One trial foreshadowed Macy's later, and legendary, prowess in courtroom argumentation, including closing arguments. As he recounts it now, "I had a case involving J.B. Smith, a truck driver from Ada. He and a gal had been married, then divorced. He was paying her $25 a month. They wound up in conflict. She filed against him for abandoning the kids, but that wasn't true. When time came for the trial, J.B.'s car broke down. I had to take him to the trial, which had been moved up to Oklahoma City, and had to borrow gasoline to do it."

As Macy recounts it, "I went up against two assistant DAs, who were there dressed in nice suits. I was dressed in western clothes and a sports coat." He remembers the lead prosecutor, in particular, who wore a $200 suit and $75 shoes. "He hit us hard. I hit hard back. They put on their evidence. The lawyer against my guy asked what he'd done with the money," accusing the man of neglecting his children. Macy knew "there wasn't any money. He was dirt poor."

When it came time for final arguments, "I said J.B. worked all day every day for very little money. I said there was only one of three things the jury and the court could do in this case.

"First, they could find him guilty and put him in jail. Second, they could find him guilty and tell him to pay a fine, but they'd have to lock him up because he had no money. The last option was 'Do what's right. Let me take him back home to Ada with me.'"

Macy then looked at each juror and asked, "Which one of you jurors is going to tell his little girl where her daddy is if you convict him?"

The jury took about eleven minutes and found J.B. not guilty, freeing him to go. Macy chuckles as he remembers, "Two of them offered to buy his lunch before we went home. That was a little bit of drama. It was a time I felt like I had done justice for a poor man." And, as time passed, Macy landed a few clients who could pay adequately, including local meatpacking plants.

He enjoyed many things about his time away from the legal work. "At that time, I had about 330 acres, at least three horses, probably a hundred cows. I didn't do much rodeo competing yet, but my friend Ken Lance had a rodeo down there. He had begun it with all the local cowboys, and they did steer roping. Eventually, he upgraded the competition, and they had one of the best rodeos in this part of the country."

Life was pretty good. "I was past master at the Masonic Lodge; I became very active in what was a very active lodge. We had twice-a-month meetings and twice a month, we conferred degrees. I got real involved in the March of Dimes and the Boys Club, helped create it there." Macy was following and even expanding his passion to help the helpless.

In the Presbyterian Church, Macy was clerk of the session, then an elder, then synod president for the congregation in Kansas and Oklahoma, a rare post for a layman in those days. He was also "stated clerk" of the presbytery, consisting of several churches in Ada, Duncan, Marlow, and other towns.

A positive professional memory from those days was "Judge Lee West, then the district judge at Ada. He was excellent, one of the brightest people I ever knew. He knew the law and had a remarkable sense of humor and a great sense of justice." He came to respect several other judges who remained important people in his life for decades, including LaVerne Fishel, Bob Howell, Joe Shumate, and Knox Bynam.

Macy grew close to the family of W.P. George, a man "I thought walked on water. He was a prince." The family ran a lumberyard, and Macy often sat in church with the Georges on Sunday mornings. He and two of the George boys, Peyton and Tom, had worked together in the Oklahoma City Police Department.

Through hard work, he steadily built his practice up from a lowly $7,500 estimated value in 1962 to about $50,000 in 1969. But Macy was restless. "Eventually, I was burned out, in part because of the very limited income. It was a situation where for five dollars, somebody got a lawyer. Sometimes it was me ... One of the judges who was cordial with me said I had 'cornered the market on free legal work.' That was funny but true.

"I had a copying machine and a secretary. I was spending too much money and time on cases that couldn't pay the bills. Every Saturday, I was always in the office. I began to realize I missed being in law enforcement. I didn't get to see much of my kids. So I just wasn't content, and I decided to make a change."

Macy interviewed for a job in Oklahoma City with G.T. Blankenship, the first Republican attorney general in Oklahoma history but no partisan. Macy mentioned to him he wanted to make a change. Blankenship ran a professional and high-quality office. G.T. complimented Macy as a lawyer with "uncommon good sense." Blankenship responded, "When do you want to go to work?" Macy, a little shocked, told him, "I'll be there Monday. What hours do you want me to work?" The state's top lawyer replied, "Just get the job done." So, in 1969–70, Macy spent a memorable few months as an assistant attorney general in the criminal division. Blankenship became a significant booster of the young lawyer and would later write a strong letter of recommendation on his behalf to the U.S. attorney general.

Macy kept his eyes open for other opportunities, just in case this one ran aground. His friend from Ada, Peyton George, Jr., suggested Macy look at jobs in Washington, DC. Macy had come to know James V. Smith, administrator of the Farmers Home Administration, an important arm of the U.S. Department of Agriculture. And that's where Macy looked first.

Smith, also an Oklahoman, "was a good Christian man, a gentleman. He had been the U.S. Representative in the old Victor Wickersham District 2, but then he lost." Macy looked carefully at several positions in the nation's capitol and received good offers. He took the job with FHA as a GS15, earning $25,000 a year. Now Bob Macy thought he was on Easy Street. He was working his way up and into the federal system; he could support his family on a nice income, and his future prospects looked bright. It was the beginning of a seven- or eight-year run of federal public service, some in the nation's capitol and some in local-level posts.

Macy remembers, "I was very fortunate. I found a house to rent, a nice place to be, and moved the family up." Learning that Smith would probably run for Congress again, Macy planned to stay at FHA for two years then move on to something else. At least, he thought, he'd get his feet wet; he would become exposed to high politics and the Washington, DC arena.

His work was varied and rewarding as a confidential assistant to the administrator. Among other things, "The agency was supposed to help with rural water systems. Multi-millions were at stake in some cases. When there's that much money, there are problems or potential for problems. That's what Jim wanted me to look into."

In one case, Macy traveled to Nebraska. At the request of both of the state's U.S. senators, Smith directed that Macy examine allegations of corruption in money distributed through FHA programs. His directions were to "go find the truth" and "find out what's really going on." Macy spent a productive month on the case, finding a variety of accounting and other issues of concern. He reported the results to Smith, who worked with the senators to clean things up.

In another situation, he was sent to dig into a matter involving a well-connected developer who was performing substandard work on septic lines in the El Paso, Texas, area. Results of the subsequent investigation "certainly got a lot of publicity," Macy notes, and the situation was corrected.

Macy found nobility and purpose in the job. He liked his work, and Smith liked him. "I always had a good link, a great relationship with Jim Smith. I was very comfortable with him." Macy had become valuable as a man who could investigate discreetly, dig out the facts, and report accurately in difficult situations, including some with delicate political connotations.

In a January 11, 1972, letter of commendation, Smith sang the praises of his assistant. Smith said Macy's assignments "have been varied and complex." Smith noted that in just one month (December 1971), the agency had received words of praise for Macy from a state director (in Texas), U.S. Rep. David Dennis, and Defense Secretary Melvin Laird.

The latter good words came for his performance on a presidential task force, the Interagency Economic Adjustment Committee, which Laird chaired. The group focused on base closings and other "necessary defense program changes," Laird said. In Laird's letter to Agriculture Secretary Earl Butz, Macy was credited—not for the first or the last time—for his "communication skills."

Laird praised the Oklahoman for taking an imaginative approach to agricultural problems and economic development. Back home in Indiana, newspapers including *The Palladium Item* took notice of the good words heaped on the native son and Earlham College graduate, reporting (January 13, 1972), "Macy helps communities diversify and strengthen their economic bases. He has assisted many areas suffering job losses because of military base closures, personnel reductions or contract cancellations." Though Macy was born and schooled in Indiana, his family was formed in Oklahoma, and that was where his heart was. Nonetheless, he was quite happy his name was being brought to the forefront in Indiana, where his relatives still lived.

It was all great feedback and support for the new federal worker. Macy was helping to run a three thousand-employee agency with a $3 billion budget and was involved in many aspects of administration other than investigation.

He had developed a knack for resolving program conflicts, including those touching racial minorities. In his two years at the agency, Macy often acted as a personal representative for Smith in meetings with members of Congress or other government agencies.

As a result of his interaction with members on the Hill, Macy was often invited to special social events and had tickets to everything that went on in Washington, DC. Betty, though very comfortable with small-town life, was in her element with the social events and was having the time of her life. She found a job at Fairfax Hospital and was excited about working with and dealing with people of high levels. Betty wasn't a socialite, Macy explains. She just loved watching them.

Jim Smith had, at some time previously, "let the powers that be know he was going to run for Congress," so Macy was already looking around for his next stop in Washington. Tragedy struck when Smith, back home in Oklahoma, was working in a wheat field. A fire started, got out of control, and killed Smith before he could pursue his dream of another term in congress.

Late in his time with Smith, Macy met Norvelle Jespersen in an encounter he considers an example of the gentle providential guidance he was receiving but not in every case recognizing it.

Macy describes Jespersen as "an ex-CIA guy and a G.S.17" who was working at the Law Enforcement Assistance Administration, an arm of the U.S. Department of Justice. Among other things, "He was a former Phoenix cop and had a degree and had been an assistant attorney general in Arizona." After time with "the CIA down in South America," Jespersen wound up at LEAA. As Macy recalls it now, "You know how you meet people and you just find that you are kindred spirits? I told him about the work I'd been doing for Smith, and within a couple of hours, he said he would hire me."

Macy went through a rigorous background check, passed with flying colors, and soon went into a new line of federal agency work. Macy would spend the next five or six years working in quite varied capacities at the LEAA.

Macy initially became associate director of the National Advisory Commission on Criminal Justice Standards and Goals. The commission drew together leaders from all levels and every branch of the federal government. As he puts it, the presidential crime commission "had the real brains on reducing crime on that project."

At LEAA, Macy served three masters, a trio of administrators, Clarence Coster, Pete Velde, and Jeris Leonard. "Members of our commission included Dick Anderson, chief of police of Omaha, Sylvia Bacon, a federal district judge, Pete Pitchess, and Frank Dyson, the police chief in Dallas. Arlen Specter was then the DA in Philadelphia and served on the commission. There was also Jack Danforth, who tried later to hire me to run his capital prosecutions team back in Missouri." The commission ultimately produced an eight-volume report of policy and procedure ideas, some of which Macy was eventually able to work on in local-level jobs for LEAA.

Macy said, "The crime commission work was good, and it was satisfying, occasionally dealing with members of the president's staff. Each of them had slightly different personalities and quirks. I learned a lot from that." The goal was to develop "a blueprint, in a series of studies, to reduce crime in the United States." Macy developed a whole new skill set, editing and producing massive reports with multiple authors to meet challenging deadlines. It took Macy and his team just fifteen months to produce the eight volumes. Each of the volumes reflected the work of a separate task force. "We had minimal experience in preparing reports, but we had lots of people with law degrees involved, some of whom had never practiced law."

In this endeavor, he worked for the first time with Ed Davis, the Los Angeles police chief, and Clarence Kelly of the Federal Bureau of Investigation, "who became a good friend. Kelley was the epitome of the FBI; husky, a bulldog, totally honest." As for Arlen Specter, the future U.S. senator, "I liked him. He was strictly a combatant, and he hated plea-bargaining. He, in fact, wanted the abolition of plea bargaining."

Macy was later director of technical assistance at LEAA. He remembers, "I was in some ways riding high. We lived in Fairfax. The kids were in Lake Braddock School, one of the best in the nation." With the infamous cost of living in the nation's capitol area, "It was an economic adjustment, but I was working in one of the top jobs at LEAA." He eventually had about three-dozen people under his supervision, an experience that proved valuable in later jobs dealing with diverse and often cantankerous colleagues.

Before long, Macy was garnering favorable attention from other laborers in the federal government vineyards. Praising his work on "working papers" for the National Conference on Criminal Justice, Deputy Director Billy L. Wayson in a February 26, 1973, letter, said without the Oklahoman, the work could not have come to fruition. He observed, "The fact we accomplished our goal is testimony to your ability at remaining objective, balancing competing interests and devising acceptable solutions." Wayson characterized himself as a "long-haired hippy freak" who became a fan of the man he characterized as a "cowboy lawyer." His letter was unusually introspective on the realities of how important government work gets done. Wayson wrote, "It's not uncommon, I think, in the petty affairs of man for those who contribute most to receive less in the short run. Competence, however, does not require press conferences to announce its existence nor self-aggrandizement to smother competitors ... The Commission's product is as much a result of your, frequently single-handed, efforts as it is the writings of national 'experts.'"

Another man heavily involved in LEAA's work, Gary Hill, wrote to Administrator Donald Santarelli on July 13, 1973, about Macy's presentation at a conference for state coordinators of the Jaycee Criminal Justice Programs. Hill's most telling comment might have been this: "His manner of presentation was such [that] each of our coordinators was left with a definite direction and outline of what to do when they get back to their various states." The fifty-one state coordinators headed back home ready to give "direct input in more than 6,700 cities," Hill said. Macy's outline of the "tools of knowledge" needed for effective crime fighting and prevention gave Hill "tremendous faith much of a positive nature will be accomplished this year."

Along with the good came the bad and the ugly. Macy remembers an issue that tested his integrity and his survival skills in government. It originated with "Bill Mooney, who worked for me, as the head of my corrections unit in Technical Assistance," as he remembered in a 2008 interview.

"There was a problem. We had a black woman, a Republican, who wanted a grant, funding to work with prisoners. It was a closed deal, a corporation. They were going to get several million dollars. You see, it was a political deal, in the bad sense. Here I was, a cowboy from Oklahoma working my way up to a good position, a good retirement. I hadn't made anybody mad yet. Bill would not, could not, sign off on the grant. After I studied it, I agreed that we just couldn't sign off on it."

One of his superiors, Jim Devine, encouraged Macy to compromise, asking rhetorically, "What's three or four million dollars?" Devine wanted Macy to sign it, but Macy told him, "Jim, it's not a good grant. Heck, I could take this money and send all these women to Vassar to finishing school for that much money!" Macy stuck to his ethical guns and with good reason.

Pressure rose when all three administrators told him, "Bob, we need this approved." But Macy could not do it and still refused. He soon discovered pressure to approve the grant was coming from elements tied to the notorious Committee to Re-elect the President, which in the 1972 campaign had quickly been dubbed *CREEP* by Washington beltway pundits and government insiders. Macy was told that President Richard Nixon's confidante "at *CREEP* wanted it signed. I told them if it was that important, the confidante could sign it himself. That was maybe a mistake, but I just couldn't." Macy refused to buckle under, not from indignation but from conscience.

Macy stood his ground, and "somebody somewhere helped me, perhaps it was divine intervention." At the LEAA, Pete Velde defended his integrity and decision making, while elements in the agency ranks watched his back, too. Even as the pressure increased, Macy refused to sign on ethical grounds, not out of stubbornness.

Just a few years into his Washington hitch, Macy was already a "player," in capitol parlance. He had seven sections, as varied as the courts, crime prevention, police, corrections, and other areas, under his technical unit. His federal career was perhaps salvaged by the wisdom of a man named Jesse James, who was "the head of my police section at the LEAA. The thing about Jesse was that he had been at Pearl Harbor. He lost one of his legs there. He had been chief of police in Charlotte. He was my closest friend in the section." James had a good sense of when to fight and when to live to fight another day.

The message from above was that Macy "just needs to sign" the dubious grant but he was not going to budge. One day, his 6'6" friend ambled in, and, as Macy recalls, "Jesse asked me where I was on the issue, and I told him."

James informed Macy, "The powers that be want to abolish your job." But James thought he saw a way forward in a bad circumstance. An LEAA-funded job working with the city of St. Petersburg, Florida, on a two-year contract seemed to James like a perfect fit for Macy. Macy had already taken a look at the position, and the clarity of James' counsel impressed him. "That way, I could retain the GS 15. It was good advice. Nothing in life is ever perfect, but that was good advice," Macy ponders now. He was able to work out a deal to keep his federal retirement and other benefits. He may not have kept the grant from being approved, but he refused to be the one to succumb to political pressure. From James's perspective, if you can't remove the fire from the pig, remove the pig from the fire.

And so an October 31, 1973, a press release from St. Petersburg city manager R.E. Harbaugh announced Macy's appointment, on a two-year loan from LEAA, as special assistant for criminal justice planning, with Macy scheduled to make the move to Florida at year's end. In a statement at the time of Macy's appointment, Harbaugh said police could only do so much to control or prevent criminal activity. "The police have no way of controlling the moral values of people living here or visiting... Although our record of apprehension is good, we can certainly improve on that record, increasing the fear of individuals being caught... in effect dulling some people's desire to commit criminal acts." Unsurprisingly, those comments reflected Macy's own views of the challenges facing St. Petersburg and cities like it all over America.

In one of our 2008 interviews, Macy recalled the mess he walked into this way. "It was a cesspool. Dope coming in by the planeloads and truckloads. The program idea to build local cooperation was good, with federal dollars provided to put together state programs. But from the start, it was getting thwarted by political purposes." Macy wasn't sure the pig had been removed from the fire, perhaps just brought to another fire. "And I didn't really care for Florida. There was no change of seasons. Besides, the marijuana was a big problem. Eighty percent of the crime occurred in twenty percent of the city."

Not for the first time, "There was a subtext to the situation there." As his effectiveness quickly grew, "The bad guys, probably the mob, dumped a body near our house that several of us interpreted as an attempt to send me a message."

Macy remembers, "The job started out okay. I was giving four or five speeches a week. We certainly made some progress putting together elements of the community with the police and the city government. I was recruiting people to help fight crime in the community, impacting two divisions in the fight on crime." Macy hired or influenced hiring in those divisions, helping to make local law enforcement work "more professional and free of politics." He observes, "In a way, it was supposed to be a chance to implement ideas from the LEAA book on community crime prevention. It was bringing resources to bear in the right places based on crime analysis.

I had support of much of the rank and file and good relations with many leaders in the black community, as well." Indeed, Macy was tireless in his outreach to black citizens. He was principal speaker at a meeting of the Delta Sigma Theta Sorority, a group of college-educated women. A news story about that community event said the black women leaders believed their neighborhoods would benefit from "utilization of Robert Macy's knowledge and expertise in the area of crime prevention." An accompanying photograph showed Macy with eleven black women as he spoke at the home of Johnnye G. Rose.

Macy remembers some of the St. Petersburg work fondly, "One of those I worked with was JoAnn Wilson of the Criminal Analysis Division. Her analysis was that I was smart and innovative, and I felt the same about her. I think most of the local people agreed with that." And her estimation proved out.

In that year, the entirety of 1974, St. Petersburg experienced significant improvements in crime rates. "I was kicking butt and taking names. But then the chief of police and the public safety administrator didn't like all the publicity I was getting."

The problem, it seemed, was "that I was getting my face on TV and my name in the newspaper. I had four or five people with me and went to a lot of town hall meetings. A lot of that work was very practical, emphasizing ways, preventative steps to fight crime, put locks on houses and your doors, put in dead bolts, street programs in high crime areas. It was sensible stuff. I developed some good relationships. But they were going to move my program into the silk-stocking areas, where it wasn't as needed. All this was happening in 1974, and I disagreed." Macy's record stood for itself. He was able to decrease the crime rate by 23 percent in the years he was there.

For Macy, the bottom line was, "I had a good impact for a while, then had to get out gracefully." He also didn't like the local environment's family impact and the pervasiveness of the dope culture despite his best efforts in law enforcement.

He remembers one interlude in Washington during the St. Petersburg hitch. "In the midst of all this, I went to see Nixon's resignation and departure. He was suffering from phlebitis at the time, I believe, and was sweating bullets when I saw him at the event. I was back about halfway in the audience when he announced he was retiring." Macy had also attended both of the inaugural balls of Nixon and, as he put it, saw a president coming and going.

His next opportunity to work at the grassroots level of "real world" law enforcement came from his native state. He looked forward to moving back home. His dad had died in 1965 and his mom, suffering from cancer, was living alone. Macy was to serve two years at the Indiana State Police Department, on detail from LEAA. It was another high-impact, high-stress, posting.

A detailed letter Superintendent Robert L. DeBard wrote on February 19, 1976, to LEAA Administrator Richard Velde described what he characterized as remarkable and unusually effective service from Macy in his early tenure in the Hoosier state.

> "This assignment has placed [Macy] and his family under severe emotional stress, has required him to be on call twenty-four hours per day, seven days a week, and has required hours and hours of overtime for which he has received no additional compensation. He has been confronted daily with complex, difficult problems and has conducted himself as a true professional, always placing the best interests of the department ahead of all other considerations."

In light of the nature of his work—focused on finding corruption or conflicts of interest within the ranks of the state police—it was not surprising Macy encountered powerful opposition in his native state. DeBard wrote, "The Indiana State Police Department, like most law enforcement agencies, does not readily welcome outsiders into its ranks. Consequently, when Mr. Macy arrived, serious efforts were made to discredit him, and, when this failed, he was attacked in the newspapers, and his assignment agreement was subjected to scrutiny and modification."

Things were rough from the start, and they stayed that way. As DeBard described, "Efforts to minimize Mr. Macy's impact upon the department have continued throughout the life of his assignment and the stress upon him has been constant." DeBard complimented him for professional conduct and "significant accomplishments." DeBard went on to credit Macy for reversing the "total lack of cooperation" that had previously characterized his relations with the Indiana State Police Alliance, the employees' organization. Serving as DeBard's liaison, Macy improved relations to the point that in late 1975, the alliance president actually appeared before the state police board and endorsed DeBard's efforts. As for DeBard, he gave the credit to Macy. "Vertical communications within the department are probably at this time the best they have ever been in the history of the Department."

The vice president of the alliance, which represented more than 90 percent of the department's personnel, echoed DeBard's analysis in a letter to Velde transmitted on June 16. Concerning Macy's task as direct liaison between the superintendent and the association, Richard L. Haseman of the alliance said, "A more sensitive and perilous position does not exist in our department." Macy had only verbal authority and responsibility, Haseman recounted, but managed to secure a "team" mentality that had previously been absent at the department.

"Macy was able to establish an atmosphere within which conflict resolution could occur. At no time was there doubt as to where Mr. Macy stood. He was the Superintendent's representative, and he functioned as such," Haseman said. But as a result of his actions, "a relationship of honest, open correspondence was created between the Superintendent and the Alliance—a situation which both resulted in relaxation of tension" between those two sides yet "also set the stage for an all out attack on Mr. Macy by those who were hoping to profit from division."

Haseman recounted that "contact with Mr. Macy was a very refreshing experience. Initially portrayed by some as a federal bureaucrat to be held in deep suspicion, he proved to be fiercely honest, decisive, and open. Feared to be shallow and vain, he was proven deeply knowledgeable in all areas of the criminal justice field and, in fact, rather reluctant to expose his credentials and other memorabilia by which we attempt to demonstrate our human accomplishment." Haseman said Macy "demonstrated an uncanny ability to function with genuine conviction, regardless of the social strata within which he found himself."

Macy always believed that "right is might," but he had to constantly prove that to others. Another delicate assignment was to respond to emergencies and any situations in which the state police department or employees might be subject to civil liabilities. Macy immersed himself in that work, communicating with troopers "on the road" and at crime scenes. In the letter recounting Macy's work, DeBard said this "provided me with valuable insights into the problems and situations confronted by the men that I am charged with supervising."

In his first year-plus with the agency, Macy designed a goals program that emphasized not only crime prevention but also detection and suppression. His vision pushed down into the ranks and was designed to elicit the input and wisdom of those on the front lines fighting criminals and their allies.

On a parallel track, Macy initiated efforts to establish better cooperation and coordination among Indianapolis-area law enforcement agencies. That led to regular meetings involving the FBI, the local sheriff, and the chief of police.

He also served as DeBard's "personal advisor and counselor" on department reorganization, "a civil rights legal action, a minority recruiting campaign, implementation of a police chaplain program, internal investigations, and disciplinary proceedings."

But what probably got him in hot water with some powerful players in the state was what DeBard called a "vital role in coordinating special investigations into corruption, vice and white collar crime, and in better defining the role of the Indiana State Police Department in combating crime."

In an April 23 memo to DeBard, Macy summarized investigations into white-collar crime that included several projects that were ongoing under his general direction. The various parallel probes were apparently touching some who were privileged and powerful, as well as their allies within law enforcement circles. As Macy reported, "We have no secretarial support, and much of the intelligence gathered is so sensitive that we have problems finding proper personnel to transcribe cassette tapes for us." Macy remembers how delicate and stressful the work was and the sordid world his investigators discovered. His investigation uncovered the heart of organized crime in Indiana.

He remembers, "There were scams all over the place. One scam was to 'raise money to build a hotel' that was needed for economic development purposes. They wound up with organized crime running the hotel. It was a Teamsters guy that ran the scam. One of our snitches got killed."

In northwest Indiana, Macy reported in his memo to DeBard, five officers were working with federal agencies in a strike force "investigating allegations of fraudulent use of federal funds, bribery, extortion, kickbacks, and intimidation of witnesses." While some details were withheld from his written memo due to confidentiality, Macy noted those indicted or convicted already included many of the higher level officials in the city administration of Gary.

An investigation of fraudulent practices in Medicaid and Medicare payments, with only one full-time officer, had surfaced claims of kickbacks from pharmacies to nursing homes, questionable doctor referrals to clinics and nursing homes, "exorbitant claims for services which were never delivered," false claims for treatment, forged signatures on claim forms, "paper corporations as subsidiaries of larger institutions for the purpose of building false overhead and exorbitant profits for parent corporations," and denials of proper medical treatment.

In an Elkhart case then being prepared for a grand jury, Macy's team interviewed seventy people who had submitted claims, finding that only three "had any basis at all for a claim. One of the persons allegedly receiving treatment has been dead for several months."

Others were confined to institutions and unable to have visited the clinic from which the false claim had been submitted.

Yet another Macy investigation focused on corporate scam operations, finding a group of sophisticated economic criminals had created paper corporations to sell stock to innocent purchasers. The operations involved "programming the business into bankruptcy from the start, with the corporate officers, directors and salesmen draining off virtually all monies from the sale of stocks and/or income from the business while it is in operation." One of the scams had managed to rip off more than 7 million dollars.

The economic crime investigation began with a tip from Phil Kruse, head of the Intelligence Division at the Illinois Bureau of Investigation, who discovered the Indiana connection and alerted Macy. Macy's investigation found the fraudulent operators had been involved in similar operations in Maryland, Virginia, Ohio, Pennsylvania, Tennessee, Kentucky, Oklahoma, and Missouri. So much of Macy's work in Indiana exposed him to organized crime syndicates. Though he didn't have much trouble from them, he certainly came to know them well, a lesson that colored many of his future investigations.

When Macy's job in Indiana was switched to a less sensitive assignment that summer, undoubtedly a result of his effectiveness, Police Alliance leader Haseman wrote, "The Superintendent, the Alliance and Mr. Macy failed to anticipate the resolve with which the divisive element would react. The simple goal of unbending public service ... has been tainted by the self-serving, frantic pursuit of personal power on the part of a very few." Macy had performed effectively with all levels at the agency. "Bob was true to their trust, slow to criticize, but sure to offer advice and counsel when the situation warranted."

In a letter to Administrator Velde, Charles Rairdon, a police specialist at the department who served as the equal employment opportunity coordinator, said Macy had performed brilliantly in securing changes at the agency that brought "some measure of justice for employees and prospective employees that might never have been accomplished" otherwise. Rairdon recalled, "In the process, he made some friends as well as some enemies." Rairdon marveled that "regardless of where injustice existed, or who perpetrated it, regardless of how high in the organization the perpetrator was, Bob Macy spoke out against it."

Rairdon said he was not surprised when Macy was edged out of the situation in Indiana because "the price of individual integrity runs high." Macy had been willing, he said, "to stand up and fight for what is right, regardless of the consequences." He had lived out, in his Indiana tenure, "individual responsibility, commitment and integrity," which he described as "Bob's legacy" to the agency. Rairdon's comment on Bob's legacy stands true for everything Bob Macy did, not just his work in Indiana.

Macy kept working in Indiana until February 1977, but by his own recollection was not as effective after the turmoil peaked in the summer of 1976. He reluctantly learned a lesson in patience by doing what he could to serve John T. Shettle, the superintendent who replaced DeBard. Shettle praised Macy for "excellent rapport with the officers in the ranks" and for representing the department superintendent "in many complex matters, both internally and with other agencies."

So Macy moved on. He went back to Washington for another hitch at LEAA's home office. Assigned to the Community Programs Division, "basically a one-man operation," he was able to achieve some good things, providing help for federal, state, and municipal employee-exchange programs.

But Macy's time in Washington was drawing to an end. It has been a good run. From January 1972 to the summer of 1977, he had worked for the Law Enforcement Assistance Administration, gaining permanent civil service status and impressing his superiors.

Macy proved adaptable as he moved from $28,142 in annual compensation to $39,419. He wasn't getting rich, but the work was good.

He nearly took a job with Cummins Engine Company, where he would have been in charge of internal and external security for the company. He had discussions with the firm about protecting top employees and their families at the company that had worldwide interests. But that was only a glancing look.

As he looked homeward and away from the nation's capital, he wrote to potential employers or clients: "In order to pursue my chosen profession, it may be necessary to accept a reduction in salary and financial security. However, the opportunity to be active in church, fraternal, and civic activities compensate for the necessary reduction in financial reward."

Macy relocated the family to Oklahoma City, where for the next three years, he worked for a variety of clients. He did better financially than he had early in his legal career in Ada, attracting some good clients who could pay their bills.

Some of the legal work was tied to men he had met years before while attending the University of Oklahoma Law School in Norman. He worked with Paul Ferguson, Ted Bonham, and Wayne Kempton, among others.

He became involved in corporate takeovers and other work. At the time, he worked in the offices of Paul Ferguson, who practiced insurance law and had been Muskogee's district attorney. Everything was fine at that office until he was approached by one attorney from New Orleans representing Louie Roussell who, Macy remarks with a grin, "sued everybody." Roussell had a controversial reputation. Some even said, Macy discloses, "he was crooked, but I don't think he was. I will tell you he never, ever asked me to do anything wrong. He might have been the meanest man I ever knew; yet he never asked me to do anything wrong, and he always paid his bills."

Roussell bought stock in the United Founders Life Insurance Company and found out it was part of the Teamsters' retirement fund. Allen Dorfman, son of Al Capone's chief aide, Red Dorfman, managed the funds. The contacts with organized crime became obvious. The First National Bank had acquired the stocks, and Macy's job was to have the stocks signed over to the principal owners, of whom Roussell was one. His friend, Bill Berry, represented the United Founders Life Insurance Company and Gerald Grimes represented the State Insurance Commission. Nonetheless, Macy wrote three lawsuits and won all three. OPUBCO published a story claiming Roussell was involved with organized crime, but the story had to be retracted when no evidence was presented. Macy insisted that Roussell never asked him to do anything unethical or illegal and volunteered to drop any lawsuit if Macy had any questions.

Everything went as planned until Macy walked into a stockholders' meeting. His heart dropped to his stomach when he recognized a room full of organized crime figures from his past investigations in Indiana and Chicago area. Macy said he "called Hays Foster, a south side lawyer, and told him to strap on a pistol and get down here." He went on to say he could just imagine the OPUBCO headlines the next day: *Macy Shoots It Out at the OK Corral.* I asked him if he was carrying a gun. His response was simple enough. "Darn right."

This meeting happened just before Macy quit. He went on to tell the rest of the story. Anthony "The Ant" Spilotro was the Teamsters' representative. He and Dorfman were highly visible at the stockholders' meeting and were well known to be up-and-coming mob bosses. A few years later, Spilotro and his brother were brutally murdered, tortured with a blowtorch, and Dorfman was found dead in Chicago with a gunshot wound to the mouth, an obvious warning from the mob to others who may talk too much. Macy quit Ferguson's law firm when he started to represent Roussell because Ferguson represented Grimes and there was a conflict of interest problem imminent. And after the stockholders' meeting, Macy quit Roussell and was unemployed again.

The private law practice was methodical and good-paying work, but it wasn't enough for Macy's idealistic side. But soon enough, events conspired to create Bob Macy's dream job. David Boren, one of the most successful governors in state history, had won election to the U.S. Senate in 1978 and would go on to serve without serious opposition until his voluntary retirement in 1994. Despite the huge popularity of Boren and Nigh, two of the most successful Democrats in state history, Oklahoma was starting to lean toward Republican politics. Former Governor Henry Bellmon, in many ways founder of the modern Oklahoma GOP, decided not to seek reelection for the U.S. Senate. With Bellmon's departure, Andy Coats, a Democrat serving as district attorney of Oklahoma County, thought he could get the U.S. Senate seat back for the Democrats. The Oklahoma Supreme Court ruled that Coats had to resign from his district attorney position in order to run for the Senate. He appealed the decision but lost and subsequently notified the governor he would resign on June 15, 1980. His opponent was a little-known businessman from Ponca City named Don Nickels. Politics in Oklahoma City was at a boiling point. It was expected to be a Democratic sweep, but instead, Oklahoma Republicans carried every office from the courthouse to the Senate. Andy Coats was buried in the sweep, along with many of his original county employees who quit their jobs to assist in his election campaign.

In Oklahoma, the position of district attorney was just one of the seven county offices. Until judicial reform, the title was county attorney, and there was one in each county. Good attorneys could certainly make a lot more money in private law practice with many fewer headaches. The county attorney also served as legal counsel for the three county commissioners, the Sheriff's Association, the treasurer, court clerk, and the county clerk.

Under Coats's administration, young lawyers agreed to stay for two years in exchange for lots of trial experience. Most of them were "preppy types" from the upper-middle class homes with little exposure to real, street-level crime. Many of the young "preppies" ended up going into private practice, but some, like Ray Elliot, Don Deason, and Chuck Black, became respected district judges.

While Oklahoma governors are relatively weak constitutionally, they do have the power of appointment when vacancies occur in statewide posts and in local jobs like the district attorney's position. Such appointees then stand for election in their own right in the next cycle.

To replace Coats, Governor Nigh, hugely popular with voters, wanted to appoint a strong prosecutor who would also, in the 1982 election, have a good shot at retaining the job for Democrats.

One day, Macy's old law school friend David Hudson, an advisor to Nigh, called to say that Paul Ferguson, another one of their old law school pals, "was interested in the job of Oklahoma County DA. Well, I said Paul Ferguson was a good man who would do a good job." The conversation continued, touching on other capable prospective candidates like Saundra Johnson, Arlene Joplin, and Jim McKinney, all respected local attorneys. Macy was intrigued, as Hudson himself, in each case, seemed to have "some reason that he didn't want to recommend any one of them to Nigh." Hudson didn't have anything particularly negative, just a sense the person under discussion wouldn't be the right fit from Nigh's point of view.

That's when the conversation went off on another angle. "What about Bob Macy?" Hudson asked Macy. "Would you be interested?" Despite his youthful infatuation with the radio show about *Mr. DA* and later, more mature visions of prosecutorial work when he worked as a street cop and went to law school, Macy insists he had "never thought about" positioning himself for the Nigh appointment. "I told David that, but he told me to think it over quickly and pressed the issue with me, saying, 'We'll need a decision right away.'" Hudson asked Macy to come the next day to Ponca City and the historic Marland Mansion, where Governor Nigh was visiting and speaking. From that point on, things moved quickly. "I saw George at the Marland Mansion, and we talked." Nigh told him, "Let's get this done by Monday."

"He said I was the most honest man he knew and told me to come by the office first thing that following Monday morning." Nigh wanted the appointment made quickly with the best person he could find. The vacant district attorney's office was a hot potato, and many other less than qualified people wanted it and were busy gathering their political cronies. Nigh knew Macy didn't bend to political pressure and was known for doing the right thing.

Macy ran the idea past John Amick and Bill Berry, friends and local attorneys. Both were well connected at the county courthouse, knew his abilities, and were attuned to the community, both politically and in professional legal circles. Both men liked the idea.

"I took counsel with my wife. I had dragged her all over the world already by that point." Bob knew she was always ready to follow, even if she wasn't particularly fond of the assignment. She had gone to Washington, DC, Indiana, and Florida, but he knew she was ready to settle down at home with her current family and close to her birth family in Seminole. Her favorite times were visiting her family on weekends and, Bob admits, his, too. And this time, she was supportive, always looking after Bob's career.

Nigh and Hudson encouraged Macy to visit, as well, with state Senate President Pro Temp Marvin York, who said immediately he would support Macy's appointment. York would later serve as capitol lobbyist for the City of Oklahoma City.

Macy went to the state capitol's fourth floor and into the governor's office for a meeting that would set the stage for the remainder of his public career. "I told Nigh I was willing to do it. They said let's have the press conference to announce it." There was just one thing. "Nigh looked at my string tie and said, 'Get Macy a neck tie.'

I told him, 'Governor, that's what I wear. I've been wearing it for ten years.' He said okay, so I stuck with it." And that's how the string tie became introduced to the people of Oklahoma.

Still, the deal was not quite closed. The two men lingered for a time over the issue. Nigh told Macy, "the only negative thing we can find is your temper."

Macy told him, "Governor, I haven't been in a fight for over a week."

The Oklahoma chief executive laughed but said: "Bob, if I appoint you, can you control your temper?"

I said, "Governor, I will."

Macy remembers, "I told him I would treat the job just as if I'd been elected to do it and that I would answer only to the public. He said immediately, 'That's exactly the way I'd expect you to do it.'"

Governor Nigh offered the job, and Macy took it. And Judge Stewart Hunter swore Macy in the next day.

In his first public statement, he told the public he wanted to be the best district attorney in city history.

Once in office, Macy had to get control of his office and provide for his safety. He established policies and procedures and hiring practices, something that had been lacking. He had to dispose of his private practice and did so with the valuable assistance of Mickey Homsey, another attorney. The office had to be restructured and supervisors appointed and a distinct level of authority and responsibility established. Macy laid down strict guidelines for his employees. "You can do dope, steal, smoke pot, or drink and drive," he told them. "But you can't do those things and work for me. I have no right to control your off-duty activities unless you act in such a way to reflect badly upon this office. Then I will fire you."

He knew he was going to make enemies. His experience with organized crime figures in Indiana proved that. During his days as a patrolman, he became very close friends with a big Irish cop named Kenny Lyles, "Bigun" as he became known.

Unfortunately, Macy's first year was not an easy one, and his appointment cost him dearly. Betty and Bob, and this is a topic Bob reluctantly talks about, separated in January of 1983. Betty was not a socialite and cared nothing for the country-club gatherings, much of which she would be expected to participate in. Medicine was her entire life. She had stayed at home with the kids until they were through grade school and then went back to nursing. The rift between two careers was too large to repair. But that's not the end of the story with Betty. Currently, she lives with Brett and his family, not far at all from Bob. They remain close, and Bob admits he sees her often.

As for Macy, in 1982, he was elected in his own right to a full four-year term. Bob Macy would be the longest-serving elected prosecutor in Oklahoma City history, and that string tie would become a symbol for a lifetime of service. What he learned from his LEAA tenure he held fast to in Oklahoma—do what's right, and right has might.

CHAPTER 6

A Man in Action

Robert Macy became district attorney of Oklahoma County on June 16, 1980. Accepting Governor George Nigh's appointment, Macy said, "I want to be the best district attorney Oklahoma County has ever had." Macy had many friends at the courthouse and an eclectic local legal practice before taking the job. He already knew there were operational, personnel, and other challenging issues to confront as soon as he stepped through the office door. As it turned out, he faced a lot more of those than expected—and he faced them in the midst of several major prosecutions and political landmines.

In those early days of his career at the courthouse, the wheels were coming off the life and career of Gene Wells, the Oklahoma County sheriff. As Macy recalls, "There was a lot of politics, rough stuff, at the courthouse. Bob Turner, the prior sheriff, had been impeccable. He didn't run for reelection. Eventually, Wells got the job."

Even though he had worked with Turner, Wells apparently had some issues that remained under the radar. The numbers racket in the developments was lucrative. It included what local officials called, "big-time action over in Green Pastures," a neighborhood on the predominantly black east side of Oklahoma City. There were allegations Wells was involved in taking payoffs to avert his eyes from the action.

Apparently, another aspect of corruption at the top was, as evidence ultimately indicated, "diversion of the money he was supposed to use to feed the prisoners. People in the office were making that money work for them rather than using it to feed the prisoners. Anyway, it was a built-in formula for corruption, and Wells was allegedly tied up in it."

At one time in Oklahoma, unbelievably, sheriffs were essentially allowed to use the federal prisoner money as they wished. Wells had an outside bookkeeper employed to keep track of his use of federal funds intended to pay for jail time in the county. For many years, money for such purposes went straight from the federal government to the sheriff. A 1941 legal case set the precedent for county sheriffs to get the direct payments. The state Supreme Court even said sheriffs in such cases were acting "as jailer for the United States."

However, as *The Daily Oklahoman* newspaper reported at the time, a then-recent change in state law barred sheriffs from making a profit from housing county prisoners. Evidence hinted that sheriffs were using the prisoner funds as the equivalent of a business profit center.

Macy remembers that a grand jury investigation was already ongoing on other matters, under the direction of Assistant District Attorney Steve Korotash, a capable attorney who had worked for Coates and remained in the DA's office to work for Macy. As the case unfolded, it appeared Wells misappropriated funds for his own use. The grand jury got a tip that, in essence, guided its deliberations and investigation to look into Gene Wells' office.

The probe shifted toward corruption in the sheriff's office, "and that was a rich vein. They subpoenaed his records. Wells refused to comply. Then the grand jury actually went into his office as a group and demanded the records." Still, he refused to comply. "Later, Wells was called to testify, but he refused."

As events reached a fever peak, including daily news stories in the three newspapers then competing in Oklahoma City, Wells became ill. As Macy notes, "Then he went into the hospital, and he died just two days later. It was certainly an odd situation. Wells was under a doctor's care, and, therefore, there was no requirement for an autopsy. Anyway, it was a mystery."

After Wells died, a better era began at the Oklahoma County Sheriff's Office, but the tumult impacted Macy's early tenure and affected his thinking for years.

State vs. Clifford Henry Bowen

Two weeks into Macy's tenure as district attorney, at 2:00 a.m. on July 6, 1980, a day after Macy's birthday, a triple homicide linked to illegally selling Dilaudid and the "Dixie Mafia," occurred at the Guest House Inn in north Oklahoma City. The summer heat had brought several of the guests out to the pool for the evening. The number of guests thinned as the night went along until only three men remained sitting around the poolside table. Conversation and cold beer kept the three men in their chairs, never noticing when a salt-and-peppery-haired stranger in a red ball cap appeared out of the shadows. Without hesitation, the mystery man shot each man twice with a .45-caliber pistol and silver-tipped, hollow point bullets, killing two instantly and mortally wounding the third, then disappeared back into the night.

Ray Peters, Marvin Nowlin, and Lawrence Evans were strangers until that night; the acquaintances shared the pool with Ray Peters's associates, Harold Behrens and his boyfriend Herman Borden, Carrie Pitchford and her daughter Dawn, and the motel's night manager, Mary Chilton, and a female friend. Harold Behrens and Herman Borden were the first to excuse themselves from the poolside party. As Behrens left, he walked up behind Ray Peters, placed his hands on Peters's shoulders, and said, "I'll see you tomorrow," then walked away with Borden. This was later thought to be the gunman's signal as to whom to target as Behrens feared that Peters was going to expose his drug business after being arrested in Pauls Valley for drug possession in Behrens's car. So Behrens wanted to permanently silence Peters before he said too much.

Mary Chilton decided to check her mail then check on her sleeping children in her room. She and her friend left shortly after Behrens and Borden. She later testified to seeing a tall man with pale skin, salt-and-peppery hair, a potbelly, and a red ball cap for an hour and a half around the well-lit vending machines as she walked past and made a mental note that he was not a hotel guest. She told police that she'd gotten a good look because she was within three feet of him as she walked by. Carrie and Dawn Pitchford left shortly after when Carrie realized they were the only two females left out by the poolside. Carrie Pitchford was on the second floor on her veranda when she saw a tall man with light skin, a puffy face, a potbelly, and a red ball cap under the well-lit concession lights. She testified that it was like he was center stage with a spotlight on him. Though neither lady saw the actual shooting, both heard what they first believed to be fireworks but realized were gunshots. Mrs. Chilton gave a detailed description to a detective, who did a composite drawing of the suspect. A few days later, Mrs. Chilton identified a man from a photographic lineup, but when she saw him in the physical lineup, she recanted because the man was too short to be the one she saw that night.

Sergeant David McBride of the Oklahoma City Police Department looked at the composite sketch, as all of the officers did. He believed it looked like a man that he and a long-ago partner, Herald Behrens, had under surveillance for organized crime in 1975. Behrens and McBride conducted surveillance for several months on two men, Jerry Ray James and Clifford Henry Bowen, until both moved from their apartments and disappeared. Around that same time, Harold Behrens resigned from the police department to set up a drug distribution ring. When McBride heard the physical description of the Guest House Motel assailant and knew of Harold Behrens's involvement, he thought of Clifford Henry Bowen and pulled Bowen's picture from the police records bureau. He then took the picture to the homicide supervisor and said he thought Bowen to be a good suspect but was told that Bowen was deceased.

Several months later McBride, still sure that the picture looked like Bowen, contacted the police department in Bowen's last known residence of Tyler, Texas, to confirm that Bowen was deceased. To his surprise, Bowen was still living in Tyler with his wife and step-daughter. He informed District Attorney Investigator Jack Mullenix of his findings. As a result, an arrest warrant was issued for Clifford Henry Bowen. Shortly afterwards, Bowen was arrested for the triple slaying and held at the Smith County Jail in Tyler, Texas, without bond.

To be sure the right man was in custody, a photo of Bowen was shown to Mary Chilton and to Carrie Pitchford; both agreed that was the man they saw that night. Three weeks later, Mary Chilton and Carrie Pitchford were flown to Tyler, Texas, to see if they could positively identify Bowen out of a lineup at the Smith County Jail. Escorted into the jail, Mary Chilton, followed a while later by Carrie Pitchford, viewed a lineup of similar-looking men and then positively identified Bowen from the lineup. After they were flown back, District Attorney Macy began the paperwork for Bowen's extradition. On November 25, 1980, Macy presented his extradition papers, signed by both Oklahoma Governor George Nigh and Texas Governor Bill Clements, to Smith County District Judge Donald Carroll. Though Bowen's lawyer, Frank Wright, fought to detain Bowen's extradition to Oklahoma, the judge granted Macy's request because Wright had not filed a writ of habeas corpus prior to the extradition request. Macy was given the okay to proceed with the extradition, so District Attorney Investigator Ken Lyles placed his own belt around Bowen's chest to clip handcuffs to it in preparation for the trip back to Oklahoma. Accompanying Macy on the trip back to Oklahoma with Bowen were District Attorney Investigators Ken Lyles and Jack Mullenix, two Oklahoma City police detectives, Bill Cook and Bob Horn, and a reporter for the newspaper *The Daily Oklahoman*, Mick Hinton.

During the trial proceedings, Bowen's attorney, Raymond Burger, attempted to discredit Mary Chilton's testimony by asking if she was sure it was Bowen she saw and not the previously identified suspect who was released because he was too short. Burger told Mrs. Chilton, "Look at the face, Mrs. Chilton; are you sure? Look at the nose, Mrs. Chilton; are you still sure?" Mrs. Chilton told Mr. Burger that it was like Bowen's image was burned into her mind and though there were similarities between the two men, the shorter man was definitely not the one she saw that night.

Though twelve witnesses testified to seeing Bowen at a rodeo in Tyler, Texas, the night of the killings, Macy uncovered a unique twist that would have allowed Bowen time to be at the rodeo between the time his witnesses testified to seeing him and the time the killings occurred. Macy discovered that Bowen's key witnesses were flying via Learjet daily from Tyler to the Oklahoma City courtroom. He sent an investigator to fly to Tyler, catch a Learjet back, and go to the Guest House Inn location to establish a timeframe. It was revealed that Bowen could have been at the rodeo, caught a Learjet out of Tyler, did the shootings, and then caught another Learjet back home.

Because of the flight risk, Bowen was denied bond first by District Judge Raymond Naifeh, then by Alma Wilson, a Cleveland County district judge temporarily trying cases in the Oklahoma County courts. But on February 7, 1981, Judge Stewart Hunter, a juvenile court justice, granted bond of $75,000 for all three counts of murder. Moments later, Bowen posted bail and walked out of the courthouse a free man. After Bowen spoke to a radio reporter, David Parrett, about "going to Texas to build some witnesses," Macy filed a petition to have the bond revoked out of fear that Bowen would flee back to Texas or his key witnesses may come into harm's way.

The February 11, 1981, headlines in the local paper read, *Alleged Hit Man Back in Jail After Bond Revoked.* Criminal District Judge Homer Smith reversed Judge Hunter's order and revoked the $75,000 bond set for Bowen just four days prior, placing Bowen back into jail. Several days later, the State Court of Criminal Appeals, in a split decision, granted Bowen a bond of $225,000. The bond was the highest ever posted in Oklahoma County. Despite that, Bowen posted bond fifteen minutes later and was freed once more.

On March 9, Bowen was back in Judge Raymond Naifeh's court and on March 13, a jury found him guilty on three counts of first-degree murder after five hours of deliberation. Bowen, in astonishment, shook his head and repeatedly muttered, "You're crazy ... you fools." After the verdicts were read, Bowen's attorney, Raymond Burger, offered "a $25,000 reward for information leading to the apprehension and conviction of the real murderer. That's the only way to solve this crime, because obviously the police are not going to." The next day, the jury's decision came down: three sentences of death by lethal injection. Bowen spent the next two years on death row appealing the decision.

On April 28, 1983, Bowen's attorneys, Steven Taylor and Jack Zimmerman, announced publicly they had evidence pointing to another man as the triggerman in the killings, a South Carolina ex-policeman named Lee Crowe, who was the boyfriend of Raymond Peters' estranged wife. It was reported that a witness had stated that, while staying at the Peters/Crowe residence, she overheard Crowe and Mrs. Peters talking about killing her husband because she didn't want her children to be around him. The two attorneys gave several factors in pointing the finger at Crowe: he matched the description of the shooter, was reported to have been seen in Oklahoma City the same week of the shootings with Mrs. Peters, he carried the same type of gun and ammunition used in the triple killing, and upon his return to South Carolina, he quit the police force. Though Oklahoma City homicide detective Sergeant Don Pennington responded by saying that Crowe had been investigated and ruled out as a suspect, the appellate court gave the state attorney general's office twenty days to reply to the motion for a new trial. On June 4, 1983, Clifford Henry Bowen was granted an evidentiary hearing in front of Judge Raymond Naifeh once more. Naifeh said he would hear the evidence and then determine if a new trial was warranted.

On September 30, 1983, the evidentiary hearing began. Bowen's lawyers, Zimmerman and Taylor, presented the evidence against Lee Crowe as the gunman and said that within weeks, authorities were aware of Crowe as a possible suspect of the slayings but did not give the information to Bowen's trial attorney, Raymond Burger. Macy rebutted, "Burger did not file the usual motion asking prosecution to turn over any material that might have been helpful to the defense either." The defense called Macy to the witness stand. He testified that two witnesses placed Bowen at the Guest House Inn the night of the slayings and ruled out Crowe when shown a photograph of him. He also said Crowe had an alibi that checked out and ballistics tests had eliminated his .45 as the death weapon.

On December 1, 1984, Judge Naifeh ruled that the evidence presented did not warrant a new trial. According to the court ruling, the death penalty handed Bowen was justified because of the "cold and calculated executions" and because the crime was "especially heinous, atrocious, or cruel." The appeals court, in an opinion by Presiding Judge Hez Bussey, agreed that no new trial was justified and rejected fourteen other contentions by Bowen's attorneys that errors were committed in his trial.

Bowen's lawyers continued the appeals process; however, a motion for rehearing was denied on March 8, 1985, and an execution date was set for June 17, 1985. Subsequently, a stay of execution was filed in the Oklahoma Court of Appeals on May 6, 1985, but was denied the next day, and a similar motion was filed in the United States Supreme Court on May 20, which was granted by Justice Bryon White, pending disposition of the petition for writ of certiorari or review of the lower court's documents. In the petition, Bowen claimed denial of due process under the constitution in the prosecution's withholding of exculpatory evidence and a denial of effective assistance of counsel at both stages of the capital murder trial. The petition was denied, and the Court of Criminal Appeals reset Bowen's execution date to August 12, 1985.

Once again, a temporary stay of execution was granted immediately after pending the review of an instant writ of habeas corpus. United States District Court Judge Thomas Brett granted the writ of habeas corpus and set aside the murder convictions of Clifford Henry Bowen on January 22, 1986. Although Harold Behrens received a life without parole sentence for his part in killing Raymond Peters on January 24, 1981, no one was ever brought to justice for the triple killings. Clifford Henry Bowen died in 1996. Though it is Macy's opinion that justice was not served for the three slain victims, he knows that some cases do not always come out with an acquittal or a guilty verdict or justice served satisfactorily. Mere men can do only their best at serving justice. Eventually, justice is left to God to serve completely.

David Shupe, now a veteran of nearly four decades with the Oklahoma City police, remembers, "It was a rough start, including with the police officers. Bob Macy immediately inherited the very tough case of John Clark," a well-liked and popular leader of the rank-and-file police officers who had been charged with murder or manslaughter by Macy's predecessor.

The Clark case began in March 1980, when he and his partner responded to a call of a disturbance at an apartment complex in the south downtown area. "When they got there, there was a belligerent man, essentially yelling 'come and get me, copper!' It was like something from a Jimmy Cagney movie. The man's girlfriend was also screaming about killing cops. He would not go with them and didn't make it easy. Other officers were on the scene." But by that time, several blows were struck to the man's head, and he was unconscious. The man was taken to the hospital and died two days later in police custody.

The case was fraught with difficulty for prosecutors. Macy soon learned the apartment owner had scrubbed the place clean. The evidence got cold because one or two days passed before investigators were at the scene. What had started out as a controversial arrest turned into a death case.

Evidence from the dead man's body indicated that one or more of the early blows ultimately caused his death, and it was unclear that Clark was the one responsible. As Macy remembers his prosecution of the case, "It was tough, really tough, but I followed through on the charges my predecessor had filed." Macy studied the file and knew the evidence was contradictory. The FBI was making noise that they would intervene, and dismissal would be considered a cover-up. No one on his staff wanted to try the case, so Macy stepped in and led the prosecution. He knew that only a wide-open trial could resolve the problems, so he planned to open the case with all the evidence so the jury could decide. In fact, he did just that. Macy put every bit of evidence his predecessor had gathered against Clark into his prosecution. Jurors had a lot to consider, and, in the end, they acquitted him in forty-five minutes. Reporters asked what he thought about that, and Macy said simply, "I think justice was served." Macy admits still today that was the correct verdict, but the case made many officers despise him for even taking it to trial.

Another police-involvement case: Highway Patrol Officer James Pishel, in hot pursuit of a speeding motorcycle, ignored a four-way stop and exploded through an intersection at some ninety-three miles per hour. Pishel and his vehicle struck a car in which the wife and two daughters of Choctaw Police Chief John Whetsel were traveling. In a wrenching twist of fate, Whetsel himself was one of the first responders at the scene of the devastating wreck, in which Whetsel's wife and one of the girls died.

Macy was certain the hot pursuit in that case was reckless, even negligent, and pursued charges against Pishel. In the end, Officer Pishel "walked" due to a hung jury, and Macy chose not to file charges again in the case. As a result of the hung-jury verdict, the state Highway Patrol rehired Pishel, who had a troubled career. Though Macy had not known Whetsel long, he was asked to carry out the hardest task ever asked of him—to carry Whetsel's little girl's coffin. Macy became a lifelong friend to Whetsel, who later was elected Oklahoma County sheriff.

Macy carried through on the police prosecutions, but he eventually managed to gain the confidence of the same rank and file that liked Clark. As Shupe recalls, "To overcome the dynamics of that very difficult situation required what he did and was inclined to do anyway, to establish a close relationship of respect and mutual support with the police. I'll tell you, police officers can be at times the most unforgiving of critics."

As indicated, it all added to a highly stressful start to what turned into twenty-one years as the county's top prosecutor. All this came in a context of Macy turning a methodical and meticulous eye to problems of crime in the city. His public life as a crime fighter, though, was not all about crime. His passion, what he calls "the fire in his belly," dealt with more than just serving out justice. He wanted to give life, at least as much as he could, back to those who had been victimized by having their lives taken away, figuratively and literally. The death penalty to Bob Macy was not an act of social vengeance nearly as much as it was an attempt to keep killers from repeating their crime and to warn others of the possible outcome of their actions, should they decided to come to Oklahoma County.

Despite frustrations illustrated in the Bowen case and the circumstantial evidence of his ties to the Dixie Mafia, Macy never believed there was a heavy mob presence in the city he came to love. Still, he knew organized crime lurked at the edges, in the shadows and along the interstate highways that criminals, like all other Americans, used to move quickly from one place to the next. Indeed, beside the Bowen case, a drug "mule" killing and the shady career of Andre DeJesus was an early sign of the mob's attempts to come into the city.

Macy remembers one case from those early months that he thought "stunk" of mob involvement. A drug "mule" carrying "product" from Los Angeles passed through the city on his way to Detroit. The man was killed in a manner that resembled a mob execution. Macy got information, a tip, that mob boss Tony Giacolini was probably involved. At least circumstantially, it seems Giacolini could have been involved, but the case was never solved. But Macy believes the case hinted, however fleetingly, at larger involvement from organized crime.

"Before I came back to Oklahoma, some believed the mob was very active hereabouts. We always heard they were trying to run drugs out of Kansas City. There was a guy named Tony Spilantro who ran junkets to and from Las Vegas to Oklahoma City. Apparently, he would burglarize the homes of rich people there then dash back to Oklahoma with the money. After a couple of years of that, one day his dead body was found in Indiana." This was the same Spilantro who was involved in the Teamsters' retirement fund from Macy's earlier days.

"Then, there was Andre DeJesus, who ran prostitution and cocaine operations and who was into pretty diamonds and jewelry. We caught him because we had an informant. When he was tried here, he was convinced he would dodge conviction. Then, after a good jury of Oklahoma City people convicted him and he was sentenced to prison, he stood in the halls of the courtroom and cried like a baby. He'd never, for a minute, thought he'd get caught, and if he did get caught, never thought he'd serve a day."

Ultimately, the mob seemingly stepped away from the city during Macy's tenure, leaving the street crime fight between and among ethnic gangs in conflict with Macy's allies in the police department.

Into that summer whirlwind of mayhem and intrigue, in the midst of controversies profound and petty, stepped the string tie-adorned Bob Macy, the new kid on the block. After surviving the bureaucratic wars in Washington and local-level postings in Florida and Indiana, Macy had a philosophy about prosecution and office management that was proven workable. He began to implement it immediately.

"The way I ran my office, cases would come in and initially be assigned to a division or to the chairman of a section. The police would bring the case. Our team leader would review all the details as they stood at that early point and make a recommendation on what the case was worth in prison/jail time and in terms of our efforts," Macy explains.

"An assistant DA would then make a recommendation, including to the defense lawyer. Let's say, based on the nature of the case and the evidence, it might be ten years, that is, a ten-year sentence. The defense lawyer then faced three choices: plead guilty and take the recommendation, go to trial and take their chances, or plead 'blind' and let the judge decide."

While not completely inflexible in considering the circumstances of a crime situation, Macy did not "really believe in plea bargaining. I tried to train my assistants to make recommendations to our office and to the defense based on the valid basis of the evidence in the case and let things go forward from there." Macy also had a standing order for his staff. "Don't promise anything you can't deliver—and answer all your phone calls."

As he built one of the best trial teams in the country and waged relentless war on criminals over the coming two decades, Macy made a science of motivating employees and repeatedly delivered lectures on the subject to the National College of District Attorneys and similar organizations.

One such presentation stressed that the political success of any elected prosecutor—and Macy, like most of his peers, faced popular scrutiny regularly—depended "entirely upon the performance of the office employees." Positive motivation, he argued, was crucial because it incited employees to perform "more effectively and efficiently." With brevity and professionalism, Macy's presentation touched themes ranging from pride in workmanship to idealism, from supervisor praise to the importance of a "team" mindset.

He notes that prosecutors' offices are unique in that the "service" or "product" is justice itself. And he points out that the "super egos of trial lawyers" had to be taken into account in establishing a strategy for employee motivation.

The undeniable impact of a prosecutor's work upon society, especially his or her own local community, provided an obvious method for helping young lawyers realize "the importance of the job itself." An effective DA has to fight to provide the best possible working conditions, salaries, and benefits, not leaving this to others. "You are their representative," he told the assembled prosecutors.

He pressed local DAs to allow non-trial personnel to attend and witness "the courtroom drama, the product of their labors" so they could witness the end result of their efforts. He advocated—and in his work for Oklahoma County practiced—"broad delegation of authority and responsibility" within office guidelines. And he said it was crucial to provide their bright young staffs the "opportunity for participation in policy and planning."

Finally, Macy believed throughout his career that it was the prosecutor's role as leader to have the right attitude toward employees, to model personal and professional behavior, establish and maintain a tireless work ethic, be willing to take a stand, and—above all—to lead by example.

For twenty-one years, these were the management principles of Robert H. Macy, and they were the basis for his professional and personal ethics.

Before long, Macy had attracted a first-class team of legal professionals. He remembers every one of them and has kind words for each. But perhaps his closest friend was his longtime first assistant, Patrick Morgan, whom he describes as "a true war hero and a great American." His military service included time as the youngest major in the Vietnam War, Macy remembers. "Anytime I was out of the office, Morgan was essentially the DA, and he did a wonderful job."

Don Deason was a felony team leader who eventually was appointed to a special judge position and is now serving as district trial judge. An eminently effective trial lawyer, he was a loyal friend to Macy and, notably, an ordained minister.

Susan Caswell was also a felony team leader who was later elected as a district judge. She became, Macy says, "a darn good judge" and married Clint Caswell, who worked on the Oklahoma City Police Department at the same time as Bob's son. In one of several overlays in the careers of Macy and his son, Clint's father, Ben, was Bob's police colleague on the police department back in the 1950s.

Macy fondly remembers Fern Smith, whom he bluntly described as "the equal of any man in any courtroom in Oklahoma. She tried more capital cases than anyone in my office. She was a lady and a professional. It's interesting that she was so soft spoken, but such a darned good trial lawyer. She always conducted herself as a lady and someone who could be trusted."

Fern's husband, Wendell, another top-notch lawyer on Macy's team, was "a truly gentle man, a gentleman all the way. He was a hero and a recipient of the Silver Star." Macy remembers, "He died of a brain tumor. It broke Fern's heart when he died." Before his death, Wendell, too, was a judge.

Finding and grooming young talent, Macy churned out a powerhouse of capable alumni who went on to serve in higher office. One was Vicki Miles-LaGrange, who he hired shortly after her return from the nation's capital as a young lawyer just out of Howard University. Despite stellar credentials and roots in one of eastside Oklahoma City's best-known and most-respected families, Miles-LaGrange had trouble finding the right job after her return home from Washington. A skillful lawyer and brilliant politician who served in the state senate, Miles-LaGrange was a U.S. attorney during the Clinton administration and then became the second black woman federal trial judge in the country. When she became chief judge for the western district of Oklahoma in 2009, she told reporters and friends, "Bob Macy gave me a job when no one else would."

Another bright star in his crown was Tommy Colbert, who Macy characterizes as "sharp in every sense of the word." Colbert went on to distinguished service at the state Court of Civil Appeals.

Tim Henderson, an ex-policeman now in private law practice, is characterized by Macy as "a superb, even outstanding litigant. If you wanted to be sure a bulldog was on the case, you gave it to Henderson." Steve Huddleston, a former assistant DA now in private practice, was "one of the handfuls I thought could have made a good successor when I left in 2001. I felt he could have filled my shoes." Judge Joe Cannon dubbed him "Magnum DA" because of his star-like visage.

Macy remains proud of the work of his legal intern office, which gave many aspiring young law students their first glimpse of the real world. The program stressed instruction in ethics and handling of actual legal problems, Macy recalls. One alumnus is Kerry Kelley, a woman who now heads the felony division at the U.S. attorney's office.

Macy grins at memories of Gary Ackley, a "great researcher and case preparer" who became one of his longtime employees. Jay

Farber, a narcotics expert, is now an assistant U.S. attorney. Chuck Black, now a district judge, learned to be "a real trial lawyer" working for Macy.

Other key aides to Macy are scattered throughout the pages of this biography.

On the other side, among the public defenders and the defense bar, Macy considered some worthy foes. "Bob Ravitz would be number one among those I truly respected and still do. He was a good public defender, a good lawyer, and a good man." Ravitz still is the top public defender in Oklahoma County.

Jim Turner and his brother, Ken, were "not only good lawyers but also good human beings and sons of former Sheriff Bob Turner." Then there was O.A. "Buck" Cargill, Jr., a criminal defense lawyer whose father was a "bag man" in one of Oklahoma's most searing political scandals, involving the bribery of Supreme Court members. For all that, Macy believes Buck Cargill, Jr. was honest and worthy of respect.

In the category of "S.O.B.," Macy puts James Rowan, a public defender and fierce opponent of capital punishment. But the latter view was not what polarized his relationship with Rowan.

Macy remembers, "As you know, I love my son very much. Several years into his career with the Oklahoma City police, Brett and other officers were involved in a bust over in Del City. As they began to enter the apartment, the bad guys inside opened up, and a shootout resulted. As soon as he heard a commotion, and before the bullets flew, Brett, who was experienced, hit the ground. Two of the other officers were hit. One was hit in the belt buckle; another was hit in the hand. But the group made the arrest, and no one died." Macy recalls his encounter with Rowan a short time later this way.

"Some time later, I was on the elevator with a couple of my investigators"; one of them was Hal Burleson. That day, "Rowan got on ahead of us and couldn't see me in the back. Rowan said to the guys he was with, 'It's too darn bad the DA's son didn't get killed.' I couldn't believe it. Well, my guys had to drag me off the elevator. I was so angry. I told Rowan the day would come that 'I'm gonna meet you somewhere, even if it's ten years from now, and you'll be hurting.'" That confrontation never took place, but Macy never forgave Rowan. Rowan denied saying anything like that, but Macy heard him.

As for the judges before whom he tried cases, "I often found myself in front of Judge Ray Naifeh. I didn't always get my way. We knew each other, but I remember how surprised and touched I was when a story got back to me."

It seems a group of attorneys were talking and someone said something negative about Macy and his style. Judge Naifeh interrupted and said, "Bob Macy's a friend of mine. You can't say something negative about him in my presence."

Macy professes, "I never knew until then he felt that way about me. It meant a lot to me, coming from a judge I didn't always persuade."

As for Judge Charlie Owen, the first black trial judge in state history and still a legend in Oklahoma County, Macy said he became "one of my closest friends in all those years." Even in cycles when he lost cases in front of the affable Judge Owen, Macy would ask him to conduct his swearing-in ceremonies—usually not too long after each of them had been overwhelmingly returned to office. Oklahoma trial judges are subjected to popular reconfirmation, and Owen was always returned to office.

As for one of the county's most disputatious jurists, "I loved Joe Cannon, as crazy as he was." Most of these judges served well into Macy's latter years in office.

Macy comments on an earlier era of jurists. "Carmen Harris, Bill Meyer, Homer Smith, Stewart Hunter, Harold Theus, Jack Parr, Dave Cook. I always thought the group that was on the bench when I first got to the DA's job was just about the best I'd ever seen."

Macy's son, Brett, a young law enforcement officer in those early days, commented in a fall 2009 interview, "Jack Parr and Charlie Owen were always in charge in their courtroom. You had to respect that."

Despite his respect for this cluster of jurists, Bob Macy had occasional conflicts with nearly every one of them, including a memorable joust with Hunter over bail for Clifford Henry Bowen in the infamous Guest House Inn murders case, mentioned before.

As the years passed, Macy attracted some of the best legal minds in the state and region and retained the loyalty and professionalism of attorneys who likely would have done financially better for themselves if they'd left for the greener pastures of Dallas, Chicago, New York City, or the nation's capital.

One such lawyer was John Jacobson, who still works at the prosecutor's office for current incumbent David Prater. During a long interview in September 2009, he reflected, "Bob Macy gave me a career and the job of a lifetime. I was a city attorney and was involved in work with the civil division of the city government. Director Richard Mitchell asked me if I was interested in working for the city. I was, and I took it. Then in 1988, I had one brief six-week shot at the city attorney's office. I realized I had made a mistake. I came back to the DA's office especially to work under Bob Macy."

Jacobson has the same memories as many other Macy alumni. "He mentored me. He always, always had time for me and for others on the staff. This explains in part the great loyalty we had and have for him. He has blessed many lawyers, many developing legal minds, with his time and energy. There are judges, state prosecutors, and assistant U.S. attorneys all over the place who got their start under Bob Macy.

"What I learned from him was that if you communicate, it is possible to solve a lot of issues, a lot of challenges. He taught us to keep informed, to listen. He certainly would listen to us. You knew if you were informed and deliberative, you could make a decision with his backing," says Jacobson.

Jacobson worked almost exclusively in the civil arena, removed from the glare of publicity and from the high-profile murders and other felony cases Macy became known for all over the country. He reflects, "It characterized the civil division under DA Bob Macy that we were always talking things through. I was his first assistant, and it still impresses me that never once did he ever cut me out of any decisions. He wanted people to voice their concerns, to say what was on their mind, to reach a good decision."

"Macy's way," Jacobson says, "was to put someone there, to trust that person to call upon their experience and the experience of others to do the right thing. He knew it was a prosecution office, but he had other responsibilities on the civil side. He took those very seriously."

Seldom remarked in most examinations of Macy's tenure is his role as a counselor and legal advisor to other county officials. Jacobson reports, "His input on contracts and other issues was very important. He counseled elected officials on when to hire and how to hire right. He defended police officers and others in the crime-fighting arena and balanced that with his responsibilities as the chief law enforcement officer. The other elected officials truly respected him because he gave equal weight to each of them, treated them as peers whose issues and needs were important."

In the areas that did garner headlines, Jacobson says, "Of course, he was tops in the prosecution of homicides, sex-crime cases, and other terribly significant crimes. I remember how, in his time here, he elevated the standing of the DA's people. They were always good in the courtroom if they worked for Bob Macy. He was a great attorney but also a superb administrator and counselor to the other public officials. He made his attorneys available when needed to assure his peers had the advice and guidance they needed. I was also impressed that he did not hesitate to tell a colleague when they were out of line or doing something the law did not support. His duty was to the constitution and to the law."

In their working with the other county elected officials, "'No' is always a simple answer when you're a counselor, but Bob Macy sought a legal way to do things. He supported us in the civil division; he was not afraid to try cases, just like the criminal division did. His colleagues and his staff knew they could approach him 24/7. They had his ear, his good will, his support. He would give them great advice."

As time passed, it was customary for not only staff but also his elected peers to seek Macy's advice before making or even considering a career change. "He was also able to give counsel at a whole other level than normal. 'What do you think about plans to run for another office, to enter private practice or some other decision that was pending?' He benefited all of us tremendously," Jacobson recalls.

Another aspect of Macy's twenty-one years in the job that might disarm some critics was his consistent concern for young people, even those who'd already made a mistake that put them on the wrong side of the law. Pam Harrell designed the juvenile programs in Macy's office when he was the top prosecutor, and she ran them with efficiency and professionalism. There is much more about Bob's and Pam's work with juveniles later in the book.

When it comes to prevention of the conditions that put convicted criminals in a "graduate school of crime," as Macy describes prison, it's past time we try something different. And the something different, among other things, is to allow serious Christians to do serious work in crime prevention. Macy remembers his work with Rev. Bill Richardson, an east side leader who stood up for some young African American males who found themselves in trouble. Macy recounts, "There was one case that involved three young men, students from Langston who were out driving one night. One of them had a gun in the vehicle and had fired a gun out of the vehicle while it was moving. No one was hurt, but there was a problem that arose. In short, they could have been in big trouble." Shooting from a vehicle could be charged as a felony.

Richardson "begged me to cut them a break. He said they had made mistakes. I had a tough call, especially on two of them. Basically, we went with ten years deferred." That sentence meant that if they violated the law again and got sent before a judge, they would have to serve a real prison or jail sentence. Macy says, "Not a one of them ever went back on me. They stayed clean. Richardson was a good man."

Similarly, on the west side of the city, at the church of Rev. Jim Vineyard, Macy ultimately participated in the parole of about three-dozen offenders, many of them youthful. Not a one subsequently ever became a financial burden on taxpayers for the costs of incarceration.

Recounting a story first told in *The City Sentinel,* a weekly newspaper in Oklahoma City in 1997, there was a Laotian immigrant man running with the wrong crowd. He and his bunch got into a gun battle with a Vietnamese gang. He was wounded, lying in a hospital bed, and no doubt headed to prison, where he probably would have learned to be a better criminal.

But his sister, a Christian, begged a member of Windsor Hills Baptist Church, Vineyard's congregation, to go pray with the lad, who became born again. With the Laotian man facing prison, Pastor Vineyard, a military veteran, went to Bob Macy. Macy intervened and asked the court to allow the Laotian to be given over to Vineyard's care, with the condition that the boy admit guilt in the shooting incident. The court agreed.

Things went well for a time, but then the boy, Kam, started skipping church and seemed headed for the dark side again. Vineyard dictated a letter asking that the man's parole be revoked, but he left off the date. Vineyard told me, "I got Kam in my office and gave him the letter. I told him all I needed to do was date the letter . . . and send it. He got down on his knees and promised me the moon, begging me not to send the letter. He didn't miss any more services." Kam stayed out of trouble, a happy ending by this world's standards.

There are many other stories. In the course of a career, a reporter and writer like me hears a lot of stories. Many, even some good ones, never work their way into print. This, adapted from a story Pat McGuigan first wrote for *Perspective* magazine, is about choices, including Bob Macy's choices.

Jolene, sixteen years old at the time, awoke in a temporary place of safety, an Oklahoma City shelter where the father who had abused her for years could not find her. Police officers and Department of Human Services workers took her there after coming to the home she shared with her father's mother and a younger sister, also the object of the man's warped "affections."

Jolene was tough. When the girls were little, Jolene's mother had physically abused the two girls. Jolene had burn scars on her hands to remind her of that pain and of the mother, who simply left one day. When the father's abuse increased as they grew older, Jolene's younger sister filed a report against the man, the girls were rescued, and Jolene was taken to that shelter. Although grateful to be away from her abuser, Jolene nonetheless did not want to stay there and for good reason.

There's a preface to the shelter story. After her mother disappeared, as the home situation fell further into the pit of hell, little Jolene responded to a boy's invitation and began to ride the Sunday church bus to Windsor Hills Baptist Church on NW 23rd Street. It became her home, at least on Sundays. Her grandma, sister, and two younger female cousins began to go, too. They learned about Jesus and the Bible.

Her father, a trucker, was gone most of the time. As the years passed, he sneered more and more about the church time his mother and his daughters had when he was away. Jolene learned to "keep church at church" in order to avoid conflict.

Jolene listened to other girls her age from a distance, laughing and having a good time. She remembers, "They dressed in such lovely dresses and always had perfect little curls in their hair and beautiful, matching bows. I had never fit in with these girls. Our lives were very different, to say the least. They were pastors' daughters, teachers' daughters, or college students' daughters. These were the types of girls who went to Christian schools, not me!" Even without her father's hate and abuse, there was no money for tuition at such a place. Every time he came home, all the money was gone, spent on marijuana and other drugs.

Jolene was grateful for Sundays at church, where she glimpsed another world. One man at church, Brother Russell, heard about her dreams of mission work. One day, he asked the girl, "How would you like to go to the Christian school here at Windsor Hills to prepare for your future?' For one of the first times in her life, she was given a choice. Jolene jumped at the offer, and Russell paid her tuition.

On her tenth birthday, October 23, 1988, she entered Windsor Hills Baptist School. She told her teacher it was "the best birthday present I ever received." She fit in academically, but "I had a harder time fitting in with the students … I was already, streetwise, tough and bossy. I had learned to stand up for myself, and I often challenged the other girls and made them cry."

But, Jolene recalls, "God gave me a friend that year by the name of Rebecca, who was an only child and took a liking to me despite my personality quirks."

After a couple of years, her patron went off to the missions in Africa. There was no one to pay her tuition. Teachers didn't have the heart to send her away, so they kept their mouths shut. She did well, growing spiritually and academically.

In her ninth grade year, a new principal discovered no one had paid her tuition. He talked with Jolene, and they formed a plan that allowed her to work in the school after hours, cleaning the bathrooms and vacuuming floors in order to take care of, in a small part, her tuition.

Thus, by the age of fourteen, Jolene lived in two worlds. Her school and church were one; the other was the place she went to at 3:00 p.m. most days, a place "full of cursing and drugs" and abuse. That "home" was filthy, with only a tiny corner of the bedroom she shared with her sister as an imperfect refuge from the harsh reality of life away from Windsor Hills. Even there, Jolene tried to avoid being in the same house as her father and often found ways to stay overnight with school friends. Then, within just a few weeks' time, the two female cousins who used to ride the bus to church with her on Sundays committed suicide. Her younger sister began to hint that she no longer wanted to live either. The younger girl was hospitalized, and counselors learned of the awful family secret the two girls shared.

That's how Jolene came to the shelter, shielded from her father's abuse but longing to return to her true home, Windsor Hills Baptist School, and to church. Other kids in the shelter told her nobody ever got out before at least six months had passed. All she had with her was a backpack and things she'd grabbed when the Department of Human Services workers and police came.

Unknown to her, the people of Windsor Hills were looking for her. When she was allowed to make one telephone call after being at the shelter for several days, she called the church. An associate pastor, Joe Finn, remembering the street smart tough little gal, asked her, "Jolene, do you *want* to come back to church and school?"

She said she was "thankful for places such as this shelter that protect children and for those who lovingly work in them; however, I was also glad not to be in need of this place anymore." She certainly and quickly said she wanted to return to the school and to the church.

Vineyard got word to Macy, describing Jolene's situation as he understood it. Macy remembers that his assistant, "Jayne came to talk to me because she'd heard from the people who were trying to find Jolene and get her out of the shelter and back into the congregation. She wrote a note to my assistant in the case we were working on."

During a recess, Macy "wrote a note to the presiding judge encouraging the jurist 'to get this little girl out of there.' She was a child in harm's way who had been rescued; now she needed to go to the next place." A busy man on a busy day, Bob Macy dispatched his secretary to the shelter. As Jolene recalls it, Macy's secretary, Jayne, arrived as "the most beautiful woman I had ever met, and she made me feel like I was the most important person she had to take care of." Jolene learned that the family of her friend, Rebecca, wanted to be her guardians.

The judicial hearing was held, and Rebecca's family assumed responsibility for Jolene. They took her home across the street from Windsor Hills Baptist School. Rebecca's parents said Jolene would be given an allowance, the same as Rebecca's. After school, the other teenagers swarmed to welcome her back home. When she walked across the street to Rebecca's house, she was escorted into her first "own room."

That night in bed, she opened letters from classmates. "I smiled and wept as I read the precious words my peers had written. They did not know why I had been gone. All they knew was something terrible had happened in my family and that I was in need of special prayer. No one ever asked me to explain the details to them. Everyone just loved me for who I was and rejoiced in having me home."

Jolene said in a 2008 conversation, "I cannot be so sure that my life would have turned out so beautifully if Mr. Macy had not stepped in and taken action." Her father went to prison. And Jolene went on with a new and blessed routine in life. She was given a choice and hope.

On May 15, 1997, she became the first person in her family—that includes parents, grandparents, aunts, uncles, cousins, and siblings—to graduate from high school. She was thrilled when her degree was presented by Brother Russell, the man who had sponsored her entry into Windsor Hills Baptist School so many years before.

At school, a young man named David, older than Jolene, had kept his eye on her for a while. They became friends, and one day she told him her story, every bit of it. She was amazed when he still wanted to spend time with her. They fell in love. At dinner with friends on the evening of October 23, 1999, her birthday, David proposed to her. Jolene accepted.

Jolene's three half-brothers, abused by her mother when they were children, wound up on the front page of newspapers. The oldest boy, just a teenager, killed his adoptive mother and injured his middle brother. Jolene often thinks about him and the two female cousins who ended their own lives.

Jolene wrote often to her once-abusive biological mother. She wanted a chance to talk, but the woman ignored Jolene, even when she was invited to her wedding. But suddenly, the mother reached out after those three sons, Jolene's half-brothers and fell into the pit. Jolene and David went to see her mother in Arizona. At first, things were tense, but at the precise moment they met, Jolene had hundreds of friends praying for the lady. Before too long, sitting in a Denny's restaurant one day, Jolene's mother said, "I never thought any of my children would ever return to see me again."

David told the woman that Jolene had already forgiven her, that God forgave sinners, and that Jesus died for her sins. Jolene's birth mother had a choice. A few hours later, she was born again.

Today, Jolene is a beautiful and mature woman. On the outside, only her hands hint at the years of abuse. Jolene thinks about the future and her past.

"Though I am still young and have three small children yet to rear, I can already look back at my life and see God's amazing grace. First and foremost, I have the Lord to thank for putting people in my path to help and inspire me ... I am thankful for a man named Bob Macy, whom I have never met face to face, but who has had a great influence on my life. He went beyond the call of duty to help an insignificant teenager." The story's ending is this. In 2009, as Macy remembers with a tear and a smile, "I did get to meet Jolene. It was very gratifying, affirming to see how things had turned out for her."

The story of Jolene and many like it illustrate the true nature of Macy. He is a man of ultimate compassion for those who cannot stand up for themselves. But for all the subtleties and nuances in the living and breathing man, Bob Macy is undeniably best known as the most effective professional death penalty prosecutor in modern America. He became so because he believed in the efficacy of the ultimate sanction, and because he worked fiercely and methodically to abide within the law and to apply a careful methodology aimed at execution of those guilty of the most heinous crimes. One sure way, he thinks even today, of keeping the criminal away from the victim is through the judicious use of the death penalty.

As he said in a speech given often during his time in office, Bob Macy believed "the closing argument in a capital case is difficult for three very basic reasons. First, it consists [of] two separate and distinct arguments, one directed to guilt or innocence and the second to punishment." He asserted the importance of not using all the strong arguments and emotion in the guilty stage, lest nothing be left for the penalty.

The second reality, he said, is that a prosecutor "is trying to convince twelve people to do something that is foreign to everything that they have been taught from their childhood to the present. No normal person really wants to be responsible for the taking of a man's life."

Third, he knew full well that closing arguments would "be viewed by dozens of liberal appellate judges frantically searching for a way to reverse the conviction and turn the killer loose." Statements of "harmless error" in non-capital cases become "grounds for reversal when the defendant's life is at stake."

A capital case prosecutor should begin preparing closing arguments "the first time that he learns the details of the case," Macy argues. Closing arguments should be rooted in the horror of the crime itself, but phrases and points should be reassembled "each night... in the order in which I intend to argue them."

Macy did not say every capital case prosecutor had to work from a predetermined template. Rather, he should "use the format with which he is comfortable." While some might work from memory, an outline, or jotted notes on legal pads, Macy typed every closing argument "word for word, just the way that I intend to deliver it." He said his first draft was prepared a few days before closing arguments and then polished three or four times before delivery.

When it came to closing arguments for guilt, the prosecutor's focus had to be "not a matter of emotion" but of logic. The cascade of argument had to support the point. "There is no doubt that he did the killing." Macy customarily had an assistant district attorney present the first part of his team's closing argument. This permitted him to observe the jury while the initial argument unfolded. At this stage, the point was to review the elements of the crime one by one and point out how the evidence proves each element. In the case of circumstantial evidence, the goal was to "demonstrate to the jury that there is no reasonable hypothesis consistent with the defendant's innocence."

The prosecutor had to take care to answer key defense arguments, not skipping critical points while not allowing defense arguments to control the prosecution's arguments. In the final stage of argument at the guilt stage, Macy concludes, the jury must be persuaded the accused was guilty "not because I say so, not because the judge says so, but because the evidence says so."

In the penalty stage, Macy asserts, evidence was still the primary weapon in the prosecution's arsenal, and "most of the emotion should be saved for the final closing." Macy didn't necessarily like it, but he recognized that in many states, it was grounds for reversal "to do anything to invoke sympathy for the victim." For that reason, he forcefully argued the two crucial factors with absolute legitimacy in a penalty argument: the crime and the defendant.

As he stressed, "The crime should be described in the most vivid terms possible consistent with the evidence." Defense counsel's attempts to argue mitigation in capital crimes provide, Macy explains, the opportunity to talk about exactly those aspects of the defendant's behavior and rejection of the idea that circumstances "caused this crime."

After careful planning of all phases of the argument to this point, Macy explains that the defense counsel's final arguments would open the door to some creativity for the prosecutor, specifically in countering final assertions of reasons the killer or other capital criminal should avoid capital punishment. After exercising this limited creative time for response, Macy says, the prosecutor should return methodically to his prepared closing, taking care to stress every aggravating circumstance and the weight of the evidence.

Macy notes that while "juries convict on logic," they "kill on emotion." In sum, "Occasionally a jury will vote for death because they logically believe that that is the only way that they can stop this animal from killing again. Usually, they will vote for death either because of hate for the defendant or love for the victim or the victim's family or a combination of love and hate."

In the final moments of argument for death, Macy says, "The crime scene should be recreated in the minds of the jury," including an explicit appeal to their common sense that the "sterile courtroom" might mask the brutality of the murder. The scene should be carefully described "in all of its gory detail" but in strict compliance with the evidence itself.

The sum of evidence and the weight of law, Macy continues, must be assembled to support the argument that the death penalty is the only just verdict for the crime committed. The final paragraph should again make the case that "the only just, necessary verdict" is death.

For twenty-one years, in dozens of cases involving the most horrific crimes, Macy worked within the parameters of the law and in keeping with the approach detailed in that speech. He had no hidden agendas, no secret plans, and no personal interest but justice. He felt no vindication or vengeance, just justice served. In fact, though allowed by law to watch the execution, he didn't. Macy was a man in action, supporting the just and righteous use of a penalty explicitly sanctioned in this nation's founding document and in thousands of years of the Western legal tradition.

Still, as Macy would be the first to admit, he's no gold leaf, plaster saint. In one of our first interviews for this book, Macy said, "Be sure to ask my friends about my temper!" Then, he proceeded to tell a story on himself. He tells of a story where his temper "almost got in the way."

This story happened during his separation from Betty, who remained his best friend. He continued to assist her on things like dealing with car repairs and other issues. Their daughter, Sheila, called to say her mother had traded cars and gotten into difficulty with the auto dealer. Macy found out a salesman at the car place had taken advantage of Betty. He called a trusted friend and said, "I'm fixing to get in trouble."

The friend said, "Well, I'll go with you."

The fellow at the dealership had tapped Betty for more money and even tried to get her fired from a job she enjoyed. Macy cut right to the point. "When I saw him I told him, 'If I wasn't DA, I'd pull you across that desk and beat you until you cried like a puppy. If you ever speak to a member of my family again, I'll beat you into the pavement.'"

The friend who witnessed the event was Clint Dedek, perhaps Macy's closest friend during that phase of his tenure as DA. In an August 2009, interview, he confirmed Macy's version of the incident and said, "If I wouldn't have been there, there would have been a heck of a fight."

Perhaps because he was for such a long time a trusted body guard and confidante for the man he still calls "the Boss," Dedek has an endless supply of good stories about Bob Macy, temper and all.

Some of the best crime fighting never resulted in an arrest, Dedek discloses. One Christmas season, Macy and Clint were away from the office doing some shopping. Dedek recalls, "There was a guy at the mall who had been hanging around little girls, making them feel uncomfortable."

Made aware of the situation, the two men determined to put an end to it. Dedek says, "I did it in a gentleman's way. I went up and told him to stop hanging around and stop bugging those little girls or any of all little girls at the mall."

The guy said he hadn't meant anything by it and agreed to stop. But then, he turned to Dedek and said, "By the way, do you have authority to do this?" Bob Macy heard that, so he walked up and grabbed the guy by the shirt.

He told him, "Get the heck out of here and stop bugging these little girls, or I'll put you under the Oklahoma County jail before I'm through."

Dedek reports, "That was the end of that." There were no more reports of similar activities on the man's part.

Dedek remembers, "To tell you the truth, Bob Macy is a tough old son of a gun. He's like a great cutting horse. The best ones, you ride them and they really do all the work. You get the credit when they win the championship, but the horse did all the real work. That's how Macy was." And, "He'd still be there at the DA's office if he could perform."

Macy literally trusted Dedek with his life. Many times, the veteran highway patrolman, who had also protected Governor Henry Bellmon, got Macy out of a room or a touchy situation on pure instinct.

Macy said, "I would look at him sometimes, and I just knew what he meant. And that was vice versa. We just understood each other." The hair would rise on Dedek's neck in a troubled setting, and he would mutter, "Boss, we gotta go." A man whom few could cajole, let alone govern, would immediately comply.

Dedek remembers one particular moment he considers representative of their unspoken understanding. "I can't say where that particular incident was. I monitored the way people in the crowd acted. There was a guy who kind of 'hung around' but didn't ask any questions, but he looked antagonistic. I was in the Highway Patrol for a long time and went to the Secret Service school. I worked at the governor's office and didn't want to let Macy face any danger. There was no fancy stuff, just common sense."

Dedek's own story is the stuff of a police novel. "When I worked for Bellmon, I had two serious threats. A man was mad at Bellmon because he hadn't pardoned him. He had given Bellmon an address and said he would be there all night singing. He was bragging about what he would do if Bellmon showed up. I found the guy and told him, 'I heard you was bragging about what you're going to do to the governor.' I told him, 'You're not going to do that. If you try, I'm gonna gut shoot you.' That was the end of that."

He remembers, "I was with Bob for thirteen years altogether. It was the best job I ever had." Speaking of himself in the third person, he reflected, "Clint Dedek was/is not gonna work for a crook or for somebody who's not for our people here or for our country. I require people I work with to be honest and fair. The truth is I'm a little tough, and I kinda like tough people." This same attitude brought many of Macy's acquaintances to long friendships. People were attracted to Bob because they liked what he stood for and how he stood for it.

Once upon a time, in the DA's office, "There was a flare-up that I tried to calm down. I had to shut the door and tell the people who were fighting in the office to come back when they'd act right. Macy called them all together. He listened to what they had to say. He was very calm and suggested a way to go forward and stay together, work together for what was right. When we were done, they all stood. Some of them hugged each other; some shook hands. They went forward and worked together so well. That memory really stands out."

He continues, "When I first met him, it was like two boys going to school together. It was fun, but it was hard work. He was a real professional. He really worked hard. I would have retired three or four years earlier. I was tired. He's not easy to work for because of the long hours he put in."

His first hitch with Macy, for a few years in the mid-1980s, was after Dedek held a good, and he admits pretty easy, job at Oak Tree Country Club. "It was a good job, good people, but it was boring. I liked to have stuff going on. Macy called and said, 'I thought you were going to work for us?'" Dedek asked, "Is there an opening?' and he said 'yes.' So that first time I worked for him two or three years."

As for the work, "We had some rough 'good times.' I'm totally a law enforcement man. I cannot tell you how hard those hours were, working for Bob Macy. I wouldn't have turned him down for nothing."

The work wasn't always tense, allowing some time for critical observation. As Dedek notes, "The thing about Bob Macy is he always tried the hard cases. He would take on the toughest cases, where he knew they were guilty but the evidence was a challenge. Bob was so strong on his closing arguments, he was a genius."

"There were times I'd watch a case and hear the defense and everything about the case. I'd think, 'Well, he is finally gonna lose.' But he could make the hair stand up on the back of your neck. He was so sharp—you talk about a great lawyer. He was great. I think that even today, he could still beat them. Some who didn't like him, well, they were crooks, dishonest people and people who were used to buying their way through life. You couldn't do that with Bob Macy."

David Shupe, the police homicide investigator for much of Macy's tenure who now serves as assistant chief of police, echoes the praise for Macy's integrity, grit, and sincere appreciation for the law-enforcement officers with whom he worked. "When I was a young detective, you couldn't walk through that DA's office without him saying hello. If he heard the voice of a police officer, he would come out of his office to shake your hand. And he had a handshake like a lumberjack, like a vice grip. I was always taken aback by the fact that a man of his stature would take time out of his schedule like that."

Shupe reflects, "From my point of view, the defense lawyers were always on Bob for his closings, his final arguments. I sat through a lot of murder trials. I was often a witness. He was emotional and made a powerful connection with the victim and the victim's family. The tears he would shed were sincere; they were real. Bob Macy is the most compelling figure I have ever seen in a courtroom. He was awfully good." And, "He was ruthless for the pursuit of justice."

Shupe remembers well "a very emotional case. We were dealing with the rapes of elderly women. Trials are usually quick, a matter of days. In that case, it took two weeks. There were two victims and a third victim the killer had tried to kill but failed." Shupe describes the dynamic in the courtroom. "I remember watching Macy and the way he connected with the jurors, eye to eye. He would almost get an emotional connection with a jury."

Yet, even the most draining and emotional cases had moments of levity. "In that one trial, the jury had a very attractive young lady and an older lady. After the verdict, as members of the jury shook hands with Macy and the officers, the older lady walked up to one of the officers who had attended and testified in the case." Shupe remembers the woman said, "Young man, if you had been looking at me like you did at her, undressing me with your eyes for the last two weeks, right now I'd be slapping you silly." One very red-faced police officer left the room.

Shupe recalls vividly one time when he was testifying in an important case. "In response to a question, I was setting a preface for the defense attorney, just explaining myself. I don't even remember what it was I said, but I said something in such a way that all of the sudden everybody, all the lawyers, were jumping up." Indeed, "It was one of those times that led to *in-camera* conferences, to side bar discussions, you name it. Macy just said to me when he came back, 'Just answer the question.'" The situation got resolved without a mistrial.

Macy "had such incredible connections with the families of the victims. I remember in one of those hard cases, Macy had the children of a victim out to his old place, the one he had in Edmond. I remember those children riding and playing, getting on the horses, and having some fun. It was really something to see him do that, to watch him watch those kids and talk to them, and the way those kids reacted."

Once, Macy had to prosecute a young man, the son of a friend. Macy said to the father, "I wish you'd not go in there. I'm gonna have to say some bad things about your boy."

He said, "Bob, you do your job."

Macy recalls, "I got the boy convicted, and we haven't talked since. I don't know how he feels about me."

Macy's greatest empathy was for the victims and families of victims in heinous murder cases. But a close second would be his compassion for the law-enforcement officers. Macy told me that Shupe once told him he had to quit as a homicide detective because "the blood got too deep." Shupe didn't remember saying exactly that but agreed. "It was the best and worst time of my life. I didn't deal with it very well. I smoked three or four packs of cigarettes a day. I lost a lot of friends because of the way I dealt with the death and the carnage."

Shupe says many of his views, including capital punishment, have mellowed after more than three decades on the force. He credits Macy for some of that. "Bob was a person who fervently sought justice, yet he also recognized the fallacy, the fallen nature, of man. He had insight into human beings. He recognized we're not, any of us, perfect human beings. He forgave the weaknesses in human beings. There are no perfect people in the world. Bob knew that. He knew there was a place for compassion and forgiveness. He was not a one-dimensional person, no matter what anyone says. With age and experience, I've found for myself a more mature worldview. That's been part of a reflective process. I was a real staunch advocate of the death penalty for the most heinous cases. As I reflect now, in some cases, I'm not as sure as I was. The years have softened me, at least somewhat."

Macy says he understands exactly what Shupe is saying. Sometimes, "there was a fine line between the ones I sought the death penalty for and the ones I fought to save." Yet, he adds he is haunted by the Clifford Henry Bowen case, where his suspicions of a Dixie Mafia connection are so strong that he believes a ruthless professional killer got away with three murders. Macy still believes Bowen committed several cold-blooded murders and deserved execution—and his continued life likely came at the cost of another human life. Bowen is no longer alive, but Macy believes the man escaped accountability for three killings.

A side to Macy that few witness outside his immediate circle of friends is his deep loyalty and affection for friends, especially old friends. As a prosecutor, he didn't waste any affection or lose sleep over killers or perverts, but he has had an abundance of care for the law-abiding, the peaceful, and the righteous majority. And he had a heart full of love for those who, in the course of a lifetime, wound their ways into his big heart.

In August 1994, the veil over that side of Macy's personality was lifted a bit in the emotional eulogy he delivered in memory of Gene Wade. Wade and his father, Percy, had become Macy's friends when he patrolled the streets of Packing Town in the late 1950s. Macy always made a point to check in at their Cattlemen's Cafe on South Agnew whenever he came to Oklahoma City during his Ada years and during his brief tenure at the state attorney general's office.

With his return to Oklahoma City in the late 1970s and rise to the district attorney's job in 1980, Cattlemen's had again become a regular stop for Bob.

In his eulogy, Macy referred to "the old oak rocking chair in front of Cattlemen's" that was now empty. He remembers the Cattlemen's of long ago, a place that was open 24/7, where Macy and his patrol partner dined for breakfast regularly, sometime between 2:00 and 4:00 a.m. in 1957 and 1958. For cops, the coffee was free and the meals half-priced because Wade had a heart for the low-paid police.

Macy's predecessor as county attorney, "my good friend James W. "Bill" Berry" had, in the late 1950s, brought liquor law enforcement into the previously wide-open arena known as Packing Town. The Wades had made their peace with that, and, with young officers like Bob Macy, he never forgot them.

Macy well remembers his role in a surprise seventieth birthday for Gene at the man's own restaurant. By prior arrangement, a throng of friends quietly gathered in the upper room at Cattlemen's. Then Macy went about and found Gene to tell him that former

Sheriff Bob Turner's widow was upstairs having dinner and wanted to talk to him. Macy led the old man up the stairs and through the door, where he was greeted and shocked by the cheers of hundreds. He turned and said to Macy, laughing, "You dirty SOB!"

Macy recalls he began, some years before, giving Wade an embrace every time he saw him. Macy describes Cattlemen's as the favorite Oklahoma City restaurant of Presidents Ronald Reagan and George H.W. Bush and of Attorneys General Ed Meese and Bill Barr.

He praised Wade for living out the reality of words like "fidelity, integrity, industry, patriotism, morality, and decency," in an era when those things are "no longer politically correct." Macy lamented the old rocking chair would remain empty but said he believed "there is another rocking chair God has been saving for a very special person. As of seven o'clock on Monday evening, that chair is now filled."

More privately, aware of the approach of his own mortality, in one of our wide-ranging conversations at his home in Newalla in the unusually cool fall of 2009, Macy remembers another friend, his fellow peace officer, Ken Lyles.

"Everybody called him 'Bigun'," Macy explains. Bob's daughter, Sheila, called Lyles "a big bear of a man" who was always kind. She always felt comfortable around the giant fellow, who was six foot four or five, and who, Macy remembers, "weighed a bunch." Macy says Lyles was a burly, old school cop who "worked the streets of Oklahoma City. I first knew him in 1957 as a policeman. He stayed with the city until he had his twenty years in."

Their daily work paths crossed again in 1980. "When I was appointed DA, I needed somebody to cover my back, someone I could really rely on. Ken looked and acted like a Boston street cop. The first few years I was DA, I made him my bodyguard. He would have taken a bullet for me. I had some death threats in those days. In a couple of cases, he actually went and talked to the guys who had been making the threats. He told them if they tried to kill

Macy, they'd have to kill him." Macy remembers Ken telling him, "I'd explain it to them that I had a wife and two children and if I was dead, they wouldn't be able to eat. They changed their mind."

In the late 1980s, "Ken had open heart surgery, so we took him off as my bodyguard, but he continued to work as an investigator. He started to have constant troubles in health and had a second open-heart surgery. It didn't 'take,' and things were leaking inside him. It was very rough."

Macy recounts the difficult days that came some time later at the end of Lyles's life. Early in his career, Lyles stood six feet four and weighed 280. His hands were as large as hams, and he was absolutely fearless. "I knew he would take a bullet for me." And Bigun remained by Macy's side until the day Macy sat by Bigun's side, holding his hand shortly before he passed away. "He was put on dialysis, and things went downhill. I was with him and his sons at the end. There were all these tubes coming every which way out of him. He couldn't talk."

As they sat together quietly, Ken "motioned to me, pointing down to his hand to hold it." Like many others, Macy could remember the times that Lyles could "squeeze a man down" when he needed to because he was so strong. And so, "I gripped his right hand tight, and he gripped back. A little later, I went down to get a bite to eat. He died during the short time that I was away." In 2009, Macy laments, "I still miss him, a lot. He was the gutsiest guy I ever knew."

But Bob also had other gutsy heroes. There was a tremendous drug war going on in south Oklahoma City, and there were five men way over their heads working thousands of hours to combat it. One was Bill Keester, an Oklahoma state narcotics officer. Macy told me he often called Keester with an "I need to know where someone is and what's he driving. Keester called right back with the information."

Then there was Warren Henderson and Wade Taylor, Jimmy Birdsong and Steve Bonny, Lonny Wright, all of whom hated drugs and hated corruption with the same passion as Macy. They were equally as fierce in beating the drug dealers as Macy was in prosecuting them. They all were willing to work long, hard, and dangerous hours because of what they were seeing happen to young people with drugs. "I saw them make three buys from the same person in one day. They'd go home and shave their beards and go buy more."

Steve Bonny had a shotgun fired at him as a bad guy was trying to back out of a driveway once. Macy says the bad guy "looked the devil in the eyes that night." He also told the story of Bonny's wife, injured in the Murrah Building bombing. Bonny climbed through the rubble to find her and escorted her and two others out. Then he found Macy. "Boss," Bonny said, "I'm going to take my wife home. I'll be back." Macy then saw his own pickup truck, with Bonny at the wheel, speeding away from the destruction.

But even their time was not all glory. Macy relates a story with a somberness that is almost frightening. Someone, he told, got high enough in the power structure that OSBI served a search warrant on the offices of the Oklahoma Bureau of Narcotics, where his five favorite investigators were assigned. Macy declined every charge they had. He laughs as he says, "They forgot to read the Miranda Warning."

"OBN," he continues, "was getting a lot of publicity and doing a lot of good, and the OSBI was used as a pawn, a bystander. Several big businessmen in OKC were becoming millionaires on the drug business."

Macy's appearance becomes saddened when he talks about what happened to them after he retired. "Jimmy Birdsong was a walking encyclopedia of crime in OKC. He became an investigator for the Medical Licensure Board. He retired and died. Taylor went back to the patrol division of the police department. Keester retired. Steve Bonny is still an investigator for the DA's office." He said he did his best to make sure there was no retaliation on them after he left. To this day, Macy stands up for them against anyone who has a harsh word about them. He finished that conversation saying, "They also tried to discredit me. I never worried about reelection. I served the public, and I was not going to succumb to a small political or corrupt group." Then he smiles. "I was never offered a real bribe. I was disappointed."

Macy went on to talk about some other lawyers he admired. "I got along good with D.C. Thomas. He was a friend. I prosecuted his clients, but he supported me in every campaign. He was honest, played by the rules. I respected him."

Of his old friend and United Founders adversary, Bill Berry, Macy says, "He supported the judges in every way. They all knew he supported them. He was a gentleman, real class, the epitome of a lawyer." From everything Macy said about Bill Berry, it is obvious he had the same heart as Macy. "He didn't defend criminal cases, just the little guy. The grand jury investigated Berry, but that was thrown out. Macy recalls the earlier case when he represented Roussell and Berry represented the United Founders Life Insurance Company. "I knew I had to be loaded for bear." Then Macy becomes solemn again. "Berry spent every night at Presbyterian Hospital with Lea, his wife dying of cancer."

By this time in gathering information for the book, the editors all have learned much about Bob Macy. His accomplishments, in reality, pale against his relationships. He is passionate beyond comparison. His fire in the belly burns every bit as fierce as it did when he was first sworn in. His loyalty to his friends is remarkable. He nurtures those friendships in ways most of us have forgotten how to. Much of his understanding of human relationships and hard work came from his family, his upbringing, and his situation early on in his life. It's not too late for the rest of us to learn how. We just have to work hard, and that is something Bob Macy was never afraid to do.

CHAPTER 7

An American Man

Bob Macy was traveling through the magnificent foliage of Massachusetts on his way from the Catholic Cathedral to the Boston Airport. His chauffeur for the drive was a veteran Massachusetts trooper he had met for the first time. Macy had just attended the funeral mass for the honorable Billy J. O'Malley, District Attorney for Brocton. Billy died as he had lived, in service to his state and country, sitting at his computer in the wee hours of the night, preparing for a day's activities. Billy left behind a beautiful wife, Amy, and two handsome sons. The boys, Bob knew, were proud of their father and of his profession.

Not too long before, Billy had succeeded Macy as chairman of the National District Attorneys Association. One of their memorable joint events had been a meeting and photograph with Attorney General Janet Reno at the foot of Mount Rushmore. After news of O'Malley's death, Macy came to the funeral as a representative of the NDAA and as a final act of friendship.

Traffic was dense, and the ride to the airport turned into a long one. As a former police officer, Macy felt a kinship to the veteran cop acting as his driver. After a few minutes, the two men felt so comfortable they talked as brothers, openly and unpretentious.

Macy raised the subject of police corruption. Unspoken was the undeniable presence of corruption in some police agencies in the Eastern United States. Both acknowledged this readily. Macy bluntly asked his driver, "What will it take to get rid of corruption in these police departments?"

After some quiet thought, the officer replied, "About two generations." Macy had to pause to think about the implications of the officer's answer.

Macy states, "I come from a city where the police department is corruption-free."

The chauffeur replied, "Our problems run deeper than law enforcement." Nothing was resolved in the conversation, but the admission of facts made Macy thoughtful.

Just two days later, he was on the road again. He had a similar but even sadder mission, representing the NDAA at the funeral of Danny Hill, District Attorney of Amarillo, Texas, and past president of the District and County Attorneys Association in the Lone Star State.

Like O'Malley, Danny gave his life for his profession—but the end came from a .357 magnum and from Danny's own hand. Hill had been an outstanding prosecutor, an excellent trial lawyer, and a credit to his profession. He had a wife and four beautiful teenage daughters, as well as a boy and girl from a previous marriage, who likely could never understand what happened to their daddy.

Only a year before, Bob noted Danny's election as president of the state association. Whereas Billy had succumbed to a malfunctioning heart, the stress of his job drove Danny to alcohol, including humiliating DUI arrests. He was slowly losing the wife and family he adored and on his way to losing a job he cherished. In the end, depression and alcohol was a combination he couldn't defeat.

As he thought of his friends and his companions in the fight for a more orderly and just world, Bob Macy realized with deep sadness what a loss the country sustained in the deaths of each within just days of each other. They left their work in their careers at a time when leadership and integrity were so directly and desperately needed.

In a 1993 speech, Macy recalled his early ties to NDAA. "Immediately after being sworn in as district attorney, I contacted the National District Attorneys Association, which speaks for the nation's 20,000 prosecutors, and told them I wanted to become active."

During two decades as Oklahoma County District Attorney and a member of NDAA, Macy worked at all levels of the group.

Early on, Bob chaired the Organized Crime Subcommittee and the Drug Control Committee. Elected as assistant secretary then as one of the vice presidents, he was nominated and won the president-elect's job in 1992. After serving as chairman of the board, he returned for a second stint in the top board spot after the death of his friend, O'Malley.

Bob was probably the most prominent NDAA leader for a large portion of his time in the association, especially 1992–95. In the last decade of the twentieth century, Macy helped lead a transformation and modernization in the role and function of America's prosecutors.

As he observed in congressional testimony in 1994:

> For many years the prosecutor function was narrowly defined as that of representing the people of this nation in the state and local criminal court systems. We played no part in either preventing crime or in administering punishment for those convicted of crime. This self-defeating limitation is no longer, in my estimation, valid. If we as prosecutors do not fully utilize all of our talents and resources in preventing crime, in prosecuting crime and in punishing crime, then we do our citizens a vast disservice.

While advocating an expansive view of the prosecutorial function, Macy retained and passionately advocated a federalist view, recognizing divided powers and separated spheres for state, local, and federal functions in prosecution. As he said, "The problems that I face in Oklahoma City are very different than those faced by my colleagues in St. Paul, Minnesota, or Boston, Massachusetts. Likewise, my solutions, based upon a lifetime of living and working in the criminal justice system on the federal, state, and local level, will be different."

He recognized the political impact and accountability that elected prosecutors like him faced regularly. "I am directly accountable to the people who elected me to office. If my solutions fail, if I fail to protect my citizens, then the people of Oklahoma City will make the decision as to my continued effectiveness. This is a referendum that each of you faces regularly, and you understand the harsh reality of Election Day."

While serving unapologetically as an advocate for increased federal aid to local law enforcement—preferably in the form of block grants without strings attached—in his congressional appearances, Macy often critiqued the substance of federal proposals presuming to dictate solutions to the states. Looking back at the 1994 Violent Crime Control and Law Enforcement Act, he said many of that measure's provisions "suffered from a common failing. All were dictated and controlled by persons who did not answer to the citizens of my district." He asked members of Congress to "help get me the means to fight crime in my community, but don't tell me how to do it."

Macy described an Oklahoma program to reward high school students with discounts or preferential hiring if they remained drug-free. Looking to other states and their efforts at crime fighting, he commented, "Midnight basketball may have great potential in some areas, but we have a midnight curfew in Oklahoma City."

He took the analogy of strength in diversity a step further. "I have a hobby unique to my part of the country. I am a member of the Professional Rodeo Cowboys Association. In my spare time, I enjoy participating in rodeos in the team-roping competition. I've managed to win a few trophies and belt buckles, and it certainly is different from my daily work, in terms of relieving stress." He continued in the testimony, "In Oklahoma, Texas, and several other Western states, our prison systems have annual professional quality rodeos with inmates as contestants. As trustees, they compete for a chance to make the show. The annual prison rodeo in McAlester, attended by thousands of people, is an important part of our prison system. While this is good for my state and our prison system, its value and effectiveness as a penal program would certainly be open to debate in Maine or Vermont."

As leader of what could be considered a trade association, Macy did not hesitate to argue for the importance of his group's interests in the competition for scarce federal dollars. He faulted criminal justice proposals of that era for not providing "sufficient support for the prosecutors, judges, and defense counsel who are critical components of our criminal justice system. All the police and all the prisons are reduced in value if those who commit crimes cannot be vigorously prosecuted in a timely manner."

Macy specifically recommended that federal legislative definitions of "law enforcement" be amended to include "not only traditional police forces but also the prosecutors." As was the case throughout his career, Macy argued for federal habeas corpus reforms needed "to minimize the intrusion of the federal courts into our state judicial proceedings." The framers of the U.S. Constitution, he argued, "did not intend that the federal courts should sit in full appellate review of state criminal proceedings."

Macy also fought for an end to frivolous prisoner lawsuits permitted to those "who are motivated by anger or greed and have nothing to lose... Incarceration is only effective when it truly is punishment and not a vacation or a calculated cost of doing business or a place to dream up ways of self-enrichment."

The NDAA, as the voice of America's prosecutors, was the proper forum to discuss problems facing those who fought every day to complete the job police officers started. Macy's long tenure of more than a decade on the board, including his unique second term as board chairman, put him in position to see the group through institutional challenges and professional difficulties.

Macy remembers one of his most effective and intense assistants, Richard Wintory, as absolutely essential to his success at the national level. "He was a bright guy who knew the law well. He was a totally committed crime fighter." Macy comments, "With Richard Wintory's help, I had the best couple of years. I attended every meeting and always had the raw materials to do well in the meetings." As Macy went through the offices in sequence, "Richard was my 'go-to' guy for staff support before meetings and at conferences. He was my primary means of contact for people outside the NDAA."

In the normal cycle, the group had three board meetings a year, with the big meeting attracting the most members in July. Presidents were able to select meeting places, and the sessions moved around the country to Santa Fe, San Antonio, and Rapid City, South Dakota. Macy held one of the regular board sessions in his hometown of Oklahoma City during his year as president and led executive committee meetings in Las Vegas, Nevada, Bangor, Maine, and New Orleans, Louisiana.

It wasn't all hard work and contentious issues. "We had one of the board of directors' meetings in Jackson Hole, Wyoming, and got the chance to travel on personal expense.

"A memorable time with Richard was when we went to the Snake River country and the Grand Tetons. He and I rented horses and rode as high as you could in the Grand Tetons then went down into the Snake River Valley."

Executive committee members were the real decision makers. "Richard was invaluable to me in setting up the meetings," Macy recounts. "On major staff meetings, Richard was assisted by Pete Adams, Deputy Director of the Louisiana District Attorney's Association."

Wintory grew invaluable to the national group itself, frequently lecturing to the membership and serving in other capacities. "At that same time, he spent a lot of time training assistant DAs."

As for Macy himself, "In 1993 or so, I flew 350,000 miles in the course of a year. I went to the District of Columbia frequently. On days I'd arrive in DC, I'd have lunch with the staff, work at the NDAA office until 4:30 p.m. or so, then head home to Oklahoma. I had many weeks where I traveled three days a week."

Some of Macy's traveling involved speaking to "as many of the state associations as I could." He worked closely with both Jack Yelverton and Newman Flanagan, executive directors in those years. Shortly before his election as president, the group moved its headquarters from Chicago to the nation's capital. And not long before that, Yelverton had decided not to stay on as the executive director. Flanagan, former DA of Boston, took the reins.

Aside from the contentious and challenging national policy issues the association faced, NDAA struggled with the difficulties of all trade associations in the ebb and flow of membership numbers and finances. In Yelverton's early years, NDAA was, Macy recalls, nearly broke with weak membership numbers, but the group surged ahead in the 1990s. During Macy's most active years, the group made progress in terms of numbers and association strength, reaching a comfortable and stable bank balance.

In interviews about his experiences at NDAA, Macy repeatedly credits Yelverton and Flanagan for the turnaround. And he points to his right-hand man, Wintory. "Richard was always there, covering my backside every step of the way. In many ways, he was like a son to me. When he knew what I wanted, he would move heaven and earth to make it happen."

Early in his federal career, Macy worked with Attorney General Richard Kleindeinst on the federal advisory panel on criminal justice. Then, from the late 1980s to 1993, he became an ally of Ed Meese, Bill Barr, and Richard Thornburgh, the sequence of attorneys general who served in President Ronald Reagan's second term and the one term of George H.W. Bush.

Bill Barr was a legal scholar "of the highest integrity. He was a civil lawyer, but there was a vacancy that needed filling as the deputy attorney general. He was not a politician. That's what they needed." Barr saw the same in Macy and described his as the "most outstanding law enforcement official in the world today."

Barr was Macy's favorite among the U.S. Attorneys General with whom he worked, but he also forged good ties with fellow Democrats at the national level during the Clinton years. "I remember when Bill left. We talked and he said, 'Every day, I felt like I did something good. I'm really going to miss that.' I've missed Barr a lot. We had a good relationship. We worked together on a report that described sixteen ways to reduce violence in the United States. I joined him for a press conference on the crime bill, held in the great hall at the Department of Justice on July 28, 1992. The first Bush saw me on TV when I spoke about Ice-T. His rap about killing cops was offensive. I said, 'If your rap about cop-killing causes the death of a cop, the fires of hell won't be hot enough for you.' Others heard that speech and joined in. I always appreciated Charlton Heston, who gave a speech later at the MCA or Time-Warner stockholders' meeting. He stood strong against that filthy language."

It was in the weeks and years after the bombing of the federal building in Oklahoma City that Macy grew close to Attorney General Reno. Later, in the mid-1990s, Macy forged strong ties with Janet Reno, even though he was not a fan of her boss, Bill Clinton. He met her in an official capacity when he was the president of the NDAA. The president had been looking for an attorney general, and Macy interviewed her as a possible appointee. He remembers one possible conflict he might have with her. She didn't believe in the death penalty, but she explained she would enforce federal law because of her position. "We became good friends, and I admire her. She was authentic in wanting to improve the criminal justice system. She always did what she thought was right. Once, the White House tried to get her to do something she thought was wrong. She told me, 'Bob, if I'm forced to vote for that legislation to keep this job, the job has to go.'"

Macy went on to tell another story that reflected her character. Washington, he said, was a town full of hidden agendas, very political. She assured Macy he wouldn't have any trouble getting Terry Nichols back to Oklahoma to stand trial, but the time period was running out to bring him back. "Bob, it's been taken care of," she assured him again. Nichols still was not on a plane. "Bob, it will be taken care of." Once again, she assured him, but he could tell the frustration was mounting in her voice, not at his persistence but at her request not being fulfilled. Then, Bob got a call from Reno's assistant. "Bob, I want you to know that Nichols is on a plane to Oklahoma City, and I just got the worst butt chewing in my life." Like Bob himself, if she gave her word to someone, she fully meant it to be kept.

Then he reflected, and I could see a real amount of pain come to his eyes. "She was a real friend at the bombing. She is a real beautiful woman. Her Parkinson's has advanced. I hate it for her." I could tell he was honest. In the final year of his career, Macy appeared in support of the confirmation of John Ashcroft, President George W. Bush's first attorney general.

In a November 1993 speech to the Northwest Kiwanis in Oklahoma City, Macy remembered a then-recent trip to the nation's capital, where he had been at a gathering for prosecutors hosted by President Clinton, Senate Judiciary Committee Chairman Joe Biden of Delaware, and Attorney General Janet Reno. In his remarks at the event, the future vice president Biden pointed Macy out in the crowd as the guy wearing the black string tie and said, "I wouldn't want to be in his county if I got arrested."

For all his status as a national player throughout the 1990s and until his retirement in 2001, Macy was first, last, and always a local prosecutor, with primarily local concerns and issues on his daily list of concerns. But Macy often reflected on the ways in which he had enjoyed a series of "golden years" throughout his life, with the time as Oklahoma County District Attorney at the top of his list of rewarding labor.

Starting on June 16, 1980, and running for a period of over twenty years, he had the happiest years. He was appointed to a job he loved by a governor he liked and respected, surrounded by a staff he personally handpicked, and supported by hundreds of outstanding police officers. Macy loved his job and looked forward to going to work each and every day. His passion seemed to be fulfilled every day.

But it was the best of times and the worst of times, as written in *A Tale of Two Cities*, by Charles Dickens. Conviction rates for Macy's office were over 80 percent, and homicides in the county were down. The prisons were loaded with thieves, murderers, and sex offenders.

Every day was a new adventure. Death threats were frequent, and confrontations with defense attorneys and appellate courts seemed common as the office proceeded with the task of making Oklahoma City the safest city in the United States.

Macy fed off those he considered friends and peers who also found satisfaction in progress made in central Oklahoma law enforcement in those years. In discussions with friends on the police force, it was found they often concluded that the mid-1970s and '80s were the best years to be in the profession. Likewise, visiting with college chums brought agreement that the years 1948 through 1958 were the best years to play football at a small college and later serve in the military. For a reason that seems obvious, Bob Macy had a fundamental effect for those best year evaluations.

The mid-80s to the early 1990s was a time when Macy was surrounded by people he loved and admired, and his joy extended beyond his immediate daily involvement with the law. Those years brought pleasure and satisfaction to Macy's life as he rode and roped with cowboy champions and movie stars. They were all different and very unique but had one thing in common; they were Macy's friends. People became the ultimate reason Macy did all he did. His career, his rodeo work, and his civil service all revolved around his love of people, helping those he could, and vindicating those who had suffered at the hands of another.

At the core of Macy's identity, then and now, were his ties to policemen and women working on the streets to push back the darkness and bring the light of law and ordered liberty.

In an August 2009 interview, Major Billy Weaver, now the Oklahoma City Police curriculum director, recalled with Macy the transformation of police work patterns, practices, and equipment since the latter's years as a police officer. The police academy, for instance, today lasts twenty-six weeks, a total of a thousand hours of training, double what the state requires. In today's six-month police academy, trainees spend four months studying in an office or academic setting, covering thirty-two categories of procedures and policies. They then pass two additional months in the field with a training officer, during which they ride through four evaluated phases.

Today's vehicles, and just about everything else, make the equipment of Macy's police years, 1957–60, seem paltry in comparison. When Bob was a police officer, there was one police channel. Officers today use handheld radios that cost $4,000 each. There's a button on those handheld instruments that, if pushed, send automatic signals to dispatch with an alert if an officer needs help. Each car has a computer that allows the officer to keep in constant contact with dispatch and other officers while permitting information research from records held in the city, state, and federal government.

Today's police vehicles, Crown Victorias, have global positioning satellite abilities so the officers can always be found, regardless of location. Dispatchers still talk directly to the officers in the field, but traffic stops are coded into the computer, sending back to dispatch those signals characterizing the nature of the situation.

While Macy covered his old West side Packing Town route with a partner, Weaver notes, "There are very few two man cars left these days." Macy remembers he thought he had reached some kind of high point when, in the late 1950s, his earnings as a police patrolman reached $325 a month. Weaver notes, "There are hundreds and hundreds of applications for every position we have" on the police force. Pay and benefits certainly "dwarf what they were in Bob's day."

Bob had to buy his first pistol, which probably cost less than $50 dollars. Today, members of the police force are provided their radio, guns, bulletproof vests, all the equipment they need, winter coats, everything, and they prepare their own reports. In the old days, Macy and his partner dictated in person or onto tape machines everything that happened on an arrest to report clerks (a kind of secretary) back at the station, and reports were prepared from there. These days, officers work eight days on, six off. In the elder Macy's earlier times, it was twenty-seven days on, four off.

It is no wonder that Macy turned frequently to former policemen when he assembled his leadership and personnel team at the district attorney's office. Clint Dedek, one of the men Macy turned to, had an impressive ability to assess situations by watching "faces in the crowd. Clint was always scanning the room and watching out for me." Dedek's "primetime" with Macy came at the height of the district attorney's state and national clout. In an August 2009 interview, the affable Dedek, now living with his wife Joyce in retirement in suburban Edmond, recalled a particular incident. "One time, we were both at the state capitol. A lot of the DAs were there meeting with the representatives and senators."

Macy remembers that moment this way. "I was talking to the commissioner of public safety in a normal conversation about some legislative issues, about getting some things law enforcement needed to do its job. That senator came up to me and started cussing out DAs, saying, 'You sorry SOBs' over and over. Well, I've told you I have a pretty good temper. After a while, I was about ready to put him down."

But he didn't. Instead, Dedek recalls, "Bob Macy looked at him, then looked at me. I said no, just shook my head."

Macy said Clint softly muttered, "No, Macy, no.'"

Dedek said the potential confrontation wrapped up quietly. "I didn't explain myself. Macy turned toward me, and we just walked away."

Macy provides the story's sequel, which he considers satisfying. "I don't remember that man's name right now. It will come to me. He was a senator and very powerful. At the next election, I went to his district to campaign and make speeches against him in the primary. He was defeated."

Like many others among Macy's closest associates, Dedek still reveres his old boss. "I just loved being with him. When I was police chief in Edmond, he gave me good advice every time I needed him. I so wanted Edmond to have a good police department, and he helped me with that."

Of his two intensive stints on Macy's staff, Dedek has clear memories. During his final hitch, "At some points, I wanted to retire, but I saw how Bob Macy gave his body and soul to this office. He was kind of like Will Rogers, just solid and decent. I learned a lot from him. It was interesting to me how he led but never browbeat anybody."

Dedek remembers an instance "that might have been in the early 1980s. Bob called me. It was when I was a captain for the

Highway Patrol. Macy called because some convicted murderers had escaped. We had to go up to Logan County because they had figured out where those convicts were hiding. J.C. Burris, then the Logan County sheriff, was part of the group that worked together that day. J.C. was just a wonderful man. Also with us was Ken Lyles of Macy's office and two or three guys from the FBI. We'd tracked those escapees down to a place out in the countryside, and there we were ready to go bring them in with the district attorney from Oklahoma County alongside us. There was also a guy who was a state law enforcement officer. He wasn't much use to us. When it came time to go in to apprehend those men, that OSBI guy said, 'Somebody needs to stay out here and guard the cars; I'll do it.' Well, Macy went in right beside me. We went up and climbed over the fence. One of the escapees, an old boy, was sitting there at a table when we looked in. The light above him was stark; it had just one bulb. We went in, and I pointed my gun at his heart. Macy pointed his shotgun at the guy's head. Then, I told him to 'put the gun on the table and put an end to this.' If he had reached for the gun, I would have shot him dead. Macy would have, too. I'm glad we did not have to shoot him."

Dedek laughs and remembers this and other moments this way. "It may sound odd, but the work we did was a lot of fun." In 1985, "the Edmond police chief's job came along. Edmond wanted to know if Macy would 'loan' me to them. Macy said to me, 'No, I won't loan you.' He said to them, 'I won't loan him but if you want him as police chief, I'll give him up. You'll have to support him because he's going to kick butt and take names.'" Dedek continues, "Well, they wanted me. A lot of the credit for that opportunity I got and for the successes I had goes to Bob Macy. He would always, always take my calls." His work for Edmond included the shocking triple homicide at Wynn's grocery store. It was a terrible crime, yet as Dedek recalls, "We had them all in jail by two thirty in the morning."

Although he never worked directly for Macy, Nichols Hills police chief Richard Mask collaborated closely with him on a series of major child sex abuse cases during the years they overlapped in office. Mask described Macy as a champion in prosecuting the pedophile cases. He explains Macy's pivotal role in his career. "Bob Macy is what brought me to Oklahoma County. In 1982, I had met Steve Korotasch, his first chair. I was in Amarillo because my mother-in-law was at that time terminally ill. He offered me a job as an investigator for the Oklahoma County DA, and that brought me to Yukon.

"Then the bottom fell out of the oil market, and revenues for such things plummeted. The only openings I could find were in Nichols Hills, and I'd never heard of it before. Bob was a close friend of Danny Hill, who I had worked with in Amarillo and wound up working closely with Bob Macy as an investigator.

"We investigated Carroll Gregg and were ready to prosecute. Macy had a meeting in his office. There was a prominent defense lawyer there known as 'the fixer' who was there begging for mercy for Gregg. Macy listened to the lawyer's story and the reasons for leniency. He turned to Shayla, the victim. She was seventeen at the time and had been sexually abused for a decade. He asked her what she wanted. She answered, 'I want him to die in prison.' Macy looked at Gregg and his lawyer and smiled and then said, 'There's your answer. Looks like a done deal to me.' That endeared me to Mr. Macy."

Later on, Macy pulled Mask into his work on another awful case of child sexual abuse. In 1999, Oklahoma City had opened its investigation of Grover Miskovsky, and Mask was asked to meet with Bob Macy's investigators into the case. Once again, they formed a strong team in an area notoriously difficult to secure convictions. Mask says simply, "As a result of Macy's prosecution and his strong case, Miskovsky will die in prison. Had Bob Macy not been in office, I'm not sure we would have ever gotten that investigation off the dime." Mask says, "There are very few people I have the level of respect for that I do for Bob Macy. It has always been a pleasure to work with him. He is what he is. If he makes a mistake, he apologizes. You're not gonna bluff him down. When he's in something, he's in it all the way."

Macy's drive was born out of his desire to do the very best at anything he tried. What so many people confuse is his determination with his job. Most would suggest, without knowing Macy's background, this determination for his job was born out of the same drive to do his best. While the determination to be the best is there, the drive actually stemmed from his convictions of "doing the right thing" and "standing up for the little guy." It just so happened that his drive for the best and determination for doing the right thing merge together into his powerhouse role as Oklahoma County district attorney. Likewise, Macy surrounded himself with people of equal passion for "doing the right thing."

"Richard Mask," he says, "brought real professionalism to that city, to that department. He worked real hard to prevent crime from coming into a community that prided itself that way."

Oklahoma City Deputy Chief David Shupe remains one of Macy's biggest fans, still remembering how impressive was Macy's performance in overcoming deep-seeded suspicions among the city's street cops. In the end, they were convinced of Macy's attitude, passion, fearlessness, and were converted into his strongest allies.

"Access had a lot to do with why Macy was trusted," Shupe says. "He never made himself unavailable to the rank and file. He sought out leaders, and he sought out the men and women who worked the streets."

Shupe adds, "I remember the case of the murder of Gary Ward. He was a policeman working security after hours at a Holiday Inn. He was filling in for a relative who was usually there at a time like that. Alvin Parker was a burglar who worked the hotels. He shot and killed Gary at the hotel. That was a tough deal. I worked that night and day for three or four days. Parker was a Star Spencer basketball star. They used to call him 'King' Parker. We got an arrest warrant and went to his house looking for a gun. I hadn't been to sleep in three days."

Shupe continues, "I remember it was icy. I was walking from the search and fell. I slid across the road into Bob's feet. I remember those pointed cowboy boots as I looked at them. My gun slid out of my hand and into his foot, and it bounced off the toe of his boot and spun on the ice. Well, the next day he filed 'charges' against me for pointing a weapon at an officer. It was hilarious, but his point was to josh me, to support me and show he was on our side."

As for the murder of Gary Ward, "We convicted Alvin Parker of murder, but it was reversed for some deficiency in the investigation. We were able to retry it, and he got ninety-nine years on a charge of manslaughter."

Shupe repeats what he said earlier. "From my point of view, the defense lawyers were always on Bob's rear for his closings, his final arguments. I sat through a lot of murder trials. He was emotional and made a powerful connection with the victim and the victim's family. The tears he would shed were real." This was less a job and more a passion. "Bob Macy is the most compelling figure I have ever seen in a courtroom. He was awfully good," Shupe adds. "And excelling at anything he tried went along with his passion."

Despite the emotion and power in some of his closing arguments, Shupe says Macy always followed the law. To be sure, "He was ruthless for the pursuit of justice." For Macy, Shupe says, "The process started long before the crime itself ever happened. His methods were based on personal relationships, on his ties to friends, colleagues, and coworkers. I'll tell you that changed after he left. It deteriorated. But it has improved some again under David Prater," the current DA. There was a fire in Macy's belly, a driving force that clearly defined right and wrong, that surely separated winners from losers. From his perspective, the victims of crimes were the winners, and he would do whatever was in his power to make that so.

In some cases, the power of transforming a victim to a winner was not possible. Even Macy was limited by the power of the law, though personal relationships he developed with victims and investigators urged him to do otherwise. Those personal relationships often kept investigations on track and morale high. In some cases, discussions between the prosecutor's team and the police working the case could get heated.

"When you work together in those circumstances," Shupe explains, "when you get into one of those deals, things get very emotionally charged. There would be arguments and if the DA told you they weren't going to be able to press charges, you'd say, 'BS!' There was a lot of hollering and sincere differences, but because of the relationships, just ten minutes later, you'd be going to lunch. There was a lot of great trust among police investigators and the DA's people." If Macy could not prosecute a case, there were always legitimate legal reasons why.

For his part, Macy says, "Shupe was the best homicide detective I ever saw. He was deadly on the witness stand."

In the course of our discussions about local law enforcement, Macy has some critical reflections on other police departments in Oklahoma County and law enforcement operations in and around the Oklahoma City area.

"Bethany was good. In some of the smaller jurisdictions, the officers were/are limited by their finances," Macy adds. "An effective police department must have financial backing," and Macy fully realizes the connection between a well-paid and trained police department and the reduction of the crime rate.

For all the success police had battling crime, there were new and constantly evolving challenges for law enforcement. As Macy recalls, "During my time in office, there were two or three major spurts of population growth, and the growth in the far northwest of the city was phenomenal." With affection, Macy remembers a particular East side leader. "I remember Mr. Goree James. He and I were often on a circuit together to convince people there was a real crime and drug problem, and it wasn't just on the East side. At the time, it seemed crack cocaine was the black man's dope. The criminals did some clever things as far as marketing. They brought in crack and gave away free samples. Once the young people were addicted, the price was sky high. It became a real epidemic in the Oklahoma City courts."

At the same time, Macy remembers, "There was an influx of Hispanic gangs on the South side and around town. Their cocaine version was 'ice'—another variety that was powder mixed. Tensions arose on the south side with an influx of marijuana and those gangs."

In terms of forces driving the south side gang surge, Macy says American economic vitality had, in some cases, been oversold to illegal immigrants who were drawn here thinking the streets were paved with gold. When that turned out not to be the case, "Some of the people began to feel they'd been duped, to feel they weren't getting their share of the money." That gave some added impetus to the gangsters.

He explains his observation further. "If you think about it, we opened the floodgates and let the illegals in. They came here to get work. They had been told things about how great it would be. Things in our culture and society were not bilingual. They had in some cases been lured under false pretenses, even by others in that population. There were false promises about how good it would be. The Mexicans were territorial and became suspicious when the new circumstances they were in were not as favorable as expected or described to them."

His understanding of "street truths" and the solid reputation he had for what is now called "street cred" (credibility on the rough edges of the culture) might partially explain Macy's phenomenal success as a politician, although he rarely spent much money on campaigning and elections. Bob Macy won countywide elections in 1982, 1986, 1990, 1994, and 1998. One of his secrets is that he never intended to run that many times. "When I took the job, I didn't know it would be that many. I wanted to be the best DA in the country, and I wanted Oklahoma City to be the safest place in the country." Once again, his inclination to be the best and his passion for helping people coupled into a twenty-one-year career doing both.

The country and the county changed a lot in the twenty-one years he served. Macy was a conservative when he started and ended his historic tenure, yet "I'm still a registered Democrat. I almost changed, but my friends said, 'We need you where you are.' So I stayed."

When pressured to explain his ties to the Democratic Party, Macy candidly replied, "Well, it's hard to say. My dad liked Ike a lot. He believed in him. At Earlham, one of my classmates was actually John East, later the U.S. Senator from North Carolina, a great conservative leader. We played football together. His wife, Priscilla (Sissy) was a classmate and friend. Conrad Joiner was also a classmate, who was later Barry Goldwater's speech writer. There at little old Earlham we had quite a group. Maybe I stayed a Democrat because I met George Nigh and his allies, my classmates at the OU law school. All except Nigh went to OU law school at the same time. We used to all get together and drink cups of coffee in the mornings."

He elaborates that he always felt comfortable with the policy views and beliefs of Nigh, the man who appointed him Oklahoma County DA and, despite his anger at some national Democratic trends, never felt compelled to leave the party. Partisan considerations aside, Macy had a remarkable run of trust with the voters of Oklahoma County. A decade after he left office, there is little doubt that, if nature allowed him the time and stamina, he would still be the dominant figure in Oklahoma County politics.

The roots of his political strength lie in the confidence voters always had in his sense of purpose and his passion. While best known for his laser-like focus on the most heinous crimes and his success in conviction and execution of murderers, Macy's interactions with citizens reinforced the habits and patterns of his office and staff.

A 1993 speech included his reflections on several non-capital crimes and criminals. Oscar James Johnson had been given a twenty-five year prison sentence in September 1988 but "was not in prison at 3:00 a.m. on February 9, 1993, less than five years later. Instead, he broke through the patio doors of a woman's home and pressed a metal pipe into her throat while demanding money from her."

As Macy noted in the speech, Johnson was on parole at the time of his new crime. In this case, "We got lucky and Oscar Johnson was captured at the scene. How many he had victimized before he was caught and how many more he would have victimized, we don't know. We do know, though, this was one victim who didn't have to be."

Earlier that same year, a series of robberies occurred while citizens were gathered in two Oklahoma City churches. As Macy reflects, "We were all shocked that people are unable to find sanctuary from crime even in the house of God." It turned out the church robberies were part of a series of crimes in which the same perpetrators had struck area motels and a pet store. "We all felt relieved when the men believed responsible were arrested." By this point in his career, it was hard to surprise Bob Macy with the facts of any crime. Yet it shocked Macy when it turned out the ringleader of the crime spree was Eugene Clayborn. Macy prosecuted him in 1988 as an accomplice to murder, putting that accomplice on death row.

After his own early release, Clayborn led a "four-month crime spree of home invasions and robberies of elderly citizens in near northwest Oklahoma City back in 1987 and 1988." Clayborn was sentenced to ten years in the penitentiary. But that's not all. He'd been convicted in 1991 of attempting to escape, but just a year later, he was paroled. Then, he found new victims.

Then there was the case of Darrie Lee Glover, Jr., sentenced to ten years for burglary in November 1990 and released after just two years inside. Two months after getting out, he walked into a Circle K store carrying a tire iron and, Macy relates with disgust, "threatened to kill the female clerk if she didn't turn over all of her money."

At times, Macy got crossways with the Pardon and Parole Board and, as he reflects now, "wanted to kick their butts." There were times, however, he had success at the parole-board hearings. One specific case comes to mind. A murderer of a police officer was given life without parole but was allowed to appear before the parole board after a very short incarceration. Macy appeared before the board and simply said, "This is an outrage!"

The response from one of the board members was, "Well, that takes care of that." The murderer remained behind bars to serve his time.

In the same 1993 speech, Macy knit together his coherent view of the implications of crime and lack of punishment, a perspective that resonated then and still does today with Oklahomans.

> Each of us is robbed every day by outlaws who carry pencils instead of guns. The clever criminal who pollutes our environment to make a buck literally steals the future of our children. The phonies who cheat insurance companies through fraudulent claims in worker's compensation, auto insurance and health and other medical insurance steal enough each year to provide free health coverage for every American who is now uninsured.

Macy was unusually blunt in dealings with criminal defense lawyers, even those he respected. But he had withering disdain for those he did not regard as honest or dedicated to the law.

One story centers around an event involving his long-time aide, Steve Korotash. The trusted aide brought to "the Boss" a well-known Oklahoma County attorney who wanted to negotiate a deal for his client. He told Macy he had a big bloc of votes "out there" he could deliver, but he had to have a break for his client. Macy comments on the conversation, "I told him he needed to tell me if there was something deficient about the case against his client, and if there was a legal reason to talk things over about the case, but that being able 'to deliver a big bloc of votes out there' was not a good reason for his office to change its approach. The other attorney was disappointed." After the other attorney left, Macy talked things over with Korotash. Macy remembers, "He asked me what I thought about the situation and the lawyer's pleas." Macy responded, "No way in hell." Laughing, Korotash replied, "I knew you were going to say that."

Macy continues, "I never linked campaigns to the job but understood the campaigns were necessary to get an audience. I raised money only so I could get the message out to the people about the job we were doing and get their support." Macy believed then he needed to make as many speaking engagements as possible, often making as many as three speeches a day. "I told my secretary to get me face to face with as many people as she could."

Macy was never a fan of the role of money in politics but recognized that the alternative to elections, executive appointment, was not without its own flaws. He never really considered himself a politician. He simply was put into a position to do the best job he could and to follow his convictions.

In a November 1993 speech to the Law and You Foundation, he recounted a reelection fundraiser in Oklahoma City which Wilford Brimley, the beloved Western actor and Macy's dear friend, had emceed. Bill Barr came to town for that event and told the crowd of his esteem for Bob Macy. "If I ever went into battle, I'd want Bob Macy at my shoulder."

One of his early strong supporters was local attorney, D.C. Thomas, of whom Bob had many fond memories. Many of those came to Bob's mind after D.C. died on April 7, 2009. "I met D.C. Thomas in law school in 1961. Bob Reynolds was at that time an assistant district attorney, 'fire-eater.' He was good and wanted to run for county attorney. There was also on the scene at the time Bob Walker and Earl Mills. They all had successful law practices. Reynolds had run for county attorney with the support of our little group." When Macy became DA, Thomas was one of his strongest allies.

In one campaign, Macy remembers, "Buck Cargill got me in trouble with Betty. There was a fundraiser over at NW 4th street. His boy sang a song for the event. That night, they had these stickers that said, 'I'm for Bob.' Somebody, as a joke, slapped one of those stickers on the rear end of D.C.'s wife. It was a joke, but then it got into the newspaper, *The Oklahoman*. My wife got unhappy that it was in there for everyone to read."

D.C. Thomas's understanding of the DA's job was based in part on his own experience as a local prosecutor who worked for one of Macy's predecessors. D.C., Macy remembers, was "honest and true, a good man you could trust." But one of Macy's most outlandish opponents was Mike Gasaway, a lawyer who has found himself in repeated trouble with the bar and with other lawyers for various ethical lapses. When Gasaway ran against Macy, he made a wild accusation about alleged immorality by the incumbent and had come up with a signed affidavit that Macy was supposed to sexually "take care of" the wife of a Gasaway client while that fellow was in prison. Gasaway brought the affidavit to Macy's office and told him that he should drop out of the race or he would give the affidavit to the press to be printed.

Nolan Clay, a seasoned reporter for the powerful *Daily*, got on the story. He pinpointed the exact time and place of the supposed proposition to the woman at the center of all of this. Clay then went to Macy with the dates when all of this allegedly had taken place. It turned out that the night the proposition allegedly took place, Macy had been in a hospital recuperating from a chainsaw accident the day before—another in a series of health challenges over the years. In any case, then and for many days thereafter, Macy was in the hospital and on crutches at the time Gasaway contended he was propositioning women.

New articles and editorials in *The Oklahoman* condemned Gasaway, contending that Oklahoma County politics had really reached a brand new low. Macy crushed Gasaway with more than 80 percent of the vote.

When Macy came into politics in the 1960s, the rule in campaigns was often "anything goes." And some things about that didn't change with the passage of the years. When Macy faced dubious foes, Bob Ravitz, the public defender who respected the tough prosecutor, used to joke that his pickup truck kept "jerking to the right" in such a way as to destroy the opponent's campaign signs.

Another time, in a race for an East side state senate seat, the Democratic primary between Vicki Miles-LaGrange and E. Melvin Porter was closely contested. In order to discredit Senator Miles- LaGrange, Porter alleged that Macy was supporting Miles-LaGrange and personally financing her campaign. It was completely untrue, and Porter knew that was the case. Not too much later, Macy and the other two were working the court of Judge Ray Naifeh. Macy accused Porter of illegal conduct in the charges he'd made.

Porter smiled and said, "Hey, Bob, that's just politics." Miles-LaGrange, a former trusted aide to Macy, won the primary and went on to a series of important jobs in public service. Once again, Macy surrounded himself with those who he not only trusted but were trustworthy and honest people in character.

In a July 2007 interview with Byron J. Will, a student of legal history, former governor George Nigh said that what made Bob Macy great was not that Nigh had appointed him the county DA but that Macy had so overwhelmingly and repeatedly won reelection. Nigh's point was that to go before the voters that many times and make it through deeply impressed him as a political matter. And, of course, few men in Oklahoma politics understood the challenges of electoral politics better than George Nigh, an excellent politician.

Macy was proud of his success in three important campaigns to pass ballot measures on public safety. After the city's founding decades, local voters began to cast highly critical eyes on spending for public schools and even public safety. Though he never considered himself a politician, rather a passionate advocate for "doing the right thing," he went to the voters and won their support "for the pay raises for police and fire, and for equipment. I was able to get approval for money for the jail and for better communication equipment for the police department. Getting approval on a ballot measure is a different kind of politics, and I'm proud of the job we did on those ballot issues."

Macy remembers, "I hadn't been DA very long when the first one came along. It was a proposal for a tax increase to pay for an additional three hundred police and three hundred firefighters and to properly equip them all. The city administration had tried to get something like this before, and the voters turned them down. I was able to work with the Fraternal Order of Police and the firefighters. I gave dozens of speeches on that subject and did question-and-answer sessions all over the county."

After one of the successful referenda, he received a letter from Debbie Blackburn, who was then director of the Neighborhood Alliance of Oklahoma City. Blackburn told Macy:

> Your generous donation of time and energy was invaluable in the passage of the sales tax for the police and fire needs. When the DA speaks, people listen. It would have been much more difficult without your assistance. History was made last Tuesday by the citizens of Oklahoma City. Voters spoke loudly and clearly for better public safety. As the director of an organization which encourages both informed citizen participation and citizen involvement in crime prevention, I am grateful to work with a public official who not only listens to citizens but attempts to work with them to find solutions to their problems... Your sincere commitment to public safety in our community helped us secure an overwhelmingly successful election. We are grateful.

Blackburn, a Democrat, went on to serve several terms in the state legislature.

Another issue was the jail, which was overcrowded and outdated when a major proposal for improvement was made in the 1990s. Although not involved in the design or administration of the jail, Macy told the public, "If you build me a jail, I'll fill it up." As he says, "They did, and I did. I was fortunate because from early on, I had the support of the people."

One of the greatest controversies of Macy's tenure centered around a plea agreement reached concerning wrongdoing in the 1990 gubernatorial campaign of David Walters. Walters, who prevailed early in that election, was dogged by allegations of illegal contributions during and after his election, and a good deal of his time in office was consumed by the allegations.

In Oklahoma, convictions for campaign violations in statewide campaigns have usually been the result of federal investigations. A well-known example of this is the county commissioner scandal of the 1980s, in which several powerful figures wound up in prison after federal prosecutions.

In the case of Governor Walters, however, two fellow Democrats delved deeply into the chief executive's fundraising patterns. Macy and Attorney General Susan Loving, a Walters appointee named to finish a term when the elected incumbent retired, guided the work of a multi-county grand jury looking at the allegations. Investigations by *The Daily Oklahoman's* reporters unearthed much of the early evidence of violations, and the grand jury did the rest. Walters was indicted for eight felonies.

For two years, mounting tension surrounded the case. Walters insisted he was innocent, his attorney argued the prosecution was selective and unfair, and many fellow Democrats, including former Attorney General Mike Turpen, rallied to support Walters. In the end, however, the governor pled guilty to one misdemeanor charge. As Macy points out, Walters "signed his name" to a document admitting guilt. The governor forfeited the "remaining unencumbered balance of his campaign funds" to the state Ethics Commission.

When the outcome was reported in the Oklahoma news media, fierce criticism unfolded. Radio talk hosts, political commentators, and newspaper columns assailed the outcome as far too soft on the governor. An October 24 front-page editorial in *The Sunday Oklahoman*, the state's largest newspaper, called the plea agreement "ludicrous" and "outrageous." While stopping short of writing off Macy and Loving, the newspaper said the accord appeared to many to be a "backroom political sellout."

Macy and Loving, however, had some defenders from the first moments of the controversy. Defenders observed there was absolutely no indication that Governor Walters was willing to resign from office, as many of his critics had hoped. That meant that prosecution of the case would have taken up another year or two. Others said the plea agreement's combination of an admission of guilt and the forfeiture of campaign resources was sufficient sanction.

In its own editorial, the *Tulsa World* described as absurd the all assertions that the pair of prosecutors had "whitewashed the governor." The grand jury itself issued a joint statement on behalf of all of its members, expressing appreciation for "the honesty, integrity, and sincerity" Macy and Loving had shown during the process.

In his own right, Macy aggressively defended himself and his colleague, the attorney general. In broadcast appearances and interviews with newspaper reporters, Macy characterized the author of the editorial in the *Oklahoman* as a "coward" for not signing his name to the criticisms of the plea.

In a notable interview with Arnold Hamilton of the *Dallas Morning News*, Macy explained that his approach to the case was the same as in every case. "I do everything in my power to see that equal justice is done in Oklahoma County. I don't look at race, creed, financial wealth, sex. I try to treat everybody the same. I try to be totally fair." By this time, Bob Macy had certainly overcome his dislike for the wealthy. They, too, he had discovered, could be the victims of horrendous crimes.

But this controversy played out in interesting ways. Both critics and fans expressed admiration for Macy. Liberal editor Frosty Troy of the *Oklahoma Observer* said the DA was a "quality prosecutor" and "the kind of guy you want. He's a bare-knuckled prosecutor. At the same time, he's not the kind of guy you'd invite home for dinner."

Irven Box, one of Oklahoma County's best known and controversial defense attorneys, criticized Macy for certain practices but characterized him as "a very worthy adversary" with "total command of the courtroom."

It was not long before much of the criticism faded as citizens reflected on the bottom line. The governor had pled guilty and the state had moved on to concentrating on substantive policy issues. Today, Macy admits he was shocked by some of the early responses to the Walters plea agreement. He explains that although he and

Loving certainly agreed with the accord, it was, in the end, a judge's decision to approve the accord reached with Walters and the governor's attorney. The bottom line for Bob Macy was then, and still is now, that the plea contained Walters's admission to the facts and forfeiture of the campaign war chest.

Just weeks after the controversy, in a November 1993 talk, he reflected:

> The good Lord has a way of reminding us of our place in His world. As you know, He gave me and Susan Loving a lesson in humility the last several weeks over the governor's plea agreement. They say the Lord puts no greater burden on us than we can bear, and while that may be true, I assure you that the last few weeks have been the most stressful and by far the heaviest burden of my career.

Macy continued, "Whether you think I did right or wrong in the agreement with the governor over his guilty plea, I swear to you I did what I believed was right as it was given to me to see what the right thing to do was."

Macy pointed to supportive newspaper editorials, including one from the *Edmond Sun*, which argued, "History will show that the deal framed by Macy and Attorney General Susan Loving was the right way to end this affair in court." As always, Macy was true to his ideals as he saw them—"just do the right thing." There was no political maneuvering, favoritism, or bending to the winds of pressure.

As time cooled some of the initial rhetoric over the plea accord, Macy said he was particularly grateful to those who told him they would continue to support him even though they thought the plea agreement was too lenient on Governor Walters.

Within days after the early criticisms in the editorials at the *Oklahoman*, publisher E.L. Gaylord instructed the writers on the editorial page to ease up and reconcile with Macy, who had always enjoyed the paper's strong support.

Editorial page editor Jim Standard asked Macy for a meeting. Macy agreed but was still angry from the slaps he had taken. Further, Macy meant it when he accused the unnamed author of the offending editorial of cowardice. At the arranged hour, Standard and a colleague arrived at the district attorney's office. When they were escorted in for the session, the gregarious Standard, tall and lanky like Macy, grinned broadly as he stuck out his hand and declared, "Hello, Bob. I'm the coward." Macy couldn't help but laugh and respond with a firm handshake. They talked things through, made peace, and the newspaper remained a strong supporter of Macy the man, even when occasionally critical, as in some aspects of the Murrah bombing prosecution after 1995.

In the end, Walters served out his term but did not seek reelection in 1994. He went on to a successful career in the energy business and power development and made an unsuccessful run for the U.S. Senate in 2000.

For her part, Susan Loving was buffeted on one side by allegations that the plea for Walters was a sort of political deal and on the other side by many Democrats for being too tough on the governor. She ultimately chose not to seek election to a full term. She became a partner in an Edmond law firm, where she is a name partner. Of the principal characters in the drama, only Macy remained a political powerhouse, twice more gaining overwhelming reelection before his 2001 retirement.

Stepping back from the particulars of that case, Macy says that in general, "I had excellent relations with the media. I felt like it's a public office, and the public was and is entitled to know what's going on." In the course of any regular prosecution, "Some things had to wait to be on the record. I tried to be as forthright as I could. I didn't have any secrets, but the media, the reporters, seemed to understand that for some things, they had to wait for an appropriate time to get my comments."

Macy said he doesn't think he ever had a problem with journalists sensationalizing or blowing issues out of proportion. His experience was that he could explain limitations on commentary by his office, so long as he promised to answer all questions at the appropriate time. Throughout his tenure, "I appreciated the editorial endorsements I got. The message seemed to be that the good old boys were no longer in control. I called things the way I saw them. The editorial writers seemed to respect that."

But Macy's life away from the difficulties of public life was not nearly so full of incomprehensible pressures and difficulties. In fact, he managed to have a better personal life than many of his peers. His fondest memories, he tells with a smile and a gleam in his eyes, are of the times he went to Seminole with Betty and celebrated the holidays with her side of the family.

Macy remembers the times in Seminole. "We'd all come in on Christmas Eve or day. For Thanksgiving, we'd go over there and all watch the games. I'll tell you, there were kids everywhere. They were a very good and close-knit family."

One incident he recalls this way. Jack Skirvin was a friend of Betty and her side of the family. One year in Seminole, while the women were shopping, Bob and Jack went out on Christmas Eve and walked around the stores. "It was cool and there were just a few people on the streets," Macy remembers. "Jack was looking at these kids who were standing there looking at the merchandise in the store windows. Those little ones would go inside and back outside, just looking at the presents. He bought a coat, shoes, and scarves for one little boy." Macy told Skirvin that was a good thing to do for that lad. Bob, then, got a $100 and joined Skirvin in the Christmas spirit, spending it to buy presents for two of those kids. Jack said, "I don't do it for those kids. I do it because it makes me feel good."

Macy remembered, "Dedek and I used to go to these cheap restaurants and fast food places. There was one down on Forty-Third and Shields on the south side. We would eat there maybe once a month. We felt at home with those poor people and the working people who came in there to eat and with whom we talked. Once in a while, usually in that season of the year, I'd stop in, have lunch and then go to the clerk and pay for everybody in the restaurant at that moment. Then, when they got ready to leave, they'd find someone had already paid for it. Clint would complain and say, 'Macy, why are you spending all that money?' I'd reply, 'Well, I'm not spending it all, because you're gonna pay for half of it.' And he did."

Macy used to deal with Roma McAlway, "a woman who was the head of my juvenile division. I'd ask her to get me a family I could help without any credit before Christmas. She asked me that first year, 'Can I pick the family?' And she did. I remember Roma told me where she was going to shop, when she took a little girl or boy to the store. I was a few rows away watching her with the kids. She gathered up coats, scarves, and gloves. I'd told her I wanted to pay for the necessities, not toys. Well, that little girl saw a doll, and she was just set on having it. Roma glanced over at me, and I couldn't help it. I nodded my head slightly to say, 'Yes.' I told her to keep it around $100, but it was a lot more than that."

During one long morning of conversation in the summer of 2009, in a particularly memorable exchange with Macy, inter views with David Shupe had made Macy particularly reflective. Pat McGuigan had closed his notebook for that session and was preparing to leave. Macy then began to tell Pat something fresh and important, he knew from his tone. The only thing available to grab to write on was an old piece of stationary headed "to be done *yesterday*." At the foot of the pages, that stationary had "r.h. macy." That reminded McGuigan of the poet e.e. cummings. Later, he asked and learned that the supply of notepads had been given to Macy some thirty years before by ladies with the Junior League in

St. Petersburg, Florida. It turned out to be an appropriate place to sketch McGuigan's notes.

Here's what Bob Macy told McGuigan:

"You have a window in time, and that's when you need to get it all done. After you spend time getting ready, you'll have maybe twenty or thirty years of productivity. Before that, you don't know enough. After that, you're too crippled up. If I was in my prime right now, I'd be running for attorney general or something like that. But my window in time has passed."

Bob Macy told McGuigan in that same conversation he has few regrets; he just wants young people, professionals who are at the start of their careers, to understand that this is the way things work out.

Nonetheless, Bob Macy leaves a legacy and a lesson all citizens must understand. He explains why he made countless speeches, more than memory can recall, to every kind of civic group imaginable. Explaining his reasons for so many speeches, Macy says, "Organized crime can never be won by law enforcement alone. To stop drugs, molestation, [and] violence on children will take a concerted effort by all. It's the public that make up the juries that determine the punishment and verdicts. Stopping crime must constantly involve citizens. The only way to eliminate violence," he continues, "is to remove the violent perpetrators from the streets and homes of law-abiding citizens. There are scum who run rampant through our city streets."

Macy knew his job and did his very best to do it all, as attested by the crowded prisons and the dozens of murderers who spent their last days on death row. Americans enjoy many freedoms and blessings, but the one freedom we seem not to have, even now, even after Macy's hard work, is the freedom from violence. But as he said, it's up to the citizens, not to a single individual, no matter how committed and how passionate.

CHAPTER 8

The Years from Hell

Historian Robert Barr Smith, in his book *Outlaw Tales of Oklahoma*, tells the story of the Buck Gang. In a chapter entitled, "Evil Incarnate," he summarizes how this gang of whites and Indians briefly terrorized a large portion of what later became eastern Oklahoma. The fundamental nature of man hasn't changed since the fall on man in the Garden of Eden, let alone since the territorial days of Oklahoma. The depravity to which those who fall the farthest are capable of continues to astonish even people who are the most knowledgeable about the evil that men do.

In a late 2009 interview with Bob Macy, he reflected that he understood, even before the massive terror of the Murrah bombing, that "Every murder, every killing, is horrible, yet as a cop or an investigator or a prosecutor, undeniably some affect you more than others. As the years passed, I learned again and again that every time I thought I'd seen it all, some new act of brutality would refocus the mind on just how bad things can get and how important it is to have a system that responds to push back the evil with justice and truth and accountability."

As was the case during his early years in office, Macy still reads a lot. Smith's *Outlaw Tales* is one of the books he absorbed in retirement.

Rufus Buck led a band of men who, in the course of a brief career of carnage, engaged, to the extent needed to finance their activities, in robbery and larceny. They were an unusually vicious bunch in that era, when Judge Isaac Parker in Little Rock and intrepid U.S. marshals were slowly carving order into the frontier. Initially, Rufus used his Indian ancestry and the travails of the eastern native tribes that had been forced to resettle in Indian Territory as an excuse for his actions, but no one bought that. The real pleasures for the depraved members of the gang came from rapes and killings, and they committed a staggering series of both over thirteen days in July and August 1895. They brutalized women of all ages, including a gang rape of Mrs. Henry Hasson. She miraculously survived to testify against the whole bunch. In their spree, the Buck Gang killed several innocents, including one deputy U.S. marshal, a brave black man named John Garrett.

In the end, the frontier gangsters managed to unite the people of the territory, including the Lighthorse, the Indian police who pursued them relentlessly. Federal and territorial posses of Creek Indians, whites, blacks, and others joined the hunt, tracking the gang down to a hilltop in eastern Oklahoma. After a day-long standoff, the Buck bunch was captured alive and taken to receive Judge Parker's tender mercies in Arkansas. They got due process and were found guilty. Less than a year after their two-week reign of terror, the five rapists and killers were hanged simultaneously on July 1, 1896.

Justice generally moves more slowly these days, as illustrated by the aftermath of a murderous spree that began nearly five years into Bob Macy's tenure. He dealt with a series of killings among the most heinous he ever faced, and it took until shortly after the end of his time in office for final disposition of one of the cases.

Looking back, you could say it was a year from hell. Between January 24, 1985, and January 30, 1986, eight of the most high-profile murders on District Attorney Bob Macy's watch took place in Oklahoma County. For some of them, it took years for final justice to come, but ultimately, each of the killers were convicted, incarcerated, and, in several cases, executed.

The State vs. Bigler Jobe Stouffer

The first story begins at the upper end of the local economic strata. Oklahoma City businessman Doug Ivens, a middle-aged man who separated and pursued divorce from his wife Velva, had developed a warm and loving relationship with Linda Reaves. Doug, the developer of the Greens Country Club, agreed to let Velva live in their former home that backed onto the golf course, while he resided in a nearby condo.

Doug was happy in his budding relationship with Linda. Macy recalls that Ivens once told him Linda was "the best thing that ever happened to me. She is different from everyone else I have ever dated, a very special lady. We are engaged and plan to get married. When I found her, I'd found the love of my life." Doug was still concerned about his ex-wife and their two eight-year-old daughters. For her part, Velva had been dating a fellow named Bigler Jobe Stouffer. While not particularly handsome, "Bud" Stouffer was a bit of a gigolo. He had developed the habit of hanging around high-end car washes, seeking opportunities to pick up wealthy married or divorced women. That's how he met Velva and, ultimately, moved in with her at Doug's former home. Ivens encountered Stouffer a few times but had no particular reason to dislike or fear him. In fact, they even played golf together just days before things took an awful turn.

On the night of January 24, 1985, Stouffer came to Iven's house, where Doug was spending the evening with Linda. When Doug came to the door, Stouffer asked if he could borrow a pistol, saying he needed the weapon because he believed there were prowlers or a burglar watching Velva's house. Doug went into a bedroom and emerged with a bank bag that contained a loaded .357 magnum Colt revolver. He gave the bag to Stouffer, who turned away for a moment. When Stouffer turned back around, he trained the pistol on Doug and fired twice. As Ivens dropped to the floor, Stouffer went to the couch where Linda was reclining and shot her twice in the face at point blank range. Stouffer then walked back to where Ivens was lying on the floor and fired another round into his face.

After Stouffer left, believing both victims were dead, Ivens was able to crawl to a telephone in his garage and call the police. In the tape from the police dispatch, Ivens can be heard telling the dispatcher, "Hey, pard', you'd better hurry because I'm not sure I'm gonna make it." Ivens, wracked with pain, was remarkable in the exchange, describing who had shot him and Linda, how Stouffer was dressed and what kind of car he was driving. A recording of that 9–1-1 call would later provide gripping and powerful evidence against Stouffer. Linda ultimately died from her horrible wounds, but Doug miraculously survived.

After the shootings, Stouffer went to a nearby post office to create an alibi for the approximate time of the killing. After his miraculous survival, Doug eventually told Macy about his beloved dog's role in the drama. Prior to the arrival of the police, the dog kept running back and forth between the main house where Velva lived and the condo where Doug had been living, barking up a storm as if trying to call attention to the fact something had happened.

Stouffer was an odd cat in many ways. After his post office visit, he went back to the place he shared with Velva. She was there with her parents and the two daughters. When he first came in, Stouffer asked if anything had happened to the girls.

Soon thereafter, he returned to the scene of the crime after police were there, asking what had happened and playing like he didn't know. Of course, the police had Doug Ivens on tape describing the guy who'd shot him. The police arrested Stouffer right there on the spot.

At trial, District Attorney Bob Macy's expert witnesses concluded five shots had been fired from the Colt Python revolver, which had one unfired round in it when it was found. Defense witnesses argued more shots could have been fired and that it was not clear every spent cartridge found came from the pistol. The defense experts also sought to cast doubts on the processing of the crime scene, implying police had focused on Ivens's narrative and nothing else.

Stouffer's defense wanted to argue a theory that Stouffer's shooting of Ivens was in self-defense, elaborating that argument from the fact that Linda had held a part-time secretary job for Phil Blair, Velva's brother. Phil and Doug held some joint business ventures, and Phil had been charged with embezzling $900,000 from Doug. The trial on that matter was set for the Monday after the shootings with Linda intended as a witness. Stouffer theorized that someone shot Linda Reaves before Bud got there and he, in turn, shot Doug Ivens in self-defense.

The state's assertion was that Stouffer shot the two so that he, through Velva, could get his hands on Doug's money in the form of a rather hefty joint estate they still shared. In one of our discussions, in response to my question, Macy said there was no reason at all to believe Velva was in on the murder plot. However, Stouffer apparently thought Doug's large life insurance policy, which had once listed Velva as beneficiary, would be the source of another big pot of money.

Bob Macy led the first prosecution of the killer with Patrick Morgan at his side. After that first conviction, counsel for the murderer was found incompetent, and Macy, in retrospect, finds it hard to disagree. Indeed, Bob recalls he and Morgan tried to find ways, in sidebars and *in-camera* sessions with the trial judge and defense lawyer, to keep things proceeding toward justice with fairness for the accused. In the end, Stouffer's lawyer was so ineffective, the trial had to be held a second time.

Today, Macy remembers that when Stouffer came in for sentencing after the first trial, the murderer had completely shaved his head, was dressed nicely, and carried a large Bible in his hand. Sometimes gregarious during the trial, he didn't talk much after the sentence was handed down.

When a second trial was required, Richard Wintory carried the ball and ultimately won the day. Two years after Macy left office, Stouffer's verdict of guilt was upheld for first-degree murder and shooting with intent to kill. He was sentenced to life imprisonment on the latter charge and to death on the murder charge. Stouffer remains on death row as of this writing.

An important sidebar in the Stouffer case involved two of Doug's best friends, Ron Shotts and Jimmy Goodwin, whom Macy called "outstanding civil lawyers." Shott was very well known as a star football running back during his days at the University of Oklahoma and for an unsuccessful run for governor as the Republican candidate in 1978. Shotts and Goodwin were infuriated by what happened to their friend, Doug Ivens, and at Stouffer himself. They were aware that Stouffer had substantial assets and wanted to assure that in no possible scenario could Bud benefit from what he'd done to Ivens. The two attorneys filed civil lawsuits to impound all of Bud Stouffer's assets. But while the battle over Stouffer's assets was going on, there were rumors that Stouffer had someone out to do a "hit" on Macy and Shotts. Macy recalls that the word on the street was Stouffer himself had hired the hit man. In any case, at one point they found a bullet hole in the driver's side door of Shott's vehicle. The bullet had somehow lodged inside the doorframe and not penetrated the inside. It wasn't clear if the shot had been fired while Ron was driving around or when the car was parked somewhere.

The State vs. Rex Moore

Another awful case, one of the most notorious of the 1980s, was the burning of Tammy Lee Moore on May 7, leading to her death two days later. Tammy Buerge met Rex Moore when she was just fourteen years old. She was a babysitter for his children, and there was, as an appeals court later noted, "More than thirty years difference in their ages." She grew up a little and then married Rex, a union that lasted nine years while she finished high school, went to college, and studied drama. She became involved in local theater, and they had two kids of their own. For a while, economically speaking, things were good due to the vibrant oil economy of the late 1970s.

But Macy said there must have been more than met the eye. He said, "Evidence in the house found after her death suggested Tammy might have been subjected to torture in some instances." In any case, by 1985 the two were headed for divorce court. Rex had accused his wife of embezzling funds from his oil-exploration operations, something Macy noted in retrospect was never proven. As they moved through the divorce process, agreements on child custody and property settlements were reached. While the accord indicated she would remain employed at his oil business, she would lose custody of her children for a period of time.

On May 6, according to court records, Rex told a friend he was happy about the agreement for him to get the children and for Tammy to continue working. Rex claimed he had "retrieved the company money Tammy had taken, and . . . looked forward to a favorable agreement on their divorce."

The next morning, some men working at the home said Rex seemed normal as he left with the two children and then returned a little later. At about 10:00 a.m., Rex ran out of the office and shouted, "Call the fire department and an ambulance." The workers then ran into the house with Rex, who said his wife was in a bedroom on the second story, where there was a fire. The workers and Rex made an attempt to put out the flames but failed. Firefighters arrived and raced upstairs. As the appeals court later reported, "Captain Barton and Fireman Edward Koch entered the burning room and found Tammy Moore draped over a couch."

About ten days before the fire, Tammy told her father and a friend that she feared Rex and thought he might harm her. His defense lawyer argued this was hearsay, but the trial judge allowed the information under the "state of mind exception," indicating the victim's concern for her safety. Tammy had related her concerns after what the appeals court called "a domestic disturbance between [Rex] and his wife."

The incident originated when Rex saw Tammy hug and kiss a male friend good-bye outside the home. When she returned inside, she saw a gun and was concerned Rex might do something to her. She hid the gun, but he found it and pulled it on her, the testimony indicated. The trial court judge refused to suppress the friend's testimony about Tammy's state of mind and about her concerns.

Tammy Moore was transported by emergency medics to the hospital with third-degree burns over 95 percent of her body. The only part of her that was not burned was a tiny spot on top of her head. Prior to alerting the workers outside, Rex had also been burned on his arms, chest, and face. He, too, was taken to the hospital.

Later, at trial, Deputy Fire Chief Tom Smith testified, "The fire was confined to a suite of rooms including the west bedroom, a sitting room, bathroom, dressing room, and a sun room. The fire involved the bedroom, the sitting room adjacent to the bedroom, and the bathroom." Smoke from the fire traveled through those rooms and others in the suite, causing significant smoke damage. The record said, "The most heavily burned area was in the sitting room where a gasoline can and a flammable liquid pattern were found on the floor." Tammy was found in the bedroom on a couch near the foot of her bed. "There was a flammable liquid pattern at the foot of the bed." The windows throughout the area were locked.

John Soos, a fire investigator, said there were two fires in the complex. The worst flames were in the sitting room near a gas can, Soos said. The second fire was in the area where Tammy was found.

At the hospital, Tammy was conscious but so severely burned that she could not talk. She had to answer questions by nodding her head yes or no in response to questions from Fire Captain George Hale and police detectives. As time passed, Tammy also communicated with hospital personnel and, her family said, with family members by using her fingers to mark letters on her sheets.

In all that torturous communication, Tammy made it clear she had not attempted suicide. She responded affirmatively when asked if gasoline had been poured on her and set aflame. Her condition grew worse and worse, and she died on May 9. Tammy told Captain Hale that she knew she was dying and that Rex had tried to kill her. While attempting to comfort Tammy, her mother said, "Everything's going to be okay." Tammy shook her head violently. In what must have been agonizing moments, she spelled out, "Rex poured gas on me," and, "I wrapped in blanket."

Later at trial, defense counsel made strenuous efforts to suppress the testimony of Tammy's father, her friend, and the communications of Tammy herself to her mother and others. The judge let the information in, and later, the appeals court said the evidence was strong enough to convict Rex, even without her final communications. The appeals panel repeated findings that "a statement made by a declarant while believing that [her] death was imminent, concerning the cause or circumstances of what [she] believed to be . . . impending death" was, indeed, admissible.

Macy says that in this, and in all the cases he ever tried, he was seeking to tell a story, to make a case compelling from the very beginning. He argued that the facts of a case are critical, but putting the facts into a story so that the jurors see and understand what was happening at the time makes the case memorable so that the victim does not become another statistic. "Every time I tried a case, the first thing was to pick a jury, then make an opening argument that tells them exactly what you're going to demonstrate from the evidence."

In the Rex Moore case, the defense counsel objected and said, in essence, "The prosecutor is not making an opening statement. He's telling a story."

Macy countered, "I'm telling you what we're going to prove, what the evidence indicates happened."

What Bob told me is that he followed the old line for not only prosecutors but also storytellers—tell them what you're going to tell them, tell them, and then tell them what you told them. As for this particular trial, Macy remembers, "Jimmy Turner defended Rex Moore. Jimmy is an excellent attorney. His real mission, his job, was to try to save Moore's life and, in that sense, he succeeded." As said before, Turner tried to argue Tammy's communication with her caregivers, her relatives, police, and fire personnel amounted to hearsay, assertions that extended into the appeal that followed Rex's conviction. The trial judge said her statements were admissible because they showed her state of mind. In the end, appellate judges agreed, but it's reasonable to think that perhaps the information Turner presented helped save Rex's life.

Turner made a strong case about the children of Rex and Tammy. "These two young people have already lost their mother. If you sentence Rex to death, they'll lose their father, too. They'll have to go through that, too." The lawyer argued, "As old as he is, he'll never get out anyway."

In our discussions about the case, Macy recalled that Rex Moore, at the time of the crime, was significantly in debt. His wells were not coming in, and the price for oil was low. He was living well but had nothing to show for all his efforts. Another piece of information that contributed to Macy's intensity on the case came from hospital personnel. When both Rex and Tammy were in the hospital, some of the nurses were upset because Rex requested a telephone be brought to his room. While Tammy lay dying in her hospital bed, he was working in his room, doing business down the hall. Macy heard stories Moore was working to promote another well, even while in the hospital.

Moore's ultimate conviction had a gratifying outcome for Macy. This was one of the most heartbreaking cases with which he ever dealt. Tammy was one of the most beautiful women Macy ever saw. According to her friends, she was a very nice mother and daughter, and all that beauty and kindness was destroyed by one vicious old man.

The State vs. Plantz and Spaunagle

Another set of murders committed by women involved the women, Plantz and Spaunagle, who recruited younger men to kill their husbands. In both cases, the motive was to gain their husbands' insurance money. In each of the cases, the killers were the women's lovers. Macy had no reservations in prosecuting the defendants when he learned the nature of their crimes. In both cases, the husbands were brutally beaten to death in their own homes. In Spaunagle's case, the husband was beaten, then stabbed, and finally strangled by a rope. In the Plantz case, the husband was brutally beaten by two men with baseball bats and then burned to death in his pickup truck on a county road. Plantz was executed, and Spanaugle waived all her appeals and pled guilty to life without parole.

The State vs. Malcolm Rent Johnson

The case of Malcolm Rent Johnson was about a serial rapist who raped and killed a seventy-six-year-old lady named Ura Alma Thompson. Johnson was convicted of several counts of rape in

Illinois and was paroled as long as he left the state. So he came to Oklahoma City.

In the vicinity of 13th and Harvey, there was a cluster of duplexes where several older ladies in their '70s and '80s lived. There had been several rapes reported in this area by these ladies. The rapist hung out in the local grocery store, followed the ladies as they walked home, and then raped them. In Ms. Thompson's case, on October 27, 1981, Johnson had followed her home, waited for her to unlock her door, and then pushed her through the door onto the living room floor. Johnson didn't usually kill his victims, but this time, he overdid it.

When the police made their investigation of Ms. Thompson's murder, they found that Johnson had attempted to rape seven other ladies during the same time. One in particular was ninety-two and was able to fight him off. Serial rapists normally take souvenirs from their victims after the encounter and, in the case of Johnson, when the police arrested him, there were several items on his fireplace mantel that belonged to his victims. Officers identified several items belonging to Ms. Thompson, including furs, a typewriter, watch, key rings, cigarette case, hand mirror, rings, a purse, and other valuables.

Macy personally prosecuted Malcolm Rent Johnson. After looking into Johnson's record, Macy found that he had prior convictions for two rapes, two armed robberies, and a burglary. Johnson was convicted of rape and murder then sentenced to death. Execution took place January 6, 2000.

As bad as the previous crimes were, Macy lost sleep over two cases because of their viciousness and nature.

The State vs. Dewey George Moore

Jennipher Gilbert was like most other twelve-year-old girls, full of love for her parents and friends, a good student, and just beginning to be allowed to go to school functions by herself.

But on September 27, 1984 around 9:30 p.m., her life and the lives of her family changed forever. As a member of the school pep squad, she was still in her uniform—a red sweater and a gray skirt and wearing red pony earrings. Little did she know that Dewey George Moore came from his brother's house—just one mile away—with borrowed rolls of duct tape and evil intentions. As he pulled up to where other cars were picking up their young passengers, Moore honked his horn several times to rush the other cars out. In a matter of minutes, Moore found his target to abduct from the Carl Albert Junior High School parking lot, a pretty, young girl standing alone waiting for her stepfather. Several witnesses saw a man with a mustache, dressed in a long-sleeved western shirt and blue jeans, grab and push the struggling girl into his 1976 yellow Buick. Though Jennipher yelled for help, no one heard her in the aftermath of the football game.

After Jennipher's stepfather arrived to pick her up and could not find her, he called her mother. The two thought that perhaps she just went home with a friend, though that was unlike her. After a couple of hours of calling Jennipher's known friends, her mother called the police to report her missing. Even though the police were on the lookout for their little girl, it was a long and torturous night for Jennipher's parents.

On September 28, 1984, at around 11:00 a.m., police found Jennipher's body ten miles from Midwest City face down in a ditch at Tenth and Peebly Road in Harrah, Oklahoma. She had been stripped of her sweater and skirt, and an earring was missing. Her battered body had adhesive and binding marks on her ankles, wrists, thighs, and throat; a piece of duct tape was wadded in her hair, and she had abrasions on her face and neck. City Detective Bill Howard testified that he observed a pattern of dots on Jennipher's arm that matched the pattern on a belt later found in a paper sack on the roof of Breeden's Grocery Store, located less than one block away from Moore's trailer. An autopsy revealed her death was caused by asphyxia by strangulation and possibly smothering.

Moore wasted no time finding new transportation. Between 8:00 and 9:00 a.m., he stole a maroon 1977 Delta 88 Oldsmobile that was parked next door to Breeden's Grocery Store in Oklahoma City. The owner of the vehicle came out in time to see his vehicle being driven away; he quickly reported it to police. Between 9:45 and 10:00 a.m., a nervous and wide-eyed Moore showed up at his work, a job he had just gotten on September 5, but did not stay. Instead, he asked his employer for his check, stating that he had to quit because he had a mild coronary during the night. Around 10:45 a.m., Midwest City police officer Joe Tuberville spotted the stolen vehicle and stopped it, read Moore his rights, and then arrested him for larceny of an automobile. After a closer inspection of the car, a pair of black gloves was found in the front seat not belonging to the owner of the car. Detectives turned the gloves over to Janice Davis, an OCPD forensic lab chemist, after finding a partial hair.

With search warrant in hand, Detective Bill Howard went to Moore's trailer park on September 29 to search his trailer and car. There he found maroon floor mats in Moore's car, wadded up duct tape outside the trailer, and a partially-packed suitcase inside the house. After he received an additional search warrant on October 4, 1984, he found various fiber samples and earring backings in a crack of the couch under the cushions.

A resident of the same trailer park in which Moore resided first spotted a brown paper bag on the roof of Breeden's Grocery Store on September 30 but did not retrieve it until he was with a friend on October 5. The pair opened the bag, revealing used, wadded up duct tape, a knife, a belt, and cigarette butts inside. The two called police immediately.

During the second stage of the trial, it was revealed that Dewey George Moore was convicted of prior felonies: 1974-Attempted First Degree Rape; 1976-Aggravated Kidnapping and Indecent Liberties With a Child; 1981-Assault and Battery With a Dangerous Weapon, Child Beating, and Larceny From a House. He still had family and friends testify on his behalf, stating that he was a good, spiritual man who was remorseful for the things he had done. A clinical psychologist testifying on the defendant's behalf gave a possible explanation of why Moore did the horrible things he did. The psychologist's claim was that he was abused as a child, had a borderline personality disorder, had homosexual feelings—deep feelings of hatred, anger, sexual confusion and bitterness—and chose children as his targets because they were easily controlled, but he was not considered to be a pedophile. The clinical psychologist stated further that Moore could not be cured late in his life but could function well in a structured prison environment. Upon cross examination, the psychologist testified that if Moore was ever to be released from prison, the chances were good that he would commit criminal acts of violence and constitute a continuing threat to society. Dewey George Moore was convicted of First Degree Malice Aforethought Murder and Kidnapping, after former convictions of two or more felonies, in the District Court of Oklahoma County, and sentenced respectively to death and 999 years imprisonment. He died in prison of a heart attack in 2008.

The State vs. John DeVooght

In September of 1982, John Edward DeVooght III was in the legal custody of his father, John DeVooght, Jr., in the state of Michigan. At that time, the younger DeVooght ran away to Oklahoma City and began staying with his mother, Linda Duke, at the home of Kathie Carter. Kathie had three daughters who also lived with her,

Patricia, 6, Dena, 4, and a baby, 2. The divorced mother worked evenings from around 7:30 p.m. until 2:00 a.m.

On the evening of October 1, 1982, Kathie left for work at the usual time and left her children in the care of her father, Warren Cox, and his girlfriend, Linda Duke. Kathie's two brothers, Tony and Tommy Cox, plus one of their wives and John DeVooght III were there also.

Earlier in the day, DeVooght had taken a dollar away from Patricia, who had told her mother and his mother, resulting in a slap in the face from DeVooght's mother.

Around 11:30 p.m., Warren Cox and Linda Duke left the house to pick up a friend at a local bar. The other adults had left earlier, leaving the three little girls alone with DeVooght—all apparently sleeping. When Warren Cox and Linda Duke returned, the kids were still there, and the adults went to sleep.

Between 3:00 and 4:00 a.m., Kathie Carter came home from work. The first thing she did was to check the children, and she found that Patricia and John DeVooght were missing. She searched the house and the yard and then woke up her father and Linda Duke, who were unaware that Patricia was missing. She called friends and her ex-husband, Gary Carter, to see if they knew where Patricia was. Kathie was nearly in shock. At 4:40 a.m. on October 2, she called the Oklahoma City Police Department and reported two missing juveniles. Officers Enos Ables and Elizabeth Graham responded to the call, and a search was started.

A short time later, Gary Carter located John DeVooght III at his grandmother's house, some thirteen blocks from the Carter residence. John was asked if he knew where Patricia was, and he replied that he couldn't remember because he drank some "choc" beer the night before. In an effort to find what was presumed to be a lost child, John DeVooght III was placed in a police car and driven around the neighborhood, hoping that something would jog his memory and he would remember where he last saw Patricia. Dena,

Patricia's little sister, had already told Gary Carter and the police officers that John and Patricia had left the Carter house together, so it was logical that he might know where she was.

At one point, Gary Carter became enraged and tried to attack DeVooght, but the officers restrained him and placed DeVooght back in the car. His mother, Linda Duke, was allowed to go to the car and talk with him.

When the search proved fruitless at about 8:30 a.m., despite the fact that several officers and many neighbors were helping, the officers decided to bring all of the persons who had been at the Carter house the previous night to the police station for interviews. DeVooght rode to the station with Youth Bureau detectives Lehr and Deeds.

After they arrived, they talked for a while. DeVooght convinced these veteran officers, just as he had officers Ables and Graham, that he knew nothing about Patricia's disappearance. While they were in the station, DeVooght's father called from Michigan to ask if his son was under arrest. Detective Deeds responded that DeVooght was only a witness and was going to be released.

As Detectives Deeds and Lehr were walking out of the station with DeVooght to take him back to the Carter residence, they learned that Patricia's body had been found murdered. They knew that DeVooght had had an altercation with her and was the last one who had seen her alive, so they placed him in a juvenile detention cell, and the case was turned over to the homicide division.

Detective Bob Thompson took charge. He first gathered all of the evidence and information from the vacant lot where the little body was found. She was lying on her back, dressed only in a little shirt. Her little legs were spread apart with her right leg at an unnatural angle because the violence of the sexual assault dislocated her pelvis. Her injuries were extensive: a dislocated cervical spine, a broken neck, a ruptured spleen, and a punctured intestine. Her little face beaten to a bloody pulp and her body covered with bruises and abrasions made her nearly unrecognizable—a once pretty little girl whose life was forcibly taken from her. Worst of all, her little vagina was ripped, torn open into the body cavity, and her anus was torn open. Both had sperm inside.

At 3:00 p.m. that afternoon, Detective Thompson interviewed John DeVooght in his mother's presence, after being advised of their rights, at the Oklahoma City Police Station. After denying any knowledge about Patricia all morning, he admitted that he remembered walking home from where Patricia was lying on her back in the field and then going to sleep in his grandmother's yard.

When asked, "Why did you do this to Patricia?"

He stated, "I don't know. It must have been because I was drunk. I drank some of the homemade stuff from the Coke bottle."

He stated that he went back to the Carter house and could see that his mother and Warren Cox were still awake and the other woman was asleep on the couch, so he waited about twenty-five minutes until everyone was asleep. He then went in the house, washed his hands, took off the clothes he wore, and then washed his red tennis shoes. DeVooght clad only in his grey shorts, walked to Grant High School, and threw his jeans, shirt, and underwear into a dumpster. He returned to the Carter house to put on more clothes and then walked over to his grandmother's.

By DeVooght's own admission, it was revealed that he took little Patricia to the field twice. After the first time in the house, Patricia struggled to get away from DeVooght, but he struck her in the face, causing a nosebleed, and then dragged her out to the field again. He didn't know that Patricia's little sister, Dena, had seen the whole thing.

During the interview, he was asked if he raped Patricia or how he beat her or if he removed her panties. He said that he didn't remember, but sometime thereafter, he said, "I don't think I choked her; I hit her with my fists." He remarked that he had hurt his little finger on his left hand while hitting Patricia. At the end of his interview, he asked if he would be tried as an adult or juvenile.

Oklahoma City detectives recovered his bloodied clothes and matched burrs from his clothes to burrs found near the body.

On October 3, 1982, an autopsy was performed upon Patricia's little body, revealing all of the injuries. The medical examiner testified that the vaginal, anal, and abdominal injuries could have been caused by an erect penis and that the injuries were inflicted while Patricia was still alive. The cause of her death was internal bleeding from multiple injuries. When he was done with little Patricia, DeVooght left her laid out there in the dark in that lonely field, engulfed in pain and to bleed to death.

John Edward DeVooght III was convicted of Murder in the First Degree and given life in prison without the possibility of parole.

The State vs. LaFevers and Cannon

Addie Hawley was an eighty-four-year-old lady and lived in similar housing as Ura Alma Thompson. On the evening of June 24, 1985, Randall Eugene Cannon and Lloyd Winford LaFevers were out drinking and rammed their car into another car, which rendered theirs inoperable. At that point, they decided they needed to steal a car. They had come upon Ms. Hawley's house and noticed it had a garage attached. The men went up to the door, and Ms. Hawley answered and inquired on what they wanted. They asked her if they could use her telephone. When she turned for the telephone, one of the men kicked the door open, while the other ran around to the back door. As she tried to get out of the house, they grabbed her and drug her back inside. She begged them not to hurt her. When they took her back inside, they told her to give them all her money. She only had $8.00 in her possession. Subsequently, they raped and sodomized her. After the act, the men wanted to drive, so they took Ms. Hawley and her car and drove to a nearby filling station. The men went inside the station and purchased a bottle of orange pop. Outside, they poured out the contents of the bottle and then filled it with gasoline. From there, they drove out to Mulligan Flats. There, the men pulled Ms. Hawley out of the car and raped and sodomized her again. Finally, they poured the gasoline all over her and set her on fire.

At trial, both men confessed to the participation in the crime, but neither admitted to the murder. Bob Macy convicted them both, and the court sentenced them to death.

Winford LaFevers was executed January 30, 2001. Randall Eugene Cannon was executed July 23, 2002.

The State vs. Fowler and Fox

The Fox and Fowler case was a triple homicide that happened in the Wynn's IGA grocery store in Edmond, Oklahoma Early of the morning on July 3, 1985, Billy Ray Fox and Mark Andrew Fowler decided they were going to rob the store. Fox previously worked in the store and knew clerks would be present at the time, early morning, restocking groceries on the shelves. What made this situation go from bad to worse was that Fox also knew the gentlemen who were working in the store and knew that they could identify him when he went in. "What infuriated me most was that there were ten thousand other stores in Oklahoma City, why didn't they go rob one where they would have known they would not have had to kill anybody? They went into that store knowing that if they robbed the place the only way they were going to get away with it was to kill everyone inside."

The men who were killed were John Barrier, Chumpon Chaowasin, and Rick Cast. John Barrier and Rick Cast were local young men early in the prime of their lives. Chumpon Chaowasin was a foreign student working on his bachelor's degree. He was working there at the store to pay for his degree. While working there in the grocery store, everyone knew and liked all three of them.

During the robbery, Fox and Fowler took the three young men to a backroom and, with a shotgun, shot both Rick Cast and Chumpon Chaowasin, each in the back of the head. In the first two shootings, Fox and Fowler spent their only two shells they took with them, and so to kill John Barrier, they beat his head and stabbed him with the shotgun. "John Barrier died a horrible death." Fox and Fowler made off with $1,200.00 in cash and $1,500.00 in checks.

Macy was called on early that morning by the Edmond police and went to the crime scene. Beings this was a triple homicide, he convinced the police chief to allow the Oklahoma City Police Crime Scene Unit to investigate, as there were more technicians available who could work the scene and they were more experienced. An informant told the police that they saw Fox's vehicle at the crime scene during the murders. When they finally arrested Billy Ray Fox, the police found the remnants of what was left of the shotgun were in the back of that vehicle.

Macy was even more angered learning that after the murders, Fox and Fowler partied all day and later that night, they fixed steaks and drank beer, all of which were stolen at the Wynn's IGA store that morning during the robbery. "If those guys (Fox and Fowler) could go and kill three people and then turn right around and charcoal some steaks, I don't want them living in Oklahoma."

During their trial, both Fox and Fowler admitted to robbing the Wynn's IGA, but both denied killing the three men inside. They were both convicted of the murders and sentenced to death. Mark Andrew Fowler was executed January 23, 2001. Billy Ray Fox was executed January 25, 2001.

The State vs. Sean Sellers

One of the best known of Macy's trials centered around a trio of killings carried out by a sixteen-year-old murderer named Sean Richard Sellers. Although the last two homicides did not occur until a few months after that year from hell, the first came on September 8, 1985.

Richard Howard, a friend of Sean's, ultimately testified that Sellers had gone into a convenience store, where he killed a store clerk, Robert Bower, because "he wanted to see what it feels like to kill somebody." For the killing, Sellers used a weapon that belonged to Howard's grandfather. Sean had no connection to Bower; Bower just happened to be in the wrong place at the wrong time to satisfy Sellers' desire. The killing was the coldest of the cold-blooded reasons. It was a test run.

Months later, Sean got his hands on a weapon owned by his stepfather, Lee Bellofatto. He used that .44-caliber revolver to shoot Bellofatto and his own mother, Vonda, on March 5 as they slept in bed. Early that morning after the murders, Sean went to Howard's house and told him what he had done, threatening to kill him if he ever told the story. Howard suggested to Sean to hide the weapon at his home, where it was eventually found by the police. Sean then devised a plan whereby he and Howard would return to Sellers' house and discover the bodies and call the police. Howard was disgusted by Sellers' delight at giving the details of the murders. Eventually, Howard could no longer deal with holding the truth of what Sean did and notified the police. Finally, Sean Sellers, age seventeen, was tried as an adult, sentenced to death, and executed.

The day before her death, Sean's mother wrote him a beautiful note telling him she loved him. Sean apparently never saw it, but Macy believes, "even if he'd seen it, it would not have made a difference. After all, he had killed the clerk precisely to see what it would be like to kill someone. The defense attorney introduced her letter as evidence, thinking it would somehow turn guilt away but it didn't." Macy recalls, "I convinced the jury as much as anything else that Sean Sellers was rebelling against his mother's supervision. The only way to get out from under her supervision, in his mind, was to kill her. His stepfather had treated him nice, and his mother loved him. But he killed them both."

One of the things that emerges from Macy's memory of the murderers he convicted is that each criminal is an individual, just as every victim is unique. "Sellers was probably the smartest person I ever put on death row. He was smart but egotistical and selfish. He was methodical and ruthless in planning the killings." Richard testified that Sean said he had to kill the clerk to see if he could actually kill someone. That clerk hadn't done anything to justify that end, but there it is. He said he wanted to find out how it feels to kill someone." As for the stepfather, "he was good man, a decorated war hero." Macy says he got to know Sellers as well as nearly anyone else he prosecuted, "and it was certainly odd. I watched two or three tapes of interviews with him. I went after him hard based on things he'd said in those videos. Sean thought he was smarter than anyone else."

At trial, Sellers "claimed he had multiple personalities, and they tried for the demonic possession defense. Sean later set up a prison ministry and computer site to say to young people, 'Don't do what I did.' I believe that was just a ploy to create sympathy. He was so arrogant and self-confident. I believe he never thought he'd die. Right up to the end, he was still thinking there would be some kind of commutation." Another thing distinguished Sean Sellers. "He never said he was sorry. The surviving members of their family really resented that. The brother-in-law of Bellofatto said Sean really planned, plotted, and carried out the whole thing. In the end, I thought he was evil incarnate. He had already demonstrated what he was capable of, what he could do, before he killed his stepfather and mother."

Toward the end, Amnesty International got involved because he was the youngest person on death row. They held a wake when it was time for his execution, and Macy didn't know if he should go to his execution. Brett, fully understanding his father's dilemma, told him, "Dad, you've done your job. Now let them do theirs." Bob took that advice to heart and never went to the executions.

The State vs. James Robedeaux

Another case Macy sought the death penalty for was the case of James Robedeaux. This case touched Macy in a unique way because of the special relationship Macy had with his own son, Brett. Both Brett and James were tall, good-looking men. Brett followed his father's advice and teachings and became an outstanding young man. James was offered the same lessons but failed to learn and chose another path, away from his father's teachings.

During the trial, Macy visited often with the elder Robedeaux. He learned the father had done everything in his power to keep his son away from drugs but to no avail. He enrolled the boy in the FFA and even started a cattle herd. However, the father lost control, and the boy was taken over by drugs. Before Macy's encounter with James Robedeaux, he had been convicted of manslaughter in the beating death of a woman several years earlier.

By the fall of 1985, James Glenn Robedeaux and Nancy McKinney had lived together for about three months. At some point in mid-September, a neighbor heard them arguing and later testified that Nancy was overheard saying, "Don't hit me any more." The relationship was troubled, and right about that time, Robedeaux met Patricia Avery at Marie's Club, soon moving in with her, just before or just after Nancy disappeared.

Carmen McKinney, Nancy's mother, used to talk to her daughter two or three times a week but did not hear from her after September

10. The last time anyone saw Nancy alive was September 22. That morning, the neighbor below their apartment, Barbara Jones, saw Nancy take trash to the dumpster. It was around 10:00 a.m. Barbara testified she heard the pair leave and then return sometime after 9:00 p.m. In an ultimately poignant recollection, the neighbor lady said she could tell the difference between the heavy footsteps of Robedeaux and the softer steps of Nancy. Barbara and her husband, Bobby, said they later heard a loud noise from above "which sounded like someone jumping off furniture onto the floor." It was loud, and the Jones' apartment shook as a result. At first, the noise was frequent, and then came less often. The noise and the shaking continued until 1:00 a.m. The appeals court later wrote, "After that night, she never heard [Nancy's] footsteps again."

On Monday the 23rd, Barbara saw Robedeaux at a storage closet in the hallway. A few minutes later, he went upstairs then left in the blue Ford Nancy usually drove. It was the next day before Bobby saw Robedeaux again. He was carrying small, dark trash bags, one in each hand. Later, when they spoke briefly, Robedeaux apologized for "being noisy," saying he sometimes drank too much and got a little loud. Bobby said the guy did not indicate there was any particular occasion for which he was apologizing.

Sometime that same week, a maintenance worker for the complex went into the apartment and saw a brownish-red stain by the bedroom closet. When he went back a few days later, the stain was gone. He also saw three dirty towels on a bathroom rack. They looked, the court later summarized, "as if they had been used to clean something up."

On September 24, Robedeaux called Joann Robinson and asked her to meet him a couple of days later in Oklahoma City. She did. They went to a pawn shop where Joann signed Nancy's name to get some tapes "because there had been a lady with him when he pawned them." Joann was with Robedeaux when he rented a carpet cleaner on September 27.

A Ford collection agent, seeking back payments on or repossession of Nancy's car, stopped by on September 25. The agent, John Farris, and his partner ran into Robedeaux and asked him directions to Nancy McKinney's apartment. At that time, he said he didn't know where that was, but just minutes later, Farris and his partner saw him getting into Nancy's Ford Fairmont. They inquired again if he knew Nancy, and Robedeaux said he did before claiming he had not understood them the first time.

Around that time, his new girlfriend, Patricia Avery, went to the apartment with Robedeaux. She waited in a pickup, while he went up to the room for about fifteen minutes. She then went up to help him carry down a stereo. Robedeaux warned her there was a bad smell because he'd left some meat out. Sure enough, when she went in, she encountered a terrible smell but saw no food or trash lying around.

Bobby and Barbara, after hearing a lot of noise from a machine upstairs, saw Robedeaux again on September 28, when he was putting a carpet cleaning machine into the back end of a pickup truck. Around that same time, Carmen, Nancy's mom, stopped by to say she'd been calling Nancy and wasn't getting a call back. She left a note asking her to call on the door three days earlier but got no response.

Not long after that, a.d. Smedley, the apartment complex owner, went into the apartment with a couple of others. He saw dark spots, like blood, in a walk-in closet and on the carpet. On October 9, he put a trespass note on the door and changed the locks. But Robedeaux prevailed upon one of Smedley's workers to let him in to retrieve his clothing. A bad smell in the apartment, Robedeaux claimed, was due to some hamburger meat he had left out. When Smedley himself went back into the apartment on October 11, he noticed the stains on the wall had been cleaned and that "the carpet was damp." The same day, Smedley's maintenance man saw Robedeaux hauling two boxes to the dumpster. After Robedeaux left, he checked things out and found in the dumpster the three towels he had seen before in the bathroom. He turned them over to Smedley, who gave them to the police.

On October 15, Smedley entered the apartment with the police officers. Inside, the men noticed "a foul odor, like spoiled meat." The police took away some of the carpet and the pad. But Smedley and the police went back in on October 24. Lifting up the bedroom carpet, they noticed more spots, and the police took that away, too. The very next day, Smedley was cleaning up the place when he wiped off a dining room table what he said looked like a blood spot. Trying to get the stains off the floor, he applied Clorox and the stain turned red, he recalled.

Smedley brought in a carpet layer to remove all the remaining carpet in the apartment. The man, John Fox, found occasional stains in the hallway and elsewhere. He later recalled the odor was so bad, he had to take off his t-shirt and wrap it around his face. Nonetheless, he had to step outside and throw up.

Lisa Austin met Robedeaux around October 18, and they lived together for several weeks until his arrest for Nancy's murder. About a month after they first met, he told her he had killed Nancy and "cut her up."

While he dodged the police for a while, he was a suspect from early on. A couple of Macy's police heroes, veteran detectives Eric Mullinex and Bob Horn, were on the case long before a body was actually found. They talked with Robedeaux on November 14, 1985, first giving him his rights then talking with him from noon until 7:30 p.m. The suspect said he and Nancy started living together in July and they moved into the apartment in August. He claimed she left and took all her belongings in early September while he was away at Red Rock. He admitted they fought, but he said he never hit her. As the appeal courts later recounted, "He stated that he had not injured himself in the apartment nor was he aware of anyone else injuring themselves ... to the extent they would have bled heavily." Robedeaux told the two detectives he had cleaned up the place, even though he didn't have a cleaning deposit to worry about. Concerning those stains in the bedroom, he said those were red Kool-Aid stains. Stains in the living room were the result of oil he spilled after greasing the hinges on a door, he said.

Mullinex then told Robedeaux the police thought he had killed Nancy. He denied it, saying she had merely left and he had not seen her. But on December 28, sixteen-year-old Charles Stokes was playing on a pipe that ran across Deep Fork Creek near Wellston. He saw a dog chewing on something. Checking it out, he found what looked like a human leg. Eventually, it proved to be Nancy's limb.

The discovery concentrated the search in that general area. On February 3, David Habben, who lived east of Coon Creek, which runs into the Deep Fork, found a human skull in his front yard. As the search went on, Nancy's brother was in a group that found Nancy's arm and hand in the middle of the Coon Creek streambed. The discovery was made west and a little south of Habben's house.

Some twenty-four years after the discovery of Nancy's cut-up body parts, Macy still remembers Nancy's brother and the other relatives who helped in the search for her body. As for Robedeaux, it was hard to understand why he turned out so bad. In his younger days, "Robedeaux's daddy felt sorry for him. He had tried to get him into 4-H. The boy had previously been convicted of manslaughter. He got out of incarceration and looked up Nancy, whom he'd previously been dating." It all flowed from their fateful reunion.

In preparing for trial, Macy learned Robedeaux "had a hell of a temper. That must have fed what he did in the murder of Nancy." Macy reflects, "It takes a special kind of a SOB to chop up the body of anyone, especially someone you'd been so close to. You can understand or at least accept how things, bad things, can happen in the passion and heat of a moment, but to do that and then go on and engage in the methodical cruelty of chopping up a body. It was awful."

Curiously, "Robedeaux was always very polite to me" during the trial, Macy says.

A memorable aspect of the proceedings, which resulted in a death sentence for the killer, was the use of one of the best forensic investigators in the world. As Macy tells it, "Clyde Snow was simply spectacular. He held the skull of that poor woman in his hands. He turned it over slowly in his hands as he looked at it." From looking at the remains, Snow carefully described Nancy's stage of life and noted inferences that could be drawn from the evidence. "He was brilliant, careful, restrained in his conclusions, a magnificent witness." In all, "we eventually used Clyde Snow three or four times in cases we tried." Once again, Bob Macy fought to uphold his promise to the people of the State of Oklahoma, gathering more ammunition in the form of expert witnesses along the way.

The State vs. John Romano and David Wayne Woodruff

John Romano was a prisoner in the Enid Community Center, from which he could check out for weekend passes. He did that October 11, scheduled for a return on October 13. Testimony revealed he had discussed with Tracy Gregg the possible robbery and murder of Roger Sarfaty that weekend, but Gregg refused to help. Sarfaty was a jewelry dealer who lived by himself at the Mayridge apartment complex in northwest Oklahoma City, where he kept jewelry, old and new and some tarnished, at his apartment. He wore rings on every finger and had buckets of quarters and other change in his place. He went regularly to the Celebrity Club, rolling in at 12:30 a.m. each morning and staying until 2:00 a.m. That was the case the last time he was seen alive, on October 12.

Roger was beaten, strangled, and stabbed five times, but his body was not found until October 16. Medical experts said he had been dead two or three days at the time his body was discovered. The details around his body were telling. Inside, opened as if he had read it, was the October 12 edition of the *Oklahoman*. Unopened outside his door were the editions for October 13, 14, and 15. The buckets of change were gone, the jewelry was gone, and a pair of slacks was draped over a door, the pockets pulled out as if they had been checked for change.

On the afternoon of Saturday, October 12, Romano and David Wayne Woodruff were shopping at Quail Springs Mall on the far north side of Oklahoma City. They had cups of beer and seemed, to witnesses, intoxicated. They spilled the beer and vomited inside a store, so security came to escort them out of the mall. At first, Woodruff refused to leave, saying he planned to buy a TV. He boasted he needed no credit because he had cash. Woodruff and Romano proved their point by emptying their pockets of quarters. A store clerk said she saw blood stains on Woodruff's pant leg and a cut on his hand.

The appeals court record indicates the men calmed down and left with the guards and their stash of quarters, about $30 dollars or less, that Romano carried in his baseball cap. The pair was kept in a holding cell for turnover to the city police after a lock blade knife was removed from one of them. Charged with public intoxication and disorderly conduct, they were taken to the Detox Center downtown. Denise Howe, Woodruff's girlfriend, came to get them and then drove them back to the mall to get Woodruff's car.

She later said she saw a bunch of diamond papers, the sort customarily used to wrap small stones, surrounding Woodruff's car. She also saw him with gold jewelry she'd not seen on him before. The necklace and several rings were "old and tarnished," a court account said. Denise knew he did not have the money to buy things like that. Meanwhile, Romano went back to Enid.

Woodruff got a call from Romano in Enid on October 16 and then drove with Denise over to the Mayridge Apartments. When he saw several police cars there, he got nervous and went back home. Soon, however, he was in custody. Denise did one last favor for Woodruff. He asked her to "clear out the house." The court papers indicate she removed pieces of rope, a pair of gloves, and a watch, all of which were later turned over to the police. One piece of rope was formed into a garrote. Medical testimony concluded the piece of rope was consistent with the wound found on Roger Sarfaty's neck.

Lou Keel was Macy's second chair for the first murder trial of the two men, and Keel handled the second case as well. Macy said it was not as hard as some. "Roger Sarfaty was flashy. The killers knew he had a high-stakes, high-dollar game and liked to gamble. Romano had gone into Sarfaty's apartment that night and told him, lying, 'I thought you should know you got a flat tire.' Of course, Romano had taken a knife and cut holes in the tire. They trapped the old jeweler and killed him." Macy reflects, "They were bad dudes, not as brutal as some of the killers I saw but definitely bad men. They were brutal to the old man when they took him out." Both were convicted and sentenced to death.

The State vs. Cyril Wayne Ellis

In some ways, Cyril Wayne Ellis was the closest thing to a one-man version of the Buck Gang, the vicious criminals who packed into thirteen days of terror a lifetime of heinous criminal robbery, rape, murder, and methodical cruelty. In Ellis's case, the trauma inflicted on several victims and their extended families and friends was even more brutally efficient. His crime spree lasted forty-eight hours.

What was called in court documents a scenario and trail of horror began on January 27, 1986. Ellis got into an argument with his fiancée, Cheryl James. Apparently for the first time in their relationship of more than a year, he struck her. He then, in a suicide attempt, took an overdose of pills. Cheryl drove him to Presbyterian Hospital on the east side of downtown Oklahoma City. He had a brief respite there and at the psychiatric ward of St. Anthony s Hospital.

Cheryl went to visit him on January 29. As she tried to leave, he forced her to take him in her car and made her drive him to the Sheraton Hotel downtown, where she was able to get the attention of a security guard. She told the guard Ellis was acting crazy and had just gotten out of a mental ward. Court records reveal an altercation happened and the police were called but no arrest was made.

Later in the day, Ellis tried to buy a handgun, falsely telling the sales clerk he needed the gun for protection for the restaurant he was opening. He didn't have enough money to buy the gun, but the clerk loaned him his own weapon for which Ellis bought bullets.

The next day he was driving down the road when he saw Cheryl in a car driven by Robert Dumas, the boyfriend of Teresa, her sister. When Ellis caught up with them, he got into a heated argument with Dumas. Dumas tried to flee to a nearby yard, but Ellis blocked him in. As Cheryl jumped out and ran for assistance, Ellis pointed his gun at Dumas, forcing him into the trunk of the car, which he then slammed shut. Dumas beat on the inside of the trunk, pleading for help and for his life. Ellis opened the trunk, said, "I see you don't want to live," then pumped two bullets into the man before slamming the trunk. Incredibly, Dumas lived through the ordeal.

Ellis drove to Dumas's house, where Cheryl had spent the previous night with Teresa and their mother. At that time, Cheryl was there with only her six-year-old daughter. Ellis used the butt of the weapon to knock out a front window and promptly shot Cheryl. She ran to the back yard with Ellis on her heels, where he shot her several more times, killing her.

Macy today cries as he remembers Taneca, Cheryl's little girl. "She was the cutest thing, and she was [an] amazing, incredible witness. She just simply broke your heart." At trial, "She described how Ellis followed her through the house, shooting at her." He methodically pursued the little girl, to assure he found her and, with the apparent intention of murdering her, he shot Taneca three times. Macy remembers that her testimony was crisp, absolutely credible, and powerful because "she was such a sweet thing." When police arrived at the scene of that portion of Ellis's crime spree, they found Cheryl dead in the backyard and Taneca clinging to life on the back steps.

From Dumas's house, Ellis went to his own home to get more ammunition. He then traveled to Consolidated Freightways on SE 15th and Interstate I-35, where he worked. He came across Gordon Moore in the parking lot, forced him to kneel down between two cars, and shot him in the face. Moore played dead, eventually recovering from his wounds. Gordon Moore later gave dramatic testimony at his trial, describing those horrible moments in detail.

Ellis then went inside the business and into the office of Carl Lake. He shot Lake just as the man was asking Ellis to leave. Ellis fired a second time, and Lake was dead. Macy says today that even justice isn't enough salve to treat the wounds created by Ellis's crime spree. "Carl Lake's wife was kind of a reserved person. It had a terrible effect on her when he was killed. For years after, she wouldn't leave the house. She was too unnerved and permanently affected."

After killing Lake, Ellis went outside onto a loading dock. He looked down and saw another worker, James Rider. Ellis shot Rider, who staggered and collapsed to the ground. Ellis shot him a second time, killing him. Ellis went back to his car to leave, but as he fled the lot, several men ran out of the business. Ellis stopped, fired at them, reloaded and fired again, and then left. In that flurry of shots, Ancil Davis was wounded but survived. In later reflections, Macy said the Ellis crime spree "was in some ways a thing that might remind you of the post office killings in Edmond, the methodical search through a house in one case, and the tracking down of people in the post office case, as Ellis did with his latter victims at the business."

In the end, Ellis was sentenced to death for each of the three killings and to terms of three thousand, two thousand, and one thousand years twice for each of the convictions for shooting with intent to kill. He died while in prison.

Edmond Post Office Massacre

Unlike the previous cases, Macy did not prosecute Patrick Henry Sherrill, an Edmond, Oklahoma, full-time, fill-in postal worker, but the case had a lifetime impact on Macy and many other Oklahomans. At the time, it was the state's largest and the nation's third-largest mass murder committed by a single individual in a single incident. The following is Macy's recollection of the events as they unfolded.

Early Wednesday morning before 7:00 a.m., August 20, 1986, an ex-Marine marksman described by fellow employees as a loner and someone who didn't like taking orders from anyone else, Patrick Henry Sherrill, drove into the east parking lot of the post office at 200 North Broadway, as he did so many mornings before. Since he was dressed in his postal worker's uniform shirt and shorts and carrying his mailbag, no one suspected that hidden in that bag were two .45-caliber semi-automatic pistols, a .22-caliber semi-automatic pistol, large amounts of ammunition, and several bullet clips. The first to be shot was letter carrier Paul Rockne, who drove into the parking lot the same time as Sherrill and parked next to him. He was lying face down in the parking lot when Macy and son first arrived on the scene.

Sherrill entered the building and headed straight for Supervisor Bill Bland's office, unaware that Bland had overslept and had not made it into his office. Reprimanded by Bland the day before, Sherrill was told to improve his job performance or find another job. Agitated by the latest of many reprimands, Sherrill spoke with a union representative about a transfer to the main post office in Oklahoma City. He was informed there would be no transfer due to Sherrill's short length of employment.

In just fifteen minutes, Sherrill changed the lives of many forever. In the wake of his rampage, no one was safe as he maneuvered through his place of employment, blocking doorways, and taking lives as he saw fit. His carnage ended with the solemn acts of turning off the lights, sitting in a chair, placing a .45 to his temple, and pulling the trigger.

Just before 7:00 a.m. in the little house on Midwest Lane, District Attorney Bob Macy and his son, Deputy Sheriff Brett Macy, were getting ready for work when the telephone rang. Instinctively, both men grabbed a phone and heard a sense of urgency on the other end of the line, "Bob, this is Joyce Dedek, and Clint needs your help. There has been a shooting at the Edmond post office." Both men grabbed their duffle bags and headed for the door. Brett suggested taking the police cruiser, since it had emergency equipment and it would save some time by running the lights and siren. Once inside the cruiser, Brett grabbed his radio to announce he was in service with the code 10–8; the channels were already chattering with emergency transmissions.

With emergency lights flashing, Brett sped down Midwest Boulevard to 2nd street, turning west to get to the post office. There was immediate pandemonium as the two pulled in front of the post office. Seeing the multitude of officers with guns surrounding the post office, some postal workers running scared while others huddled on the ground screaming, and one person lying on the ground apparently dead, Bob and Brett immediately started assessing the situation. Brett put his extensive experience as a mental health deputy into use and suggested getting more ambulances for the hysterical. Bob began searching for his old friend, the Edmond police chief, Clint Dedek, a veteran officer who served twenty years as a highway patrolman, eight years as commissioner of public safety, and ten years as Macy's chief investigator in the Oklahoma County District Attorney's office. As Macy made his way across the crime scene, he suddenly saw Tom George, his old friend from Ada who was the Oklahoma City FBI Assistant Special Agent in Charge (ASAC). Spotting Macy, Dedek made his way to him saying, "We've got multiple shots fired and at least one down. I don't know who or how many have been wounded! The last shot was heard around seven eighteen, and we cannot establish communication with the shooter."

George interjected, "We need to make entry if this is federal jurisdiction. I will find out for sure." He then contacted Oklahoma City FBI headquarters. In a matter of minutes, he was informed that it was state jurisdiction. It is imperative that properly authorized officers work the investigations in crime scenes where officers from more than one agency are involved. Failure to establish jurisdiction could result in part or all of the evidence being suppressed.

As the post office became surrounded with emergency vehicles, local residents, postal employee family members, postal inspectors, and media, Dedek did a masterful job of maintaining control. He asked Macy to handle the media and concentrated on gaining entry. With a copy of the building blueprint provided by the postal inspectors, the officers discovered there was a postal inspector's passageway on top of the building, which was the safest way to enter the building without the shooter knowing. Learning the passageway was locked with the key in Oklahoma City, Dedek asked a postal inspector to make haste to retrieve it.

At 8:30 a.m. four highly-trained Edmond tactical team officers opened the door and entered the building. Macy watched these brave young officers, with their body armor and assault rifles, as he realized there was a very real possibility of one of them dying. Everyone held their breath until the long-anticipated words of "shooter down" were heard. Dedek, Macy, and Mayor Pro Tem Randel Shadid followed the SWAT team inside to get a firsthand assessment of the carnage. Bodies, spent cartridges, and empty cartridge clips were scattered throughout the building.

Realizing the magnitude of the situation, Macy took control and began instructing officers to quarantine off the crime scene, get the wounded and dead identified and either to the hospital or morgue, interview witnesses, and handle the families of victims with extreme care. After victim identification, while working with local clergy and postal inspectors at the Edmond City Hall, Macy had the heartbreaking task of informing victims' families whether their loved ones had made it out safely or not. Each victim's family was seen separately; breaking the news never got any easier. Macy still recalls today, "It was hours and hours of hell!"

Hitting close to home, one of Macy's assistant district attorneys, John Foley, came to Macy and said, "Boss, I know you are not supposed to release the names yet, but Paul Rockne is my best friend, and I just have to know if he was a victim. I will not repeat anything until you tell me I can."

Macy stepped closer to him, feeling tears well as he uttered, "Yes, John, he was," then held him while he sobbed. In that moment, Macy felt as helpless as the casualties of the day's events. He, like so many others that day, could not make sense of the heinous act of one man's rage turned rampage as he unabashedly took the lives of fourteen, wounded six, and forever changed the lives of so many on that warm August day.

Sherrill's Victims

Patricia Ann Chambers, 41, part-time clerk Kenneth W. Morey, 49, rural carrier

Leroy Orrin Phillips, 42, rural carrier Patricia A. Gabbard, 47, clerk

Jerry Ralph Pyle, 51, rural carrier Jonna Gragert Hamilton, 30, clerk

Paul Michael Rockne, 33, letter carrier Patty Jean Husband, 48, supervisor

Thomas Wade Shader Jr., 31, part-time clerk Betty Ann Jarred, 34, clerk

Patti Lou Welch, 27, clerk William F. Miller, 30, rural carrier

Judy Stephens Denney, 41, part-time clerk Richard C. Esser Jr., 38, supervisor

Shot but Survived

Mike Bigler, forty-seven, rural carrier, shot in the back on his right shoulder but was able to return to work only to quit in the following November that same year to become an evangelist.

Joyce Ingram, forty-six, clerk, was unable to return to work because a bullet shattered her upper right arm, leaving her with about 75 percent use.

Bill Nimmo, forty-two, rural carrier, was the most seriously injured of all, spending five days in intensive care after a bullet struck his left arm and chest. He was able to return to work the following February.

Gene Bray, fifty-five, rural carrier, out of the injured, the person employed longest at the post office—twenty-one years—shot in the back and returned to work the following December but placed on light duty due to his injury.

Steve Vick, twenty-five, rural carrier, the youngest person employed at the post office, competed in triathlons before being shot under the left arm. He returned to work the following November and had begun working out again.Judy Walker, forty, clerk, shot in the back but returned to work the following February, was unable to adjust to the noise in the building so she quit after breaking both of her legs in a moving accident unrelated to work. She could not watch TV or movies any longer because of the violence in them.

In some ways, dealing with horrors such as those recounted above was all in a lifetime's work for Bob Macy, but in other ways, he makes it clear today, he never really grew accustomed to the depravity and the carnage. Long before he read about the horrific career of the buck gang from Oklahoma's early days, Macy learned the depths of human evil. Nonetheless, and years afterward, he still thanks the Buck Gang's capture and trial for showing him how to overcome the carnage and make life as right as possible after the onslaught of evil. Against that evil, he believes, must stand the police, the prosecutors, and other law-enforcement personnel. In the modern era, they displace vigilante action or personal revenge, taking the place the citizen posses of old who had to track down killers themselves to assure that justice was done, whether from a wild oak tree or, preferably, a court of law.

Macy, at first, was startled to hear how some admirers characterized him in those years. Eventually, however, he accepted and was even content with the populist shorthand some people in the young state of Oklahoma used to describe him and his allies. Most memorable was the father of a murder victim, who told him, "Mr. Macy, people like me don't know how to deal with people like my daughter's killer. We rely on you to figure that out. We need you. You are our hired gun." Little did they understand that Bob Macy was pursuing his own passion of justice and standing up for the weakened and victimized. It just so happened his passion and his "hired gun" image rode the same trail. He spent years in hell to purchase with his career and his life some peace, domestic tranquility, and justice for the decent and law-abiding people of Oklahoma County.

CHAPTER 9

The Cowboy Side of Life

Bob Macy's earliest experience with a horse came when he was just a boy. A neighborhood father brought a pony home and turned it loose in the community there on the river. Because there were no fences, the pony was free to roam wherever it wished. The local kids rode the pony, and some even claimed ownership by rights of time spent on its back or amount of food offered it. They loved that good-natured pony, and Bob said it the best-natured "critter" he had ever seen up to that point in his life. Neighborhood youths jumped on its back and pretended to be shot and fall off while the amiable pony just grazed away. But the city government made the people in the neighborhood get rid of it, breaking everyone's hearts.

It was some time later that Macy's experience with horses expanded, when as a teenager he began to work on farms just outside of town. In those days in that area, no farmer had a tractor. Therefore, all the heavy work on farms was done with a team of mules or horses. Heavy equipment, if it was used at all, operated off linked chains and pulleys attached to a drive wheel pulled along by the animals and rolling on the ground. The size of the equipment being used dictated the number of horses and mules needed for chores. Horses were needed so the farmer could use corn planters, wheat drills, fertilizer spreaders, cultivators, mowers, balers, combines, and threshing machines and to haul the grain to and from storage.

Macy's first job working on a farm was running a blower for a threshing machine. Horses were used to bring shocks of grain from the field to the thresher, but the creatures spooked easily because of the noise. It was part of his job to control the horses as they neared the thresher.

Bob remembers, "When I worked for my uncle out on the farm, Scout was my horse." His fondness for Scout in particular grew into his lifelong love for horses. Already aware of his affinity for horses, in the spring of 1947, Bob began work as a stable hand cleaning stalls, feeding, and exercising saddle horses. He met several horse enthusiasts in his work and gained a reputation as a good horse trainer. He farmed sixty acres of land for a horse trainer named Henry Johnson and rode as second whip guiding the hounds during a hunt at the Traders Point Fox Hunting Club.

Johnson had two jumping horses, one of them a Belgian named Irish. In their rare free time, Johnson and Macy practiced the horses in jumping routines. That summer, Macy was able to talk Johnson into allowing him to enter Irish in the jumping contests at the county fair. Macy and Irish entered every jumping contest they could, he recalls, and won several. Macy remembers, "Irish was old but had the heart of a champion and gave one hundred percent every time we competed."

A distinct memory Macy shares is of his father being there for several of the jumping contests. In one of those, Macy won the open jumping class and was feeling quite proud of his accomplishment. The young man's chest swelled with pride as he asked his father, "How'd you like that one, Dad?"

Red Macy replied, "I was hoping the other horse would have qualified because then old Irish could have gone six inches higher." It deflated Bob's pride-filled ego a bit but taught him the importance of being humble and striving for even greater heights.

Today, Macy recalls, "I was working as a riding stable hand with those hunters and jumpers, a line of work that continued later at Earlham College in a bit different form and lasted me for several years. I learned I was good with horses. I've always been good with horses. So I worked with horses in steeple chase and fox hunting situations at the club, and became good at training."

While at the fox hunting club, a member contracted with Macy to train two steeple chasers. The man provided Macy a small cabin next to the stables. Bob lived there and worked at three different jobs for a full year. As time went on, Macy developed a friendship with the man who had taken him under his wing and encouraged him toward a better life. The old man told him he had too much talent and ability to waste his time as someone else's hired hand. That encouragement planted an important seed that took root when Macy's opportunity to go to college emerged.

After football gave him the chance to attend Earlham College, the school comptroller asked him to work with the twenty-seven Morgan horses the college owned. It was a dream come true for Macy to work with those majestic animals and break six or seven colts a year. That turned out to be hard work, but his love for the animals shown through. A man named Ed Goebel allowed him to use two jumping horses when he taught jumping classes. His "whispering" technique was fruitful. "You talk to the horses, rub on them, and tell them what you wanted them to do. It was wonderful."

After Earlham, Macy did not have much opportunity to be around horses until he moved to Ada, Oklahoma, in 1961. Then, with a growing family, he bought a small acreage, a couple of horses, and even a few cows. Although his past love for horses remained, Macy had never considered rodeo until the Ada years. Mostly, he used his horses for stock work, strictly to assist in checking the cattle. As time passed, Bob's holdings in Ada grew from his initial five-acre start. "I had twenty acres and 330 acres on contract. I ran about a hundred cows and had at least three horses."

It was in Ada that he formed a relationship with Ken Lance in the late 1970s, who had a Professional Rodeo Cowboys Association (PRCA) competition that attracted excellent cowboys from across the region. "It had begun with all local cowboys steer roping. He upgraded the operation. Actually, he had one of the best rodeos in this part of the country," Macy fondly remembers.

The rodeo part of Bob's life took off in the late 1970s when Brett was about thirteen or fourteen years old. That's when he discovered "play days" at the local arena. The boy needed a partner to compete in team roping and cutting competition. Bob was happy to give it a go.

The two began practicing and occasionally won as they got better. Before long, they both realized they needed a higher-quality horse to win more often. They bought and trained quarter horses. Brett's horse was an excellent animal with a couple of minor flaws. He had been hit in the eye with a rope prior to Macy's purchase of the animal. This caused him to be a bit skittish. So he developed a tendency to buck, but Brett had the ability to keep the horse calm. For himself, Bob bought a dark red gelding named Bobby to ride in competition alongside Brett and his horse, Ronnie.

As time passed, Brett developed masterful skills on horseback. He even joined the rodeo team at Southwestern State University in Weatherford. He was a bulldogger for the squad. A short time after his parents separated, however, Brett came home to be with his dad after the third semester. For years thereafter, Bob and Brett were inseparable, competing in a multitude of roping events all across the Sooner State.

As they grew more serious about the rodeo, Bob purchased a tract, where he built a roping arena. Bob, Brett, and some of their friends used the facility to hone their skills. Eventually, Brett began working at the Oklahoma Bureau of Narcotics as a dispatcher. He went back to college full time, leaving less time for rodeo. At his place, Bob assumed sole responsibility for the horses and the cattle.

Brett turned twenty-one and began working full-time processing crime scenes for the Choctaw Police Department in eastern Oklahoma County. Brett eventually got his bachelor's degree and started working at the Oklahoma City Police Department.

Even while Brett was not active in rodeoing, Bob continued roping and competing. He had finally achieved, it seemed, the longed-for title of "Cowboy" and wore it proudly. In daily life and in the rodeo arena, he embraced the Code of the West. He didn't fully realize he had been living the Code of the West from the time he was a youngster. Two decades of memorable experiences outside his professional living as a prosecutor flowed into the years as he became known as, at least to some, "Cowboy Bob."

As time passed, Brett got back into the rodeo scene with his dad. One Sunday morning in those years, Bob and Brett got up early and rode to Roy Cooper's ranch in Durant, Oklahoma After a three-hour drive, they were greeted at the door by Roy and his wife and invited in to have a late breakfast.

Shortly after they got inside, Lane Frost, holder of the title of World Champion Bull Rider, pulled up pulling a horse trailer with a cloud of dust in his wake. The family and guests greeted Lane and invited him in. They had barely started back in, just reaching the front porch, when another truck hauling a horse trailer came rolling in. The driver of that truck was world champion bronc rider Monty "Hawkeye" Hawkins. Monty bailed out of his truck to be greeted by the cluster of new and old friends. Finally, they all got to sit down to a breakfast of pancakes and plenty of sausage.

As they were eating, Bob leaned over to Brett and said, "You'd better remember this, as there won't be too many times in your life when you get to sit down to a meal with three world champion rodeo cowboys." Roy Cooper, himself, was a world champion roper.

Later that morning, Clay Tom Cooper pulled in with his horse trailer in tow. As he unloaded his animal, he told the assembled cowboys he wanted to sell the horse so he could get in hand his entry fee for an upcoming rodeo. The day progressed, and Bob took the opportunity to ride the horse, soon realizing it was of superior quality, although it was not registered. The horse was nearly twenty years old and the asking price of $1,500, as Bob recalls, seemed too high. Bob half-jokingly asked the young Cooper if he could pay half the price he was asking. After a thought, Clay Tom agreed. The deal was struck. Macy says the horse was one of the best he had ever owned and that it won him more money than any other mount.

A friendship that began in 1971, when Macy was an assistant county attorney in Ada, blossomed in the rodeo years. Ken Lance, a full-blooded Chickasaw Indian, became Bob's friend after the two met through Ken's brother, who worked in the sheriff's department. After a few years, the two began to compete in PRCA events in Texas, Kansas, and Oklahoma. "Roping with Ken was a sheer pleasure," Macy recalls fondly. Ken had his own arena in Stonewall, where he held a PRCA-sanctioned competition that ran four days every year. That event required a lot of manpower to keep events underway and on track. Ken's friends, like Jerald Powers, Brenda Rebels and her sister Karen, John Flood, Hoot Gibson, and Richard Grey would come to Lance's arena during their own vacation time to help in running the events.

Bob enjoyed his stays with Ken, whom he remembers as a delightful man with nothing bad to say about anyone. He was well liked on the rodeo circuit. Bob often saw young cowboy competitors come up and express their admiration to Ken. A common belief was that Ken could calf rope, trick rope, and team rope with the best in the rodeo business. A real champion cowboy, Jim Shoulders, once joked, "Ken may not be the world's best cowboy, but he sure tries to be."

One day, Bob, Brett, world champion steer roper Kenny Call, and Ken Lance were practicing team roping at Lance's arena. Everything was going well until Kenny and Bob made one particular run. Macy's rear girth broke, and his saddle slipped forward.

At that moment, the horse bucked. Bob came down on all fours. His rope settled down on his neck, and his horse took off at full gallop. Realizing that if the rope got taut and he lost his footing, he would probably be strangled to death, Bob sprinted alongside the horse, even as Kenny came alongside with a knife to cut the rope. He managed to stay upright and sprint alongside the horse the whole length of the arena. Ken Lance caught up to the horse and grabbed its head. To this day, in Oklahoma bunkhouses, Bob Macy's friends can narrate good stories involving him and horses, but the most memorable was the time he outran a galloping horse to save his own life.

Wherever there was a Ken Lance rodeo, a dance was sure to follow. One unforgettable night, the dance was held under a large tent there on the rodeo grounds, featuring local bands. As always, the event drew a large crowd. That night, Bob was at the dance sitting and visiting with his friends Lance, Hoot Gibson, and Richard Grey when a fight broke out. Two roustabouts were drunk and eager to destroy each other or perhaps the makeshift dance hall itself. Not wanting to see the good times ruined or anyone get seriously hurt, Bob employed his law enforcement police training and maybe even some old wrestling skills. He jumped in to save the day—or night. Bob grabbed the obvious aggressor from behind by the back of the fellow's belt. His intention was simply to drag and escort the man away from the scene, but he pulled a bit too hard. As a result, they both went flying backwards and into some tables, something that must have looked like a cowboy movie.

Although Cowboy Bob did not get hurt and successfully subdued the drunken fighter, he didn't walk away without a memento. Some blood splattered on Macy's fine western shirt. In all likelihood, his shirt had more than a splatter of blood on it. He didn't notice how he looked until he went home to greet Brett. When his son saw the blood, he began to ask questions. After some explanation, Brett was satisfied that his father was really okay. Then he began to laugh. For months after, he told professional friends of the night his dad came home from a dance wearing a blood stained shirt.

Bob's friendship with Ken grew stronger as the years passed. Ken would sometimes drive to his friend's place in Oklahoma City years, showing up with a freezer full of homemade ice cream and a greeting of, "Hi, Cowboy!" to start the feast. One memorable occasion came when rodeo legend Jim Shoulders and Macy were parade marshals at the Chickasaw Annual Rodeo in Tishomingo. Additionally, Macy and Ken Lance were asked to be celebrity team ropers and lead off the day's competition. Because the two-day event was a good distance from home, Bob asked to borrow one of Ken's horses.

When they opened the competition, Ken, an excellent roper, caught only one horn at the moment Macy caught both heels of the calf. The rope, stretched tight, pulled loose from the steer's wagging horn. At that moment, Macy's heel horse suddenly released from the rope, falling over backwards. As events unfolded, Bob could see he was in trouble, about to get smashed by the saddle of his mount. In an instant, he managed to throw himself backward and to the right. He avoided catastrophe but hit the ground hard enough to see stars. To this day, Macy is thankful for his athletic training in younger years and, as he puts it now, his hard head.

As they hung around the rodeo scene, Ken and Bob made a "bachelor's pact" as health problems of various sorts mounted. The promise was that the one to live the longest would be the pallbearer for the other. Years later, in 2006, when Ken passed away, Bob was unable to keep his promise to his old friend. Bob was in the hospital recovering from another spinal surgery when he got the news. Ken Lance had died alone at home of congestive heart failure.

That was one of the most heartbreaking pieces of news Bob received in his retirement years, as friends and relationships passed from the scene. It tore him apart, he says. Bob had to sit while Brett gave the eulogy and Pake McIntyre sang, "Strawberry Roan." Bob still remembers his old friend with tears, saying, "I miss my old partner."

Even with melancholy recollections like that, Bob Macy's mind lives with visions of happy times in and around the rodeo business. He says today, "My work with all the Ben Johnson and Eddie Gaylord charities was a result of being in the right place at the right time." Although the district attorney's job required numerous speeches and appearances, Macy kept his personal life personal for the most part. He never played in the local golf tournaments or various sports fundraisers and never belonged to any country club. Bob never wanted his name to be used for political favoritisms. Any time he made a speech, it was for a purpose he ardently believed in.

The exception to his comparative insularity was his involvement for and with cowboys. His friendship with Ken Lance began long before very many people knew who Bob Macy was and continued until Ken's death. That relationship was a prelude to Bob's involvement with big-time rodeos, professional cowboys, and projects that raised millions of dollars for worthy causes including children's medical research. Bob Macy's name was not to be used for profiteering unless it was backed by his own action that helped fund causes close to his heart.

E.K. Gaylord II, son of one of Oklahoma's richest men, Edward L. Gaylord, publisher of the *Daily Oklahoman* newspaper, had constructed a rodeo arena north of Oklahoma City. The Lazy E Arena near Guthrie was truly state-of-the-art. It was completely enclosed with underground turn lanes so neither weather nor movement of stock had any effect on roping. The Lazy E was a cowboy's dream. Young Ed Gaylord was quite liberal in his use of the facilities, and lots of local cowboys wound up practicing there.

Brett and Bob both were often among those practicing in the arena. During that time, Bob developed many great friendships with a diverse crowd of highly-ranked professionals within the cowboy circles. The crowd ranged from steer ropers like Rod Harness, a premier competitor from Pawhuska, and Billy Montin, from Fittstown, to roper and lawyer Garland Bloodworth and Shawn Burchett, among many others. One of Macy's closest and dearest friends was a young cowboy named J.D. Yates. Though Macy was in his fifties and J.D. in his thirties, J.D. was the best cowboy. J.D. is also a world premier quarter horse trainer. He and his father, Dick Yates, first won the national final team roping while J.D. was just a boy.

Every year, in addition to other events, the Lazy E hosted a timed event championship, the 89ers' Day Rodeo, ranch competitions, roundups, and the Ben Johnson Pro-Celebrity Team Roping Championship. The Lazy E was only five miles from Macy's home in the eastern part of the county, and he spent as much time as he could at the facility with his cowboy friends.

The younger Gaylord had become involved in motion picture productions and activities and eventually drew lots of those performers to the Lazy E for nice events. Early on in their friendship, Macy and Gaylord were riding around the Lazy E with a group of professional cowboy contestants and some of the prominent actors who had come to Oklahoma for the Pro-Celebrity event to raise money for charity.

Macy told Gaylord, "What you guys do is a real help," referring to the children and others the benefit was for.

Gaylord startled Macy when he replied, "What we do is make-believe. What you do is real."

It was some time after that Bob was practicing with the cowboys when Gaylord rode up to him, saying, "Bob, I need a favor."

"What's that?" Macy asked.

Gaylord said, "I'm putting together a group of movie actors and rodeo cowboys to raise money to do research for children's cancer. I'd like you to rope with us."

Macy's response was, "Ed, I'm not a celebrity."

Gaylord immediately replied, "Bob, in Oklahoma, you are."

For the next fifteen years, Macy roped several times a year in those fundraising activities. His best new friendship was the one he formed with legendary film actor Ben Johnson, winner of the Academy Award for his performance in *The Last Picture Show* but probably best known for his powerful portrayal in *The Wild Bunch.* In a somewhat ironic turn, top cop Macy was drawn in by the law-abiding Johnson as a member of his own "Wild Bunch" that included both professional actors and professional cowboys.

The "Bunch" included, at various times, Wilfred Brimley, Buck Taylor, Buck's son Adam, Jerry Nalls, J.D. Yates, Roy Cooper, Jimmy Cooper, Paul Tierney, John Miller, Ben Miller, Barry Corbin, Rex Slim, Dick Yates, plus a lot of other movie stars and prominent athletes. Others included John Brimley, singer Red Steagall, Larry Wilcox, and Steve Ford, son of former President Gerald Ford. Many of the original "Bunch" participated in the roping competitions for most of the years Macy was involved. The ropers were pretty well divided between true professionals and the skilled but amateur cowboys. Other regulars in the "Bunch" as it waxed and waned over the years during which Macy participated included Dean Smith, Mike MaGaha, Gary Gist, Reba McIntyre, Bill Montin, Kenny Call, and Phil Line.

Before long, a routine that proved both thrilling and therapeutic unfolded for the powerful district attorney of Oklahoma County. Each year, there would be three or four pro-celebrity roping events, and he took part in as many of them as he could.

The selection of partners was an interesting process. When all entries had been received, each contestant's name was put into a hat and drawn out in an attempt to balance the teams in their experience. The first time Macy participated, he arrived late. The names had already been drawn out. When he found the ropers' list, he learned that his first-ever professional partner was Roy Cooper, the seven-time champion calf roper. Today, Macy solemnly remembers, "I can't begin to tell you how it felt just to be in that arena."

At each of those pro-celebrity affairs, the ropers came in on Friday night for a dance, an auction, and a fundraiser. At these events, Bob Macy had the opportunity to visit and actually get to know many of his Western heroes of both the arena and the big screen. On Saturday mornings of the competitions, there would be an early breakfast. The ropers practiced until noon, then rested during the afternoon, so they could come back at 6:00 p.m. ready to compete.

As the years passed, Macy became acquainted with more and more of the movie stars and rodeo cowboys who came to the Lazy E. Other friends he made included Dale Robertson, Doug McClure, and, of course, Oklahoma's beautiful country singer, Reba McIntyre. This was how he first became friends with Wilford Brimley, certainly among the most memorable and long-lasting of his adult friendships.

The two met at the Lazy E when Wilford was in town for a pro-celebrity event. They first met, Macy believes, at the time the Sean Sellers case was making headlines. As the awful particulars of the case became known, Sellers was claiming he was demon possessed, creating a lot of news media interest in the prosecution of the case.

Because Wilford had so far to travel, flying in from Salt Lake City to Oklahoma City, he would use one of Gaylord's horses to compete. He was riding a strange horse, so he spent considerable time in the arena simply getting acquainted with the horse he was going to ride. It was during one of those sessions that Macy and Brimley got to know each other. The pair had lengthy conversations about Sellers's crime and the legal case against the killer.

Brimley began to consider a motion picture about the case and about Bob, in which Wilford planned to play Macy. They became fast friends discussing the case during riding and competing sessions at the Lazy E and later in Utah, Brimley's home. During the Sellers murder trial in Oklahoma City, Wilford watched Macy work the prosecution. Unfortunately, Brimley could stay in Oklahoma City for only short stints because of his filming the weekly program *Our House* in California.

Wilford soon invited Macy to come to Utah to visit him at his home. When Bob made the first trip to the Salt Lake area, he met Wilford's family. Wilford and Lynne had been married many years and had three sons. In his early days of acting, Wilford had gone through some hard times, including battles with diabetes and alcohol. While the boys were small and Wilford was drinking heavily, Lynne supported the family by working in a convenience store. By the time Bob met Wilford and Lynne, they were doing well.

Ultimately, Wilford, Lynne, and their sons, Jimmy, John, and Bill became like part of Bob's own family. Wilford never tired of catching Bob up on the happenings at the acreage, which included indoor and outdoor roping arenas.

Bob remembers the first time he met Lynne. He had traveled to Salt Lake City to meet the Brimley family. Bob found the city beautiful with the Rockies in the background and the streets wide enough for a sixteen-horse team. Macy was standing curbside when a Ford Bronco rolled up. It was Lynne. The next thing he knew, they were deep in the city's traffic as she handled that Bronco like an expert. As they got acquainted, she told the Oklahoman, "Wilford got called out, so I'm going to drop you at the ranch." Their trip from the airport to the town of Lehi took about forty-five minutes. Lynne pointed out all the points of interest along the route, including the state penitentiary. By the time they got to the Brimley ranch, it was turning dark against the nearby mountains, which made them majestic, as Macy remembers.

Nestled in the midst of the ranch buildings was an older farmhouse, where Bob was left off. His room was fully equipped for his stay, including the kitchen, which was fully stocked and had an

Olympic-sized swimming pool out back. At the old house, the only other living soul was one of Wilford's dogs.

Early the next morning, Macy got up, showered and shaved, and got ready to greet the morning. The place was totally deserted. He had a bowl of cereal, drank some orange juice, and decided to step outside to explore the grand ranch facility. Bob walked along and picked up a heel rope. He threw out fifty loops; then an old Dodge pickup pulled into the drive. Out stepped a miniature cowboy who approached Bob with a hearty handshake. "I'm John," introduced the little man. "Dad got called out for a shoot and won't be back for a day or two."

Macy spent the next few days getting to know John and the other boys and riding into the mountains. On the weekend, Macy and the boys joined a bunch of neighbors, roping for hours. That evening, Bill got his guitar out and passed the time with some very pleasant music.

On future visits, if Wilford was away from his home, John or Bill would saddle up some horses and take Bob on a mountain ride into the Rockies, coming back down only for Wilford's return. The passing years just made the friendship closer and closer between the two families. To this day, Bob still considers the whole bunch like part of his family.

Jimmy Brimley, the oldest, is still single. He lived with Lynne until the time of her death. He lived on the ranch but never got caught up in the cowboy life. Instead, he was the businessman, an executive for an airline, and a talented man, one of the best stand-up comics Bob ever heard. Jimmy, if he let his beard grow, could become the spitting image of his father.

The second son is John, a little guy Bob described as "a hell of a cowboy." For years, he and his dad operated the family horse ranch in Utah. John did most of the work, breeding, breaking, training, and then selling their colt brood. John has a wife and three kids and became one of Macy's favorite people. He was a gentleman, a friend, and one of the toughest individuals Macy ever met. On one occasion, several people were working with colts on the Brimley ranch. A colt reared up and struck John, who was nearly bald, on the top of his head. The blow opened up a cut and gash across the man's scalp. A vet told John he would need to have the wound stitched, so John asked the vet to do it on the spot. After a rinse of the wound, John was given thirty stitches without anesthetic. Then, he went off again promptly to work with the colts.

The third Brimley son is Bill, built like a Mack truck and about as stout as a bull. Bill has a small band that plays at local places in Utah. He tried to make it in Nashville but never caught on there. Bill is a devout Mormon, as was his mother, Lynne, and has four children. He served two years as a missionary for the church and became articulate in four languages other than English.

Macy always found Brimley extremely proud of his sons, "and he should be," adds Macy. Wilford likes to tell of an occasion when a big guy jumped on John. John says he is a lover, not a fighter, and the big guy started to get the best of him. Bill stepped in to say, "You're pretty good at whipping little guys. Let's see how you do with a big'un." Bill then proceeded to thoroughly whip the big guy.

Brimley raised his sons right, to be proud, to be honest, to work hard, and to be proud of hard work. This is what Bob found so attractive in Wilford's friendship. It wasn't that he was a movie star. By now, the glitz and glimmer of famous people had faded in Bob's eyes. He saw what most of them really, really looked like. But there's one thing above all I've learned about Bob Macy, and that is his devotion to his true friends. True friends to Bob aren't people who flatter him or glow in the residual of his work. They are people who share his passion in helping make the world a right place to live. Wilford Brimley was such a friend. He raised his sons right, and he devoted his time and efforts to make right in the world. And Bob raised his son right as well. Brett is as devoted to the little guy, the one crying out for help, as he is to his father. For both Bob and Wilford, "it's been a hell of a party."

Some of Macy's most memorable days were spent with Bill, who liked to saddle up some horses and ride high into the mountains nearby. They'd drive in as far as they could then take the horses higher into the mountains above the snowline. Some of the trails they traveled were not more than twelve inches wide, Bob remembers, and looking at the sheer drop down the side of the mountain often made his stomach churn.

In the next few years, Macy spent many restful days and nights at the B-7 Ranch. Once assured Macy knew what he was doing, the Brimley family turned him loose to rope and ride and do as he pleased. At the B-7, Macy learned "what you see is what you get."

The Brimleys were unassuming and unpretentious. They were together as honest as Wilford was alone. Wilford Brimley is an honest and decent man who loves his family and respects his neighbors. A former Marine who once worked as a bodyguard for Howard Hughes, Wilford's movies were doing quite well by the 1980s. With hits such as *The China Syndrome, Cocoon I* and *II, The Natural, Electric Horseman,* and *The Firm*, he was making a good living. He also did well in real estate and advertisements. For years, he bought and sold ranches in New Mexico, Utah, and Montana, leaving him well off. But then Lynne grew ill. She had a disease that hardened all the organs in her body. The illness began with a loss of elasticity in her organs and progressed into dialysis three times a week.

Eventually, she was also diagnosed with a deadly brain tumor. When Bob made the trips to see the Brimleys, Wilford made sure Bob got to see Lynne as much as possible. Her children loved her very much. So did Bob. The tumor was so malignant that finally, she and her family decided nature needed to take its course.

When she died, Macy went to her funeral. There were a number of movie stars attending. People like Tom Selleck loved her as much as Bob did. Over the years, Brett also got to know many of the movie stars and champion cowboys but as people, not celebrities. When Brett and his wife, Quinna, had their baby girl, they named her Ryen Lynne in honor of Lynne Brimley.

Lynne wasn't the last person in the "Bunch" Bob knew and respected to die. When Buck Taylor's son, Adam, died, Bob gave the eulogy. Adam was married to Annie Lockhart, daughter of June Lockhart, when he was killed in a motorcycle accident.

During the fifteen years Bob worked with the pro-celebrity roping, he had too many friends to remember. There were literally hundreds of people he became close with and who remained friends with years after they were no longer able to work on the event. Besides the good friendship, Bob fondly recalls the good comradeship. He remembers one special occasion after a pro-celebrity event held at the Red Salt Palace in Utah. After it was over, twenty-five or thirty of the competitors went to Brimley's B-7 Ranch for a cookout. They were all sitting around talking when someone started singing. Two of those singing were Red Steagall, an old balladeer, and Walt Lamar, an artist. Most of the people, though, were cowboys. They sat around singing until the wee hours of the morning, and everyone hated to go to bed even then. Macy says he soon realized he'd never been in such an atmosphere of love, respect, and affection.

The Macys and the Brimleys have a unique, even enviable, relationship. Wilford raised his sons the same way Bob raised Brett, all admirable sons of admirable men. The old men see in each other what dear friends ought to see, the truth unvarnished by limelight or notoriety. Bob couldn't care less if Wilford were poor and unknown. By the same token, Wilford sees Bob for who he is, not for what the media makes him. These are two men and two families who have grown close because of who they are, not what they have done. Wilford, Bob admits, is a hard man to know. He's a loner and has few true friends. But the friends he has, he develops and cherishes deeply. The same can be said of Bob Macy. They both have people who like to be seen around them. But these two old men, brought together by a common fire in the belly for helping others, stand far apart from casual acquaintances. At the end of one of their recent phone conversations, Wilford closed by saying, "Remember, I love you." I am sure that didn't need to be said. I'm sure Bob already knew it. And I'm sure Wilford knows Bob loves him just the same.

Like his father, Brett always had a cowboy's habits and a heart for the little guy. In 2002, several months after Bob's retirement as Oklahoma County District Attorney, the two joined a group of residents in Ada, where the locals had formed a coop to raise money to help people in the region meet medical expenses and obligations resulting from catastrophic illnesses. Brett and Bob both served on the board of directors of that group.

Additionally, Brett became active in the Special Olympics and other groups addressing the needs of those with mental and other challenges. As Ryen grows up, Brett began to escort her to father/daughter dances, and Bob got to see it all.

In his own reckoning, these years just prior to retirement were the greatest days in Macy's life. He was at the top of his profession and in the midst of his three and a half years atop the National District Attorney's Association (NDAA). He served one year as president of the Oklahoma District Attorneys Association and was twice voted the outstanding state prosecutor. Spanning those "cowboy years" were his years of personal friendship with six attorneys general and three FBI directors.

He had the lauds of the country's law enforcement community, yet his cowboy life helped complete the other important aspects of living. He had two good roping horses and a half dozen saddles. At least once a year, he went quail hunting in Apache, Oklahoma, with a bunch of old athletic stars and locally famous folks like Maury Tate and Garth Brooks' folks. At least once a year, he and Brett drove to Buffalo, Oklahoma, to hunt deer, again for a worthy cause.

There is no doubt that Macy's life was full to the brim. He had wonderful friends, professional success, personal accomplishments, and a great legacy to pass along to his children and the people of the State of Oklahoma. In our interviews, Macy said his favorite movie was the film *Lonesome Dove.* At the end, as Gus is dying, he looks up into his partner's face and says, "Woodrow, it's been one hell of a party." Macy reflects, "If I were to die today, I could look into Brett's face and say, 'It's been a hell of a party.'"

CHAPTER 10

A Man at Rest—Dreams, Memories, and Resolve

The sun begins to sink slowly in the west as the old cowboy leads his horses into the barn. Macy pulls the saddles off and places them on the rack, hangs up the bridles, and puts the saddle blankets in order so they'll air out. Everything is orderly along the fence rail.

As the old cowboy stops and stands by the gate, he remembers a speech given to the Texas County and District Attorneys Association in 1992, nine years before his retirement. It foreshadowed the future and his state of mind as the evening beckons this particular day...

> Standing before you today is the luckiest man on the face of the earth. I live in the only place I have ever wanted to live. I have three children and five grandchildren who bring joy to my life daily. My only son is an Oklahoma City police officer. I live on sixty acres of land with twenty-five head of cattle, four horses, and Bandit, a female Blue Heeler, and still enjoy roping with my son. I also enjoy associations with a bunch of old movie actors, including Ben Johnson, Barry Corbin, and Wilford Brimley.
>
> Equally as important, as I stand here before you, professionally I have surpassed all of my dreams. I now hold the only job that I have ever wanted. I have held that job longer than any of my predecessors. I won my last two

elections by seventy-three percent and over eighty percent. Now, I have the honor of standing before you as president of the National District Attorneys Association, the greatest prosecutorial organization on the face of the earth.

On July 5th, I celebrate my sixty-second birthday. I could kick back, draw my retirement and social security, and spend the rest of my days with my cowboy friends.

Those of you who saw the TV miniseries, 'Lonesome Dove,' the story of two old retired Texas Rangers, might remember the scene where Gus lay dying, looked up into the face of his best friend, and said, "Woodrow, it's been one hell of a party!"

My life has been so full and so far beyond my wildest dreams that, if I should die tomorrow, I would look up into the face of my best friend, who happens to be my son, and honestly say, "Brett, it's been one hell of a party!"

In spite of my age or how tired I might be or what ten years of football and twenty years of rodeoing has done to this old body, I can't retire or even slow down, because as I look around me, I see everything that I have spent a lifetime fighting for being threatened.

I told you all that I have had a good life, probably better than I deserve. The trail that I have chosen has taken its toll and has made me wonder if I have the strength and toughness to ride point for the next year over the rocky and treacherous terrain that I know lies ahead. It might be easier to turn my horses out to pasture, hang up my spurs, and let someone else lead in this battle. But I can't bring myself to do that for two reasons.

First, if I quit now, all of the work that I have done and all the sacrifices that I have made will have been for naught. You don't spend years building up a prize herd and then sit back while rustlers steal you blind. The work that we have commenced must be brought to fruition.

Second, some of you have heard me say before, we prosecutors have a dream that we have lived by, and we know that just over the next ridge lies that dream—a nation of cities and communities living in peace and safety, places where any man or woman and every child can walk or play in any street, alley, or park in absolute safety. Our children and grandchildren, yours and mine, deserve that.

One of the best men I have ever known and am proud to call friend is Red Steagall, "The Texas Troubadour." He hails from West Texas. During Operation Desert Storm, President George H.W. Bush invited him to a breakfast at the White House where he was to recite the Cowboy Prayer. Before he did, Red told President Bush, "Mr. President, I have a message for you from America's cowboys. They asked me to tell you that our bedrolls are packed, our carbines loaded, our fastest and best horses are tethered up close to the bunkhouse, and we are ready to ride."

I liked that. It left no doubt as to where we cowboys stand when it comes to serving and defending the greatest nation on the face of God's green earth.

Today I ask you, the prosecutors of the great state of Texas, to become active in the NDAA, to put aside petty differences and turf battles with other federal, state, and local law enforcement agencies so that we may stand united and committed, just as Travis and Bowie did at the Alamo. I also ask that, as we look out across this great nation we all love so much, we send out a message to our beleaguered cities, to the victims and the families of victims, to our valiant police officers and to society's most vulnerable citizens—the young and the elderly. Hang in there, because it is the dawn of a new day, and unlike the Alamo, help in on the way. The prosecutors of the Lone Star state have mounted their fastest and best horses and are riding hell bent for leather into the battle to preserve for all future generations the tradition of freedom, which lies in the heart of every true Texan.

A cow moos, and the dog barks to bring the old cowboy out of his dream-like state. Bob Macy is back in the here and now in Oklahoma. He looks down to see Bandit wagging her tail, so he bends down to pet the old girl. Macy begins to walk slowly back to his farmhouse, and his mind slips back to that speech given so long ago. He remembers the standing ovation, fellow prosecutors lining up to shake his hand, and being escorted back to his pickup truck by the executive director of the Texas County and District Attorneys Association.

Macy remembers—and he's on the long drive back home from Texas, time that gave him a chance to rehash the speech, especially the remarks about retirement and old age. He had considered his doctor's advice to give up his lifelong love, confessing to the doctor that maybe he had seen one too many bodies.

Back in the house, Macy passes a treasured picture of himself with Ben Johnson, his dear friend, standing together at a rodeo, and he pauses a moment to remember those good times. He looks around, grabs a glass of juice, then proceeds to the living room and turns on a lamp to reveal the countless awards, plaques, and mementos of days gone by adorning his walls. He switches on the stereo to listen to the soft tones of Frank Sinatra and sits in his favorite recliner. It's a routine but not a bad one. His mind slips back to yesteryears as he starts to drift off to sleep.

The speech still fresh in his mind, Macy recalls his angst with great detail. In 1992, he had weighed his options and wondered if the time was right to retire. He had accomplished more professionally than expected and received honors he didn't know existed. He was one of the leading death penalty prosecutors in the country. He had appeared before Congress, helped draft federal crime legislation, served as assistant director of a national crime commission, and was honored by three presidents who had named him to presidential commissions. He knew the governor would not have a problem picking a replacement, since there were plenty of qualified candidates.

Although it was strongly advised in 1992, Macy did not retire. He felt compelled to keep putting the bad guys away as long as he could. In 1995, hours following the bombing of the Murrah building and the identification of the killers, Macy was approached by a number of Oklahoma City residents asking him to promise to get the death penalty for Terry Nichols and Timothy McVeigh. For fifteen years, Macy had gone head to head with the criminal element of Oklahoma County, so it was only natural that, in this crisis, the citizens would expect him to protect them. It was a complex investigation and prosecution, involving many state and federal agencies, with several assistant U.S. attorneys assigned to the case. FBI Director Louis Freeh was personally supervising the investigation. Macy had neither the authority nor the personnel to carry out a local investigation, so he made his entire office available to support the federal officials.

Despite decades in law enforcement, Macy was bewildered as he watched federal judges appoint more than fourteen lawyers to defend the bombers who attacked his city. He had served on a federal task force with future vice president, then Senator, Joe Biden, who had recommended that in a death penalty case, the defense was entitled to not more than three attorneys with unlimited funds for investigation and defense. In the bombing case, his amazement grew as he asked, "Do you waive the rules based upon the number of victims?" As events unfolded, it seemed clear that politics had played a role in the selection of defense counsel. Many things in the process concerned Macy.

Early in the investigation, allegations of conspiracy involving several other people surfaced. After a petition circulated, a grand jury was empanelled to hear the allegations. Assistant District Attorneys Pat Morgan and Susan Gump were assigned to support the grand jury. Anyone who had any pertinent information was called before the panel and statements were taken under oath. The panel was a source of controversy, with some of the activists using the proceedings to feed conspiracy theories. Macy remained absolutely convinced McVeigh and Nichols were the guilty parties and, among other things, that particular grand jury found further evidence against McVeigh and Nichols.

After the federal court trial in Denver, McVeigh was rather promptly, in comparison to most cases, executed. Nichols was a different story. From the time of his arrest until conviction, various groups and organizations interfered with efforts to assure state prosecution of Nichols for the majority of the murders of those killed on April 19, 1995.

As the process advanced, three federal agencies seemed to be blocking a transfer of the accused from Colorado to Oklahoma. A direct order from Attorney General Janet Reno was issued to get Nichols into the proper venue, resulting in a rather humorous series of events mentioned earlier. The Oklahoma Supreme Court and the Oklahoma County legislative delegation blocked funding for the prosecution, with the opinion that it would cost too much to prosecute Nichols in local courts.

Macy was furious. He had asked, "How do you put a price on the prosecution of a murderer who killed nineteen babies?" He had sent several individuals to death row for killing one baby and wondered what the appropriate punishment for a mass murderer of children was. He asked, "Where is the justice for the families of the 168 killed in the explosion?"

Though it was met with resistance, the state trial for Nichols proceeded under a state district judge, Judge Steven Taylor, in Pittsburg County. Veteran trial lawyers were not surprised when they heard the case was assigned to the county where the reputed pro-criminal defense attorney practiced, but Macy and his team persisted.

Sandra Elliot and Fern Smith, the assistant district attorneys who'd prosecuted Nichols from the beginning, selected a jury and presented evidence with the help of other assistant district attorneys from Macy's office, Pat Morgan, Susan Gump, Lou Keel, and Richard Wintory.

After several weeks, Terry Nichols was found guilty on all charges. Deliberations were very brief before conviction, yet it became clear the jury was not going to return a death verdict.

In the sentencing, with execution off the table, Judge Taylor showed no mercy to Nichols, handing down 160 consecutive life-without-parole sentences and saying, "You are a terrorist, one of a kind. No other in history has killed so many." With that, Nichols was escorted to a federal high-security penitentiary.

Macy considered the sentencing a double-edged sword. He would have liked to have had a death sentence for Nichols, but he was satisfied that at least the coconspirator was not set free and would spend the rest of his life behind bars.

It was as fresh as yesterday, and the memories poured through his weary frame. Macy, the retired old cowboy, shifted his weight in his recliner, awakening just enough to see the sun fading through the window blinds. Then he drifted back to sleep.

His restless mind then went again to the past, past the bombing, six years in an eyelid's blink. It was the day of his retirement. Mounting physical ailments and unavoidable major surgery had led him to June 30, 2001, a date that brought change to Bob Macy's life, as he turned another of life's pages to begin the final chapter.

He walked into Governor Frank Keating's office to present his resignation personally. After some discussion, Keating reluctantly accepted, after Macy explained he thought it was time to retire after working over fifty years of his life. He continued, "I have grandchildren who I would like to enjoy before I get too old!"

Keating smiled and said, "Bob, you are the best district attorney I have ever had the pleasure of knowing. Are you sure?"

Macy nodded and said, "I know I have been elected five times and still have three years left on this term, but I feel it's time to hang up my spurs. Besides, I will be out for a while when I have spinal surgery, and it isn't fair to the citizens to have someone who is less than one hundred percent capable of handling the job."

With that, Governor Keating consented and immediately assembled his staff to find a replacement.

When the end of his hitch in the county courthouse came, Macy decided to wait until the weekend to gather his personal belongings from the district attorney's office, saying he wanted to avoid disturbing the staff routine.

His time there was bittersweet. On the one hand, he was forfeiting a job he had cherished and enjoyed for twenty-one years and leaving behind office personnel who had become like family. On the other hand, his own family was growing with grandchildren. He was seventy-one years old and feared he might miss the opportunity to be a part of their lives. Various physical ailments were mounting up in his tired old body. Brett had encouraged his decision to retire. He knew it to be the right choice, although it was a difficult one, perhaps the hardest he had ever made.

As he gathered things together, Bob's mind that day raced through an accounting of a life's work—his work. He served twenty-one years as DA, twelve years in private practice, two years in the military, four years as a police officer, and several short-term jobs, including advice to congressional panels like Joe Biden's Senate Judiciary Committee. He had succeeded in getting his bachelor's, master's, and law degree while working full time. He thought of being admitted to practice before all Oklahoma courts, the federal courts for eastern and western Texas, the court of military appeals, the U.S. Tax Court, the Tenth Circuit Court of Appeals, and the U.S. Supreme Court. It all added up to an accomplishment that few could call their own.

In the office that summer day in 2001, as he packed his boxes, Macy thought back to when he served two years as an Oklahoma bar examiner and when he was a Mason and a past-master of his lodge. He realized those were among the many fulfilling jobs he had over the years.

He thought of serving with the National District Attorneys Association as assistant treasurer, vice president, committee foreman, and president-elect. He remembered the unanimous vote to elect him president and the time he served as chairman of the board of directors and the additional time he served in that capacity when his predecessor passed away unexpectedly. He cherished those days in the not-so-distant past. He was very proud when he was elected as the Outstanding Oklahoma District Attorney of the year twice and two presidents of the NDAA presented him with the President's Award for outstanding performance. All of it raced through his memory as the boxes became filled with plaques and awards. There was more of Bob Macy in what he had done than in what he had left undone.

The dream, the trips of memory from his last day in the courthouse, faded into a brief, quiet, and restful sleep.

Macy awoke before dawn. He turned on the TV but glared right through it, thinking of the dream, the memories. He sighed and then looked out his window to watch his herd of Black Angus cows and admire his Angus bull. Sharing pasture space with the Angus were two aged longhorn cows.

The sun is not yet fully up as he admires his animals, the longhorns, not the best for eating but carrying the genes and heritage of forbearers that were tough enough to survive the long drives to market in Oklahoma's younger days. Being tough enough to survive, that was certainly something to be proud of.

Outside he hears the diesel whine of a New Holland tractor and turns to watch the silhouette of Brett dump a round bale of hay into the steer's pen. As his son pulls the tractor into the barn, Macy walks out to greet him. While he waits for Brett to emerge from inside, he checks the water tanks to be sure there's enough water. Then, father and son walk together toward the farm house. The two talk about their day's events as they walk toward Brett's pickup.

Brett, living across the road from his dad, is preparing to go home to bed after work.

"I'll probably see you tomorrow, Dad, if not later today."

"Have a good day, son."

The younger Macy rolls into the driver's side of his three-quarter ton pickup and drives out the lane and under the sign that reads, "String Tie Ranch." By the time Brett drives onto the road just inside the far eastern corner of Oklahoma City, near the town of Newalla, the sky is alight with the colors of another magnificent Oklahoma morning.

The old cowboy strolls back to the farmhouse to eat some breakfast. But as he sits at the table, he cannot help but reflect on the night's dreamy reverie.

In the years since Bob Macy's retirement, the world seems to have gone to hell. Corruption, sexual, and other forms of immorality, abuse of public office and base deception seem at an all-time high. In Oklahoma, it reaches into every branch of government, into both parties. Scandals involving the auditor and inspector, county commissioners, sheriffs, judges, congressmen and women have shaken the confidence and hope of the Oklahoma voters.

Even more damnable, in Macy's considered view, is the erosion and even corruption of our educational system. Almost weekly, some school official is indicted for embezzlement for school funds or a pedophile is rooted out from the schoolyard or classroom, long after the damage is done to the developing psyche of a previously innocent school child.

The national news brings into our homes a series of disgraceful, embarrassing sexual liaisons touching governors, attorneys general, and others, and untruths from cabinet members or other high-ranking public officials, the ones who asked and begged for our trust to elect them.

Macy reflected on it all in a 2009 conversation about the future of the society he served. He spent several minutes thinking before he replied to the question. But when he spoke, he spoke with the authority of someone who had spent years contemplating the right answer. In fact, he had. "I'm of the opinion that we've not yet reached the depth of our depravity." The words of a Massachusetts trooper who drove Macy to the airport after Billy O'Malley's funeral might seem even optimistic. "It might take a couple more generations" to recover the moral compass.

Is even "a couple more generations" sufficient in light of the current leadership of the country? Where do we start? From whence comes the leadership so desperately needed? Macy has a few suggestions, honed during years of contemplative retirement.

For starters, "Law-abiding citizens must support the kinds of candidates who will serve honorably and who will keep their promises of reform and good government. Citizens must protect those brave politicians willing to seek office in the midst of a culture where the virtuous face vicious attacks upon themselves, their families. Somehow, laws of libel and slander must be made substantive again, while protecting legitimate freedom for news gatherers and commentators. Only thus will we find qualified candidates, persons of integrity to run for every level of political office." That fire in the belly that inspired Bob Macy must be ignited in others.

Actions have consequences, Macy believes. He contends, "Candidates who knowingly and deliberately violate election laws should not only forfeit office but be forever barred from seeking public office. We must become a law-abiding society. Laws must be enforced, including speed and traffic laws and tax laws that provide the government with the revenue needed to run and provide essential services. Acts of violence must be prosecuted and the perpetrator removed from society. Respect for law and order erodes without the ultimate sanction of just capital punishment. Sexual predators must be identified and removed from society and from casual opportunities to destroy the lives of the vulnerable and the innocent." Macy believes leadership to reform society can come from two professions we have always looked to for the protection of ourselves and our loved ones. At one local level, in law enforcement, "there are thousands of young men and, increasingly, women who take to the streets of the great cities night after night, placing themselves in harm's way." They do so "in order for you, me and those we love to be safe."

At both the local and state levels, he sees hope in the ranks of the district attorneys who are charged with deciding which crimes to prosecute. But there are many reforms needed to make them work properly. Any officer responding to an emergency call must be adequately educated and trained. As it is, many of our smaller departments are poorly compensated." This is a problem, Macy believes, that can be fixed.

Macy also says there should be "a single bureau of prisons and jails, operated independently of law enforcement." The judicial system, in his words, "needs to be modernized. District judges throughout the state receive the same compensation, regardless of the workload. One might carry ten times the case load of another, yet they are paid the same."

Macy also thinks, "Any hope of reformation for society must go deep. Priorities have to change in order to recover the sense of progress and positive forward motion that we have lost. Every parent must realize their most important job, their singular gift, is to rear and teach their child, to be a role model for children."

Macy, the crusty, aging conservative, sounds a bit like a Democrat, which he still is in party affiliation, when he speaks again. "There's something inherently wrong with a society that pays principals, superintendents, and teachers in schools meager salaries while professional athletes, singers, and actors are overly compensated for entertainment." It's a sad day, he thinks, when the names of famous stars and athletes influence our value system far more than our teachers who helped form our ethic and moral judgments from childhood.

Macy saw many people come and go in four decades of public service and in those twenty-one years as Oklahoma County District Attorney. When he talks about them now, the names flow like a roll call, with positive or sympathetic assessments of each.

U.S. attorneys included Tim Leonard, Bill Price, Joe Heaton, Vicki Miles-LaGrange, Pat Ryan, and Robert McCampbell. U.S. attorneys general spanned the years from Kleindeinst to Ashcroft. State attorneys General ranged from Jan Eric Cartwright, Mike Turpen, and Robert Henry to Susan Loving and Drew Edmonson.

The catalogue of sheriffs included the noble Bob Turner and the troubled Gene Wells and friends like J.D. Sharp and John Whetsel. Chiefs of police included the likes of Tom Heggy, Bob Wilder, and I.G. Purser, Lloyd Gramling, Dave McBride, Sam Gonzales, and M.T. Berry.

Those were all tough jobs requiring tough people. Some weren't fundamentally changed by their tenure, remaining pretty much the people they were before assuming office. Others grew in their work. Just a few, like Loving, became heroes in Macy's eyes.

Bob never cared much for the politics of being Oklahoma County District Attorney, but he was more than good enough at that, too. He was the best he could be at anything he attempted, and politics was part of what he had to do to fulfill his passion. The legendary attorney James W. "Bill" Berry, northeast Oklahoma City leader Tim Tolliver, John Warren, Jackie Cooper, and a few other friends made sure he had the political necessities, most fundamentally transparent financial records and scrupulous adherence to the law. He says he often misses the people but not the politics of the county courthouse.

In July 2001, when the citizens of Oklahoma County held a retirement party for Macy, around six hundred people were in attendance. The monies collected from the banquet were contributed to the Youth Cornerstone organization, the group Macy helped start during his time as district attorney. His former assistant district attorney, Kelley Bassey, helped to organize the retirement event.

Macy's retirement has not been entirely a matter of introspection. It has included tangible honors and echoes of his vibrant and vital past. The most important intangibles take on tangible form every time he sees one of his beloved family. For Macy, in the twilight years, there is the embrace and hugs of nearly grown grandchildren and his ten-year-old granddaughter running into his arms to whisper, "Papa, I love you." He cherishes time with his son, Brett, and his daughters, Sheila and Teresa, and the constant and devoted friendship of his former wife, Betty.

Then, on November 5, 2009, the staff of Youth Cornerstone pulled together a tribute to the retired Macy. A cover note to a book full of glowing tributes observed, "There was a sociological survey of fifty people over the age of ninety-five. They were asked if they had life to live over again, what they would do differently. There were many answers, but all fell into one of three categories: they would have reflected more, risked more, and invested in something that outlived them."

Praising Macy, the tribute continued, "Looking back at your twenty-one years of serving as Oklahoma County District Attorney, today we acknowledge and reflect upon your life, thinking about the many risks you took and just one of life's investments in something that will, indeed, outlive you."

The group said Macy's work with Youth Cornerstone proved he was much more than a "hang-em-high" personality. They called him "a man of heart, integrity, and great vision. One area that greatly evidenced your commitment and empowering nature is Youth Cornerstone. Your knowledge that education and individual attention is one of the best ways to keep kids out of the criminal justice system, combined with your ability to bring people together and do the hard work has brought us the distance." This had been one of Macy's life lessons he learned growing up. Education, hard work, and individual attention by his mentors kept Macy on the right side of the law, the very right side.

At the event, as he listened to the founding director and still board member Pam Harrell, Macy couldn't help but remember the time, more than two decades before, when he met the young school teacher. He was returning from an out-of-town trip in 1987 when, as fate would have it, an attractive young lady took her assigned seat next to him on the plane. The conversation turned to truancy, juvenile crime, and such issues. They found similar views about treating the root causes of juvenile crime as a means to avoid the nightmare that young criminals become in the adult system.

Days later, Harrell called. At first, when his secretary said someone was on the phone, Macy didn't remember her name. But when prompted, "It's the woman you met on the plane," he took the call. She asked for a job, so Macy asked her to come by to talk about it sometime.

"She came in, we talked some more, and I told her I wanted to hire her to run the program," Macy explained. At the time, there were about two dozen agencies touching juvenile delinquency and truancy issues in the county. "The first thing I did was get Pam to contact each of them and set up a meeting."

At that meeting, what two years later formally became Youth Cornerstone was formed and, as they say, the rest is history. Today, the group has a professional staff, an eleven-member board of professionals, and has diverted some 27,000 youngsters away from the criminal system and into productive lives.

At the celebration, David Henderson, a board member, told Macy his "vision for Youth Cornerstone has touched and inspired countless youth and young adults." Cheryl Hawkins, who worked in the DA's office for Bob's entire tenure, wrote, "There are many things you leave as a legacy to the District Attorney's office, but I believe that Youth Cornerstone may well be the one thing that makes the biggest difference in the lives of Oklahoma County citizens."

Harrell wrote, "As a single mother and elementary resource specialist, I was struggling when we met, but you offered me an opportunity I couldn't turn down—an opportunity that would change my life and hopefully that of many young people in Oklahoma County. Little did we know that when you turned John Foley and me loose with your vision of keeping young people in school and out of the juvenile justice system that two years later [in 1989], we would begin to turn Oklahoma County truancy upside down with the help of multiple agencies. And here Youth Cornerstone is twenty years later, still fighting for those kids because of your vision. You have my utmost respect for being a man of vision, commitment, integrity, and action."

Such words were, of course, immensely gratifying, as was the pleasant afternoon spent hearing such stories repeated and meeting many of the young people the program is helping today.

Another notable event, certainly the most significant in terms of deserved honor, came on December 6, 2009. Surrounded by his family and friends, in a room crowded with hundreds from the younger generation of police, patrolmen, and investigators, Macy was included in the inaugural group of inductees into the Oklahoma Law Enforcement Hall of Fame.

At the ceremony in Chandler's National Guard Armory, which will serve as the headquarters for the museum and hall of fame until a permanent home is built, Macy entered the hall along with University of Central Oklahoma President W. Roger Webb, retired Oklahoma Commissioner of Public Safety, and former Fraternal Order of Police national president and retired Oklahoma City lieutenant Richard Boyd. The late Bob Lester was also inducted.

Of special meaning to Macy was that he was inducted along with three posthumous honorees: Bill Tilghman, Heck Thomas, and Chris Madsen, legendary crime fighters from Oklahoma's early history.

Macy and other distinguished honorees led the inaugural class of inductees. Introducing Macy to the crowd of several hundred attending was retired Oklahoma City police Chief Bob Wilder, a dear friend of Macy's. It meant a lot to Macy that Wilder handled the preface to Bob's induction. During our interviews, a year before the induction, Macy talked to me about Wilder's father. "Before my cop years, Bob Wilder was a police officer. We'd been cops at just the right time, when politics wasn't affecting the streets yet. It was just the right mix of hard-nosed career cops and younger, more idealistic cops."

The younger Wilder came from a police family. Besides his "top cop" dad, his mother was a jail matron, and his own daughter is now a police officer. With his son, Brett, and his wife, Quinna, both Oklahoma City police officers, Bob related well to the Wilders, cut of the same cloth in the police family.

In his speech, the older Chief Wilder's son, a retired police chief himself, noted that Macy was considered the nation's top prosecutor as both president and two-time chairman of the National District Attorneys Association. Early on in his DA years, the late civil rights leader Hannah Atkins dubbed Macy "Mr. Integrity." As Wilder noted, "Integrity, industry, and honesty were the watchwords of Bob Macy's tenure."

Wilder reported that former U.S. Attorney General William Barr described Macy as "a great American and one of the most outstanding law enforcement leaders of our time." Barr also memorably said that if he ever went into battle, he'd want Bob Macy by his side. Former U.S. Attorney General Janet Reno also publicly praised Macy for his hard work and dedication.

Wilder recounted highlights from previous honors, given the longest-serving DA in Oklahoma County history. "He was the recipient of awards from the Religious Alliance Against Pornography, the Law Enforcement Alliance of America, The Oklahoma City Police Department, the civic leadership of Oklahoma City, the Oklahoma Literacy Council, the Oklahoma Bar Association, the International Association of Arson Investigation, the Southwest Oklahoma Peace Officers Association, the Oklahoma Association of Chiefs of Police, and many others." Wilder summarized by saying, "In his twenty-one years as Oklahoma County's District Attorney, Bob received nearly every local and national honor available to a prosecutor."

Then Wilder quoted from an award given Macy by the National District Attorneys Association, honoring his decade of service as an officer and leader. The group hailed him for bringing to the national stage "a unique extra element: the spirit of the cowboy and the flavor of the Old West: courage, candor, courtliness, and an uncompromising sense of right and wrong."

Wilder concluded his speech to the crowd. "Those who know Bob Macy best know that his most cherished award is the champion team roper's buckle that he won in the 1990 Ben Johnson Pro-Celebrity Event in Houston. That award is special to him for two reasons. First, he won it competing against some of his friends who happen to be top-notch cowboys. More important, he won the buckle while participating in one of the many annual events through which he and his friends raised millions of dollars for children's medical research, cystic fibrosis, or other childhood diseases. His interest in young people is further demonstrated by the fact that much of his time, even in retirement, has been spent designing and implementing truancy and antidrug programs or speaking with school students in Oklahoma County and elsewhere."

Macy was touched just minutes after the hall of fame ceremony evolved into a reception and a sort of reunion of law enforcement greats. Webb walked toward him saying, "There's my hero," and then gave him a firm handshake. Moments before, in a final prayer,

Oklahoma County Sheriff John Whetsel prefaced his closing benediction with praise for "my hero, Bob Macy."

I was proud to be there and watched as dozens of admirers, both those he knew and some he didn't, stood in line to give Macy a handshake, a hug, or in the case of some of the ladies, a kiss. There was a young man, a city officer who sang the national anthem on the day of Bob's retirement party in 2001. There were Donna and George Nigh and his pal David Shupe, former police officers, law partners, and many others.

G.W. Paull, described by Macy as "a jet jockey in the Air Force" before becoming a lawyer and serving as top prosecutor on Macy's team, was present. He is yet another in a long line of attorneys who could have made fortunes in the private sector but who devoted years to public service under Macy's leadership and influence. Paull specialized in white-collar crime, recovering ill-gotten gains, ending multimillion-dollar frauds and embezzlement and recovering stolen financial resources. Paull admitted to his wife, an assistant U.S. attorney herself, when she asked him when he was the happiest in his career. He replied without hesitation, "When I was assistant to Bob Macy."

I was startled by one story Bob, an assured and confident man, told me about an exchange with Paull years before at the time of his retirement.

Macy asked G.W., "I wonder if they'll remember me when I'm gone."

G.W. replied, "Bob, you're already a legend. We'll never forget you." At the age of eighty, Bob has accomplished every goal in his life, and he did it without compromising his ethics, integrity, and values. And about being remembered, he says it's not about what he has done. It's about what others can do. The last time he was in Washington DC, he said many congressmen came up to shake his hand. They didn't remember his name, but they remembered his string tie and what it stood for. "It's about integrity, standing against the lawlessness of the frontier, and the frontier keeps taking back more of the civilized land." If there is a lesson to be learned, and I think there are many, it is that people can stand against insurmountable odds and prevail. But it's much like drawing a line in the sand at the Alamo. It's not a line that defies crossing; it requires crossing. One man can't do it alone. And Bob had many friends helping him and many more carrying on even after his retirement.

Warren Henderson, his pal from the state's drug enforcement team, was there, and Bob reiterated his high opinion of the man as "one of the greatest street cops who ever lived." Also, there were Ken Nash and his wife Marie, his training officer from the city police department and one of the few cops of that era who, like Bob, went on to get a law degree.

Also attending was Danny Booth, a retired policeman who was in the horse patrol, whom Macy called "just about the toughest human being I have ever seen. Once I saw him get kicked in the head by a bull, then jump up and keep going!"

Todd Lamb, a Republican leader in the state Senate who at the time of the Chandler ceremony was seeking to become Oklahoma's lieutenant governor, presented Macy his hall of fame plaque. Bob marveled, "I saw Todd a bunch when he was a little guy. I have known his dad, Norman [a former legislator and advisor to many governors], very well. Shaking Todd's hand made me feel like our legacy will be honored and remembered."

While helping to feed the cattle at Bob's place later on, Ryen told her father, Brett, "Poppa got twice as much attention as anyone else at the party." She was more than right. Bob was the center of attention, not because he demanded it but because the crowd demanded it. He had spent his career doing what his passion demanded, and the people there knew it, saw it, and understood it.

In an interview after the Chandler event, Macy reflected, "I've spent almost my whole professional life focused on one thing, and that's crime and erasing crime. I was lucky to have an in-depth education and then invaluable experience and mentoring. This is my profession, and I couldn't help but remember I had promised Governor Nigh and the people of Oklahoma I would be the best district attorney I could possibly be. I'll tell you, receiving this honor and being put in the same category as the 'guardsmen' is kind of the crowning jewel in my lifetime of work."

He continued, "I keep telling young people to recognize they have a window of opportunity to make an impact, to make a difference. Our country, our system is in a lot of trouble, but it's not insurmountable. We have to hitch our belts, get tough and take a stand. Those young people can find, support, and elect the best people they can find. We have another chance to make a better world."

I asked Bob what advice he'd give to young people thinking about careers in law or public service. He answered, "There is a tomorrow. You have to live with whatever you do today. Do what's right."

The old cowboy is content in his retired life, at least in the restless way a man like Bob Macy can be content when he's not wrestling down a steer or a bad guy. But it's a different time now, not completely a bad time, though. When the weather cooperates, Bob Macy sits on the porch, watching his cattle and remembering a good and consequential life. Maybe he'll finally find time to pursue some of his other passions.

When we talked about that happy hall of fame day as Christmas 2009 neared, Bob referred with terms of endearment to his daughter, Teresa, a beautiful blonde woman who looks to me most like her mother, Betty. Bob later told me, "She is perhaps the most decent person I know. If she could relieve the suffering of the world, she'd do anything to make that happen."

Teresa was also at the event looking on as her dad greeted admirers. In our conversation at the hall of fame event, as we watched Bob greeting so many people, Teresa told me, "One of my clearest memories of my dad is the incredible creativity and artistry that most people never saw. I remember his paintings and his writing such beautiful prose."

Life has changed for Cowboy Bob, sometimes in ways he wishes it wouldn't. His hands aren't as firm as they once were. Sometimes, they seem to take on a life of their own and move about in his lap as if tapping to a tune only they can hear. His eyes, though still piercing, have lost some of their luster and don't always focus well enough to see as clearly as they once did. His hands and eyes can no longer work together to complete a painting, but the prose is still in his heart.

No longer are the days when he rolled out of bed at 6:00 a.m. to do the farm chores before driving to work at 7:30 a.m. Gone are the times when he was called at home in the middle of the night to respond to an emergency call from a local law enforcement officer.

His mind wanders still. Gone are the days when nothing happened without him being a part of it. Gone also are the days of responding to "Code Three" calls, seeking to encounter and make right what the violence, whether manmade or natural, of the modern world brought forth. When he was the chief law enforcement officer in Oklahoma County, he connected with his chief investigator to in-depth work on an important case or race through the night at speeds over 100 mph in the company of bodyguards or police officers in an effort to apprehend a vicious criminal before he could flee. Closed forever is the window in time when he was surrounded by employees and friends in local law enforcement. Gone, the courtroom combat and fervent search, seeking justice for all, the long nights working past midnight, sometimes until dawn, crafting the words and the arguments that might yield the proper verdict.

Gone, too, the days in congressional committee hearings and briefings by cabinet members. Gone, the celebrity roping, competing with movie stars and professional cowboys, and friendly competitions with his pals.

In the public eye, Bob Macy is gone, but in the public memory, he is not forgotten. He's retired but is not dead. If that tired old human frame would allow, he might still be out there tracking down and then assuring punishment for the wrongdoers. As it is, he is still a man of resolve. He is still the old cowboy living the cowboy ethics. He always was. His job was more than a job. All his jobs were. They were his passions. They were those moments in his life when everything in him that screamed for justice and compassion and standing up for the ones who could not stand on their own, for taking a stance against those who desired to knock others to the ground. Those were his passions. And Bob Macy was one of the luckiest men on earth whose passions and careers were one and the same. He lived more than the role of district attorney; he lived the life of cowboy, the man who stands against the wild frontier, who tames the wild and makes it hospitable for the more civilized of us. He sent sixty men to death row and refused to participate further in watching them die, refused to participate in making justice mere vengeance. We, the genteel and civilized ones, could not do that. We couldn't stand against the wilderness. We couldn't take out our guns and tame the wild. We had to hire that out. We had to hire a Cowboy Bob to be our hired gun. We paid him to fight for us, to stand in our stead, and to stand up for us.

But the pay we offered was so little compensation for the price Cowboy Bob paid. Betty went her own way to make a mark in the world after her own fashion. Sheila and Teresa have settled into the civilized world Bob fought for. Brett follows in Bob's footsteps, and where those new footsteps will lead is anyone's guess. But there is a shadow he follows, a very large and great shadow much larger than the tired frame that once cast it. The fire in Bob's belly that drove him to be the very best at what he did, not for his sake but for his passion, still burns hot and fierce.

For years I, as one of the editors, have known Bob Macy but from the sidelines. We spoke a few times, and his presence was intimidating and reassuring at the same time. He stood tall and handsome and proud but not aloof. His dark suit and white shirt set off the notable string tie, and we always knew he had a .45 automatic hidden under his coat. We were cops, and we knew he needed it. He was the veritable image of the Old West marshal, ready to jump into the fray at a moment's call and positively take a stance for righteousness and decency and lawfulness wherever he stood. And wherever he stood was the right place. We had no reason to doubt that. He was the kind of district attorney one wanted to stand behind, certainly never in front. In a moment, I'd gladly be on a Bob Macy jury. But I'd have to think long and hard to ever want to stand in front of one.

He spoke cautiously, but he spoke often and with words that came from his heart rather than just from the law. But his heart and the law were one and the same. He found his niche as district attorney, a place where he could make a difference, not in buildings or statues or even in actions but in living legacies of lives changed. But to say that his career was the beginning of his legacy is entirely incorrect. His legacy started years before, perhaps somewhere along the White River or Williams Creek. Perhaps it started on the floor of a small shack with a bunch of brothers crowded together around a coal stove for warmth. Maybe it gathered strength in the ranks of a football team standing together against the odds or in passing down lessons to airmen in Lawton. His legacy certainly found its proper footing in his cradling his newborn daughters and son and in his conversation on a plane years ago with a young school teacher.

I've come to know Bob Macy in a very unique and privileged way. He's no longer the image on the television news or at a news conference as the majority of Oklahomans have come to know. I have become one of the most fortunate to come to know Bob Macy, the man behind the image. And I have learned so much. During hours of interviews, Bob sat staring forward recalling answers to my questions. But one such time spoke more of Macy than even Macy could say. He was telling me about Betty. I said, “You still love her, don’t you?”

He turned to look at me, and I saw deep into his faded eyes and without hesitation, much quicker than he answered any question, he replied, “Oh, yes, I do.” I saw beyond his words. I saw the kind of passion that has driven him so hard these many years.

The great educator, Parker Palmer, makes the distinction in one of his books between vocation and avocation, making a living and making a life. I can honestly say Bob Macy is one of the few who did both at the same time. Any biography of Macy must include a laundry list of accolades and accomplishments, honors bestowed upon a man who, by all rights, should have the ego of a rock star. He was surrounded by movie stars, famous people of all calibers, historical names that, by simple proximity of their acquaintances, promise eons of notoriety. But that honestly isn’t the Bob Macy I have come to know. He didn’t surround himself with famous names; he didn’t lurch himself into their circles in order to become known. He followed his passion of working tirelessly for the underdog, for the helpless, for the abused and used, and they, the more famous names in our culture, chose him to lead them in the passion they, too, saw in his eyes.

Bob Macy is old and tired and broken now. He’s recovering from two broken hips and he is having to learn to walk all over again. And his walk is not nearly as stable as some years ago. But his stance is just as firm. It has truly been “one hell of a party.” But unlike Gus from *Lonesome Dove*, Bob Macy is not a dying cowboy flat on his back on the prairie. His party will live on in countless lives he has changed. There is more of the real, authentic Cowboy Bob Macy in that championship buckle than in all the plaques and accolades of his illustrious career.

“Boss”

What is a boss? In the Oklahoma County Courthouse for twenty-one years, the word had different meanings for different people. For employees, it meant endearment, respect.

In June 1980, the staff of the Oklahoma County District Attorney's office had a decision to make—not a big one but an important one. What do you call a man who has just been appointed by the governor to run the largest prosecutorial office in the state? Of course, the easiest thing to do would be simply to call him "Mr. Macy," and many did. After all, half of his staff were also prosecutors. As far as secretaries and support staff, "Mr. Macy" would be appropriate. But what about Ken Lyles, Clint Dedek, and Louis Swindler, who worked the streets with Bob Macy as fellow law enforcement officers years before?

This decision seemed so insignificant, and yet it was at the heart of the organization. The word "Boss" is such a little word but holds such a big meaning for Bob Macy. Ken Lyles, a retired OCPD homicide detective and one of Macy's dearest friends, suggested the title of "Boss." Some of the staff thought the name was too informal. Others thought it was disrespectful. A vote was taken, and the title "Boss" became the salutation among the employees. The senior personnel and ADAs were satisfied the name was formal enough. The support personnel were used to calling their supervisors by that name. Those who objected soon learned the word gave just enough informality to really be effective. Personnel working close together preferred to use last names, such as Macy's secretary, Jayne, who simply called him "Macy."

Identification cards and badges were issued to all employees and ADAs. And over the years, the personnel at the Oklahoma County Court's office were highly respected and were often met with praise and remarks from business owners. The reputation of the office grew higher and higher, and Macy employed the highest caliber of employees to carry the badges and cards. If someone violated his code of conduct, that person was quickly terminated.

In the early years, Macy wasn't as noticeable but by his ten-year mark in office, he'd become acquainted with all the employees at the county office who greeted him as equal and friend. The result was that Macy was addressed by all county employees as "Boss," as mentioned in Wilford Brimley's introduction.

So what is a "Boss?" An official who treats his employees fairly and with high respect, a person who is loyal, industrious, respectful, and dignified, and a man who earned the title so thoughtfully bestowed upon him his first day on the job and who showed daily his leadership capabilities. Some people have to work to become the title they carry. But Bob Macy gave new meaning to the word "Boss."

> In spite of the fact that he and I are the best of friends and we care a great deal for one another, I don't ever want to stand in front of him in a court of law. Because in that situation, nothing counts to Bob Macy except the truth, the right for the sake of right, and justice—equal justice for all. I have sat in the courtroom with him on many occasions. I have watched him prosecute some of the vilest human beings I have ever been in the presence of. I've seen him keep his composure, I've seen him so well prepared, and I've seen him conduct his trials and his legal matters in a manner that is awesome.
>
> Wilford Brimley

On the desk at Earlham College:
A friend is not a feller who is taken in by a sham. A friend is one who knows our faults and just doesn't give a damn.

"If there is a wrong, you fight it.
If you don't, you become a part of it."

"To avoid controversy,
say nothing,
do nothing,
be nothing."